SUPERIOR HUMAN RELATIONSHIP

SUPERIOR HUMAN RELATIONSHIP

Dr. V. N. Pathak

KALPAZ PUBLICATIONS
Delhi-110052

Superior Human Relationship

Rs. 790

ISBN: 81-7835-338-5

Published in 2005 in India by
Kalpaz Publications,
C-30, Satyawati Nagar, Delhi-110052
E-mail : Kalpaz@hotmail.com

Laser Typesetting at : Shiva Infosystem, Delhi
Printed at : Mehra Offset Press, Delhi

Good husband-wife relationship is the key to good child-parent relationship. Our children are our future. Are we, as parents, really concerned with the kind of relationship we have with our children? With seven hours of TV a day and five minutes with his father and twenty minutes with his mother, an average child is heading for adulthood that is going to witness an epidemic of divorce, child neglect, community ruin, and loneliness. In the process of evolution, we have covered a long way from animal society to human society. With the broken homes and fractured families multiplying at an amazing speed, can we now even sustain humanity, what to think of moving ahead from humanity to divinity?

Dedicated To–

Dedicated to Late Shri Ganesh Mal Ji Choraria whose principle based values have been demonstrated by his children notably by Dr. Nirmal Choraria, CEO, Nirmal Children Hospital, Ring Road, Surat.

Content

Preface

It is now realized that 85 percent happiness and success in life come from superior human relationship. People need people for survival yet people kill people. Why do people cause violence to others? Because they want to torture/punish their own self. This has a lot to do with their childhood. Nearly 7 out of 10 people are moving restlessly on or off the track carrying a heavy negative baggage. They are not aware of the many ways they are adopting to hurt others in a bid to take revenge from their one or both parents. In their childhood they were made to realize repeatedly that they were offenders, bad and unworthy. They accepted that they were so. Now they have grown into adulthood, but their old recordings of unworthiness have not stopped. These negative recordings force them subconsciously to satisfy their old belief that are bad, and to prove this again and again they continue to indulge in undesirable behaviours.

In almost every relationship workshop that we conducted from under the tree to 5-Star Hotels, participants invariably asked one question, "Have you written a book?" I tried to meet their demand by producing 12 audio cassettes but it did not serve the purpose. I then suggested them to refer to standard books written by western psychologists, but the feedback was mostly not positive. Our masses need something in print that could explain things in a simple language free from highly technical terms and jargons, something akin to their cultural background, something acceptable to the Eastern mind and something also affordable. Realizing their needs, I decided to write this book.

If the feeling of love in your family and elsewhere has died or is dying, you have people yelling, criticizing, blaming and fighting, and you have tried your best but found yourself empty and alone, then you seriously need to look into and work on your attitudes towards your own self and others. Family is the building block of society and parenting basically is a life of sacrifice. We all need to learn and practice the laws and rules that govern our relationships in the family and also elsewhere.

This book has chapters on knowledge about self, basic attitudes for relationships, husband-wife relationship, child-parent relationship, emotions (the real fabric of relationship) and tests and techniques. It's purpose is to strengthen your relationships with husband/wife, parents/children, loved ones, and boss/subordinate. We all have to serve, contribute and make a difference in lives of people so that they become better and stronger persons to make this planet a joyful place to live in.

Thanks to the modern information technology, this job of book writing became so easy. My understanding of the subject has been affected most significantly by Dorothy James, William James, Anthony Robbins, Robert Schuller, Bernie Siegel, Zig Ziglar, Albert Ellis, Walter Doyle Staples, Brian Tracy and others. I read the books authored by them repeatedly to find an integrated approach to solve my problems. I trust this book advances the cause they all so unselfishly serve: the development of human potential.

The repetition of messages received from the psychological literature coupled with emotional intensity and the valuable help rendered by thousands of participants to our more than 250 workshops and my wife Usha Pathak, caused a significant change in my perceptions about human relationship. Valuable help in compiling this document was received from Dr. Ambika Chandani, former Associate Professor of Sociology at JN Vyas University, Jodhpur; Mrs. Sangita Choraria, Dr. Nirmal Choraria,CEO, Nirmal Children and General Hospital, Surat; Vinod Choraria, Chief, Hospital Management, Nirmal Children and General Hospital, Surat; Mr. Vimal Poddar, renouned builder of Surat, Dr. Pradeep Martin and Dr. Sushma Iyer, CEO, H3 Healing Hands Hospital, Surat, and Vineeta Singhania. I am sincerely grateful to these persons in particular Dr. Nirmal Choraria who made our stay at Surat so useful. I owe thanks to our loving children Manish and Richa and their spouses, Ranjana and Mukul Gaur respectively, and our grandchildren Anushka and Samarth for their patience and encouragement.

V. N. Pathak

26 January, 2004

1
Relationship with Your Own Self

What kind of relationship do you have with your own self will determine the kind of relationship you will have with others. You cannot respect, like and love others unless you respect, like and love yourself. You cannot forgive others unless you forgive your own self. Everything that happens outside you, first happens inside you. Interpersonal relationship is a mere reflection of intra-personal relationship. Interestingly, others will love, like and respect you to the degree you love, like and respect your own self. Establish good relationship with your own self.

A childhood belief that you are inadequate can lead to a lot of self sabotaging behaviour later in life. Every body feels ugly and inadequate, as a result a sense of peace eludes most of us. It is a suffering from a compensatory disorder. Substantial structural damage to our psyche is done in our childhood and the old damage persists in the later life. As one unknown author so rightly expressed it:

If a child lives with criticism, he learns to condemn.
If a child lives with security, he learns to have faith in himself
If a child lives with hostility, he learns to fight
If a child lives with acceptance, he learns to love
If a child lives with fear, he learns to be apprehensive
If a child lives with recognition, he learns to have a goal
If a child lives with pity, he learns to be sorry for himself
If a child lives with approval, he learns to like himself
If a child lives with jealousy, he learns to feel guilty
If a child lives with friendliness, he learns that the world is a nice place in which to live

This should not mean that we are not responsible for our life. After the age of around 14, we all are fully responsible for our life. Instead of blaming our parents or other elders, we must realize that we alone are responsible for whatever happens to us because we have been granted the great freedom, "The Freedom to Choose". Benjamin Disraeli rightly said, "Man is not the creature of circumstances, circumstances are the creature of man.

Freedom to Choose

The winners use freedom to choose, while losers are hardly aware of this freedom. Freedom to choose is the greatest gift given only to mankind. It means that between you and your circumstances, between you and your disease, between you and behaviour of others, and between you and poverty, you can always choose to be happy or unhappy, strong or weak, and winner or loser. Follow the great principle of Freedom to Choose. It will revolutionize your life.

Strangely, the principle of freedom to choose was discovered not in a cozy room of the home but in the cell of a death camp. Viktor Frankle, the noted Professor of Psychology was a Jew so he was captured by German Nazi officers and imprisoned in the concentration camp. He was tortured daily. He did not know whether he would be alive next day. Even his father, mother and sister were killed right before his eyes. One day, naked and alone in his cell, he looked as an observer at his very involvement. He became aware of the freedom his Nazi captors could not take away. He began to become self aware. He thought Nazi could do whatever they wanted to do to his body, they could control his entire environment, but they could not control how all of this was going to affect him.

He found that only he could decide within himself how all the torture was going to affect him. He discovered that between stimulus and response, he had the freedom to choose the kind of response he wanted. He started projecting himself into different circumstances like lecturing to his students after release from death camp. He described himself in the classroom in the mind's eye, and gave his students the lessons he was learning during the very torture. He exercised his small, embryonic freedom using his memory and imagination. His freedom grew more than the freedom of his Nazi captors. He soon became popular to all in the concentration camp. He became an inspiration even to some of the guards. He helped others in finding meaning in their suffering and dignity in the prison existence. He discovered the fundamental principle about the nature of man, and the principle is that between stimulus and response, man has the freedom to choose.

In the concentration camp, Viktor Frankl lived because he wanted to live. Most died, he observed, because they wanted to die. They lost their will to live because their minds became consumed by the tormenting misery of their existence. He, on the other hand singled out any small incident of positive meaning and let his mind dwell on that. His frightful experience in captivity revealed to him that electric fences, chains, locks and cells do not deprive an individual of freedom. "One's ultimate freedom is the ability to choose one's attitude in any given set of circumstances," he discovered.

Viktor Frankl's discovery tells us that not until you have achieved the ability to choose your attitudes, have you achieved the freedom to be your own person, reaching out for any goal or dream of your choice. Without this freedom, you are the captive of every habit, situation, circumstances or surroundings in which you find yourself.

What an incredible gift, then, this is – the ability to choose the thoughts that dwell within your mind! You can choose your thoughts and by doing so, choose the pathways of your life. For your life is merely a reflection of your thoughts.

Freedom to choose has 4 components: self awareness, conscience, imagination and free will. Of these, self awareness is the most important component as without it the other three components cannot be used. Self awareness is also the foundation of life of human beings as it is closely related to and determine consciousness, loss of which really means the loss of life.

Self Awareness

Awareness requires living in here and now, and not in the elsewhere, the past or the future. The decisive question is, "where is the mind when body is here?". The more you become aware of the extent you are influenced by prior experiences, the more you will test your assumptions against the reality, listen to others and be open to their perceptions

Self awareness is a unique gift that only human beings have. It means the process of separating oneself from one's own life, thoughts and feelings and observe them. We must develop the art of separating our own self from our thoughts and feelings and observing them every moment. It is necessary to know what thoughts and feelings are arising from within so that one could separate oneself from them and gain better control over these powerful inducers.Self awareness is essential for effective listening. It helps in:

1. Distancing you from your own self
2. Knowing your emotional world
3. Knowing your strengths and limitations

Besides self awareness, the other valuable gifts that humans possess are imagination, will power and conscience. But, these gifts cannot be used in absence of self awareness. We need to realize that only continuous observation of thoughts and feelings that arise in our mind can render us the ability to control our thoughts and feelings. In absence of self awareness, we become blind to thoughts and feelings that automatically grow in our mind and are not able to examine them. In this situation, we do not get space to know what the other person is thinking or feeling. This insensitivity leads us to disrespect, judge and reject others .The level of self awareness can be tested through communication with others, using JOHARI WINDOWS. To develop self awareness, ask yourself every moment the following 7 questions:

1. What am I thinking?
2. What am I feeling?
3. What am I seeing?
4. What am I listening?
5. How am I listening?
6. How am I speaking?
7. What am I desiring?

Allot one hour daily for self awareness to begin with. Gradually increase the time so that you spend your entire day with self awareness.

What is a Personality?

Some 18,000 descriptive words relate to personality. It is an intricate pattern of glands, concepts and social goals. Gestures, facial expressions, speech, gait, skills, physical and mental potentials plus thinking and feeling habit patterns are some of the constituents of personality. A personality constellation constantly develops with new experiences. To evaluate a personality, you have to answer:

1. How does a person look and act?
2. What does a person say or do?
3. With what thoughts and attitudes does a person respond to situations, to other persons and to himself / herself ?

At the hub of your personality constellation is the feeling about yourself. This is your self concept. It unifies many facets of your personality. It is the focal point of all personality determinants. It is the genesis of your motivators influencing your reaction to the world

Childhood Recordings and Personality Formation

For almost 100 years, psychologists have agreed that our past experiences do determine who we are, and how we act. Memories are recorded and stored as we age and with time they create more and more influence on us. Psychological pressures in the atmosphere in which a child grows leave their mark on the psyche of the person. Your personality today is indeed the product of your whole past.

In homes, children are usually a handy scapegoat for an emotional tirade. Parents frustrated by their own personal problems give a child the feeling that he is worthless. At an early age, the child just takes it all personally. Once he incorporates these feelings into his inner portrait, a vicious cycle develops. He suffers from low opinion of himself which makes it more difficult to succeed in the next step. Thus he proves to himself that he is worthless and so his self depletion multiplies. The process continues until absurdity of clinging to these early feelings is realized.

Recent researches show that recording in the brain begins three months after conception and continue for about 28,000 hours, roughly first five years. Based on these recordings are formed our ego states.

Ego States

In a given individual, a certain set of behaviour patterns corresponds to one state of mind, while another set is related to a different psychic attitude, often inconsistent with the first. These changes and differences give rise to the idea of ego states. An ego state is a system of feelings accompanied by a related set of behaviour patterns that at any given moment each individual in a social aggregation will exhibit. Individuals can shift with varying degrees of readiness from one ego state to another. Ego states are normal physiological phenomenon. The human brain is the organ or organizer of psychic life and its product are organized and stored in the form of ego states. Personality comprises three ego states: Parent Ego State, Child Ego State and Adult Ego State. These ego states can be identified by analyzing the non-verbal and verbal languages.

Parent Ego State

The person exhibits signs like, pointing finger, furrowed brow, hands on hips, foot tapping, folded arms, and wringling hands. He/she uses words like, once for all, always, never, how many times have I told you, lazy, nonsense, absurd, disgusting, shocking, stupid, how dare you, cute, there, there, now what? Not again.

In this ego state, the person does spontaneous judgment on others and criticizes others, telling weaknesses rudely and directly, ……" you can't cope with your problems," "How can you… ", "Go take a bath….", "I like… the best ", "Our family tries to avoid…." "Now look here", "The first thing that you have to do is…" " Try to understand…." "My … is best", "When I was a young man…" " The sooner a man learns…." " If you would…", 'I know the best' Look at yourself you are not OK…", Taunting, teasing, " Why don't you…", " You dirty…."

The person is punishing others. This ego state comes on spontaneously. You cannot give positive strokes through Critical Parent Ego state.

Child Ego State

In this ego state, a person exhibits attention-asking behaviours like beating, throwing, breaking, weeping, crying, shouting., feeling miserable, inferior, sexual abnormalities, aroused feelings, hate, jealousy, anger, feeling hurt by criticism, shaky, embarrassed, seducing, not accepting compliment(thinking that he/she does not deserve it), maintaining position that was established in childhood, fearful, and worrying. The person is feeling unloved, unsecured, neglected; and is looking for positive strokes. Other symptoms are: tears, quivering lips, temper tantrums, high pitched voice, rolling eyes, nail biting, nose thumbing, and giggling. The person cannot postpone gratification and easily feels hurt. His/her action of anger and cry comes out of hurt.

The person says, " I am not fine, I am not OK, I am not attractive, I am not capable, Look at me…, So what's matter with you…? Are you blind..? Don't get mad at me., I want… I must get….." The person does not care for consequences. This ego state comes spontaneously. You cannot give positive strokes through this ego state..

Adult Ego State

This is the most desirable ego state as positive strokes can be given only through this ego state. In this ego state a person realizes that to be loving is most important. In this ego state a person does not allow Parent or Child to come on straight, using the choice to decide how to respond to a stimulus in a complementary way. The person examines: Is it a fact? Does it apply? Is it appropriate? From where this idea is coming? What is the evidence? The person uses words like, "What?" "Why?" " How?" "When?" " Where?" " Who? " "Please!" " Thank You!" " You mean…" "Let us…." " In my opinion…..," " I think it is……," " May be….., " "Possibly…" . " I see…" The person's eyes blink every 3-5 second, he/she has straight furrowed face, and his/her face has expressions of curiosity. The person estimates probabilities, thinks of consequences, and postpones gratification. The person is concerned with preservation of individual. This ego state does not come spontaneously. You can give positive strokes only through this ego state.

At gross level, personality has these three ego states,but more precisely, Parent Ego State comprises two ego states called Critical Parent and Nurturing Parent. The Child Ego State comprises three ego states called Natural Child, Little Professor and Adaptive Child. Thus our personality has following six ego states:

1. Critical Parent
2. Nurturing Parent
3. Adult
4. Natural child
5. Little Professor
6. Adaptive Child.

Critical Parent

This ego state is characterized by behaviours like, criticizing, pointing mistakes rudely, blaming, angry, protecting, preaching, morality, and sticking to rules. Its level should be less than 5 according to the egogram scheme described in the last chapter.

Nurturing Parent

This ego state is characterized by behaviours like helping others at any cost, making sacrifices and enjoying hardship to comfort others, The person has great compassion for humanity and he/she cannot feel comfortable while others are suffering. Its level should be 12 or more.

Adult

In this ego state, person postpones sense gratification, and makes right decision at right time, his/her self awareness level is high, objectivity is high, the person is realistic, and he/she is able to control undesirable levels of other 5 ego states. He/she strikes balance, and has high predictive ability. A person whose adult is high always keeps result in mind. Adult should be as high as possible and it should come with a high speed. An ideal level of this ego state is 18.

Natural Child

This ego state is characterized by deep interest in outings, picnicking, socializing, having hobbies, some excellence in extra curricular activities. Its desirable level is between 15 and 22.

Little Professor

This ego state reveals originality and creativity. It should be at least 12.

Adaptive Child

Characteristics of this ego state are: feeling unsecured, anger shooting up suddenly and cooling down promptly, throwing things, pushing, breaking, hitting a person who is dependent/weak. If the person is not expressing anger violently, then he/she is suppressing the anger and heading for depression and other ailments; the person is attention-seeking (look at me), crying, throwing tantrums, demanding love, care and respect, dominating, worrying, feeling guilty. The person is over submissive to his/her superiors, and over polite to persons having power, but rude and cruel to others if they err. If the level of this ego state is 15 or more, then the person is suffering from one or more of the following ailments:

Gastric acidity, gas problems, peptic ulcers, sleep disorders, insomnia, unidentified headaches, migraine, asthma, high/low blood pressure, hypertension, irregular heart beats, unidentified skin diseases, tumours, depression, fears, phobia, panic attacks, anxiety, sexual abnormalities including under/over sex drive. This ego state should be 5 or less than 5.

An ideal personality should have Adult ego state as the strongest ego state. Only adult ego state can control other five ego states, which are mainly the recordings made in our childhood. For analysis of your ego states, use Egogram given in the last chapter. However, you have to realize that like most psychometric tests, egogram test may not provide absolutely correct information. But should we expect such an accuracy while assessing a highly complicated system such as human nature? Nevertheless, the test gives fairly reliable indication about the strengths and limitations of personality which can be gainfully used in personal development.

Stay in Adult Ego State

The knowledge about ego states can empower you to improve your relationship with others in almost all situations. No one can stay in one ego state permanently. We all keep shifting from one ego state to another. However, most people including you remain in parent or child ego states most of the time, which come spontaneously and do not allow you to give positive strokes needed by others or even your own self. To become successful in life you must acquire the skill to stay in adult ego state most of the time. You have to free your adult ego state from the slavery imposed by parent or child ego states. Until you achieve this, you behave merely like a tape recorder controlled by the recordings of parent or child ego states. Using your adult ego state, you can also help others to shift from their parent or child ego states to adult ego state by giving them proper positive strokes.

To use the knowledge of ego states, take following steps:

1. Become immediately sensitive to your Parent and Child signals. Ask, "Who is coming on?"
2. Become aware that this is my Not OK Child or Parent
3. Count up to 10 so that automatic response coming from Parent or Child is delayed and Adult takes control over the transaction.
4. When in doubt leave the transaction, so that destructive reactions of Child are curtailed
5. To tackle signals from Parent, ask:
   (a) Is it true?
   (b) Does it apply?
   (c) Is it appropriate?
   (d) Where did I get this idea from?
   (e) What is the evidence?

6 Separate quickly the Parent and Child from Adult so that separated Adult becomes autonomous & strong.

7. See a little boy/girl in another person and talk to that boy/girl in a loving and protective way.

8. Ask what is important here? Allow Adult to work as probability estimator.
9. Act immediately to delay automatic responses of Child and Parent.
10. Develop high speed Adult
11. Make sure that your Adult works better and faster.
12. Remember that Parent hookers are everywhere. Be alert. Only Adult can control Parent and Child.

You Can Change Your Personality

Exercise 1: It will be rewarding to know characteristics of your personality. The better way to do this will be in a group of people. Collect friends, relatives or people known to you. Request them to participate in the following two exercises. Ask participants to form a team if they are ten or less in number and group into different teams if they are more than 10 . Ask each participant to fill up Table 1.

Put a check mark in column one after the five characteristics you feel best describe the general type of personality you portray most of the time. Then place the names of each of the other members of your group in one of the other columns and check the five characteristics you think best describes each of them.

> Knowing others is wisdom.
> Knowing yourself is enlightenment

Discuss with participants the following points. If there are more than one team, then appoint a Team Leader for each team and ask the Team Leader to discuss the points in the team.

1. You identified your own and others personality characteristics. Your personality is the way you appear to others. It is one of the fundamental forces that shapes your life. Your personality is a reflection of your attitudes. Your personality communicates your attitudes about others and yourself. What surprises you got from the exercise?

The science of Kinesics (non-verbal communication) tells us that these attitudes cannot be masked. Psychological studies have proved that 93 per cent of communications is non-verbal. The influence of your personality is not what you say, but the tone of your voice, your facial expressions, posture, reaction to others. What information did you get from this exercise?

2. Compare one by one characteristics marked by others for you. If there is a difference, ask each member to describe what non-verbal communication led him/her to the conclusion.

3. Ask each member, "How can I non-verbally communicate the characteristics I would like to express?"

4. Request each Team Leader to share the experiences and views of his/her team.

Exercise 2 : Assessment of your strengths and limitations

1. The participants to group into different teams and list their own strengths and limitations.
2. Each member to list his/her strengths and limitations
3. Continue thinking and writing during the entire time.

Table 1. Personality Characters M =Name of Member

Character	*Self*	*M1*	*M2*	*M3*	*M4*	*M5*	*M6*	*M7*	*M8*	*M9*	*M10*
Agreeable											
Calm											
Cheerful											
Confident											
Considerate											
Creative											
Decisive											
Dignified											
Direct											
Enthusiastic											
Gentle											
Helpful											
Intellectual											
Modest											
Sincere											
Soft-spoken											
Trusting											
Understanding											
Witty											

Strengths	*Limitations*

Discuss the following with your team members.

1. Which of your lists is longer? What does this mean?

2. Successful people build on their strengths rather than being overly concerned about their limitations (which they have, just like everyone else). People who fail are governed by their limitations. What do you feel about this?

3. How the limitations that you have listed are affecting your life?

4. What would our lives be like if we built upon our strengths and refused to let our limitations make us feel inferior?

4. Each Team Leader to share the experiences and views of his/her team

To achieve personal significance, you have to recognize your signif ance as well as deal with your limitations. To recognize your significance, you have to see that you are special and unique. You are the only you there will ever be regardless of how popular or unpopular, how rich or poor, you are. Indeed, you are special. You are not useless because you exist! You have to identify and put to work speciality, uniqueness, giftedness and abilities for your own personal wellbeing as well as your sphere of influence

Identify your ambitions and the differences you can make in your and others' lives. You must believe that you can fulfill your destiny otherwise unhappiness and a sense of failure will fill your life. You can define your destiny by understanding:

1. Your unique bent (gift, abilities, opportunities, concerns, and passions).
2. Pressing needs in your world.

To deal with your limitations, you have to:

1. Admit your weaknesses
2. Look for opportunities to grow
3. Keep adjusting

Limitations/weaknesses are not that difficult to change. We can even benefit from our weaknesses. Everyone is struggling with something, it is therefore okay to admit your weaknesses. People are usually afraid that their thoughts, attitudes, private behaviours and vulnerabilities will be rejected if truly understood by others. Therefore, individuals develop masks to to conceal who they are But people respond to vulnerabilities quite differently. They respect you more when you admit your weakness. The fact is that when you admit your mistake, you become free to grow and provide openness to help others grow.

We cannot always control the outcome, but we can always control our behaviour and our decisions. Our job must be to concentrate on the roots (right principle) of our life and not on fruits. The fruits will eventually develop by our proper concentration on the roots. This principle had been beautifully narrated in Shrimad Bhagwadgita where Lord advises that you have to concentrate only on your efforts and not worry for the results.

We must constantly look for areas to change and ask for help. Find people who will build you up. Also create levers that will help you grow. You also have to keep adjusting. Indeed you are going to fail repeatedly. Remember that failing does not make you a failure. A failure is a person who does not learn from his failings and stops making efforts towards the goal. Successful people remain undaunted even after many failures, they come back time after time and change the course of history. Remember that what you see is what you will be. You are unique and significant. Now live like it.

Take the following exercise. Complete the following statements:

A. I am unique/special because:

1.
2.
3.

B. I can make a difference in following ways:

1.
2.
3.

C. I must fulfill my destiny(reason for being) by:

1.
2.
3.

D. My three major weaknesses/limitations, I need to admit to myself, to other and to God are:

1.
2.
3.

E. In this year, I will look for opportunities to grow in the following ways:

1.
2.
3.

Place the answers somewhere so you can review them daily. Memorize the following creed. Repeat it 5 times a day:

I will take charge of my life and make a difference.
I will take problems as positive opportunities
I will centre my life on universal principles
I will actively pursue my mission
I will keep all vital areas of my life in balance
I will put others first and honestly serve them
I will cultivate my character, personality, soul and spirit
I will keep adjusting to needs
I will never, ever, ever quit!

We have to build on our strengths. Make a list of your 15 qualities identified through these exercises. Read this list daily as frequently as you can. Use both feelings and thoughts while reading the list. Remember that thoughts without feelings are powerless and feelings without thoughts are without direction. Read this list with full belief. Belief changes expectations. Expectations change the attitudes. The subconscious mind works faster on anything that is believed by your conscious mind, and this is how you achieve a change in your personality through power of belief in your goodness.

Law of Belief

Your belief is the product of all the thinking that you have done. Believes are latent and deeply buried in the subconscious, but they are powerful forces that govern your life. The beliefs represent your conscious decisions that you made in past about yourself and your circumstances.

These decisions get repeated subconsciously as you grow, and they constantly guide your thinking, behaviour and performance. Indeed your performance is the reflection of your deep-seated beliefs. Who you are? The answer is: what your mind believes you are. According to this law of belief, your belief system causes you to make judgment and interpretations of the event that in turn generate your expectations and behaviour, and that your belief system being based on inaccurate information that arose from wrong interpretations of past experiences, is almost always incomplete, and therefore unreliable. We live with many false beliefs like, if you didn't do well in the school, you will not do well in life. All research in the area of psychology of achievement have clearly proved that there is no direct correlation between academic achievement and life-time earnings. Take another false belief: protect what you have otherwise others will take it away, and never give first. The false belief makes you selfish and put you in the prison of your own making. You are deprived of help from others, because you get what you give.

Remember that it is your personal belief system that creates your reality. Irrarional or false beliefs cut you off from searching many opportunities in life and deprive you from the excellence that is awaiting you.

You create your world through your beliefs.

According to famous psychotherapist, Ellis, circumstances are activating events, say A. We blame activating events for causing us to feel and act. Let us call these behavioural consequences say, C. We usually feel that A=C. For example,

A (I did not get promotion) = C (I feel rejected) or

A (I lost the contest) = C (I feel incompetent)

The fact is that A does not cause C. If you believe that A = C, then this wrong belief will give you frustration and misery. Remember that the correct causal relationship between an event and our feelings is,

A + B = C, where B is our personal belief system. Your belief system causes you to make judgment and interpretations of the event that in turn generate your expectations and behaviour. These thought patterns (judgments & interpretations) collectively form our attitude profile, e.g.,

Activating event A (I did not get promotion) + Belief system B (I am a capable person, my turn will come) = Consequence C (I feel good about myself and my future prospects). Ellis has rightly said, "*People and things do not upset us, rather we upset ourselves by believing that they can upset us"* As a matter of fact, it is your manner of thinking (attitude) that determines how you feel and behave. All causations are internal (mental), not external, therefore, we must look inward for a solution. We must accept responsibility for the right/wrong beliefs that we finally adopt. We are misinformed about many aspects of our and other's lives and things. We accept many things that are not true. False beliefs are fatal but we live with many false beliefs. Let us now realize that our belief system is almost always incomplete, and therefore unreliable. *The breakthrough in your life will come only with the sincere realization that your belief system is largely unreliable.*

Man is only what he believes

There is only one person who causes most of your troubles. That person is "You". You are responsible for the choices and actions that have put you in your present circumstances. Since you are responsible, you can change the things for which you *are* responsible. But human beings have a tendency to avoid responsibility by passing it to someone else. We pass the responsibility through blame. If someone drops a glass, and you ask what happened, the person will say, "It slipped." Not, "I dropped it." It slipped means that the glass is responsible for its own falling. We don't just admit we did it. We pass the blame. We try to get out of responsibility.

You are responsible for all of your experiences of life. Events beyond your control will happen in your life, but how you are going to be affected by these events is in your control. Since you have the freedom to choose the way you are going to be affected, you are fully responsible for the way you feel, think and act. No amount of illness, poverty or bad behaviour of others can influence you to become happy or unhappy because the freedom to choose the way you are going to affected lies with you and not with external events. This freedom makes you 100 per cent responsible for your feelings, thoughts and actions. Whether you react or respond to a situation is in your hand and you are fully responsible for your response/ reaction.

When you accept responsibility then you are in charge. You can change your thinking, attitude, emotions and behaviour. You can plan a course of action. You can claim your power and shine because you are willing to say, "I am responsible." Be "Response-Able".

The San Francisco Double Blind Experiment

At a school in San Francisco, the Principal invited all the teachers to submit their work –reports and resume for selection of 3 best teachers of the school. The documents submitted by teachers were scanned and 3 best teachers were selected. A function celebrating their achievements was held and the salary of these teachers was raised. After the award ceremony, the Principal called these teachers to his office and asked them to teach 90 best students of the school (30 students per teacher) for one year. The Principal informed that these best students will be selected by his office confidentially. The best students were selected and the teachers taught them for one year. The result was a miracle. The students topped not only in the county but beyond. The Principal invited the three teachers into his office and following conversation happened in the meeting.

Principal: Congratulations. It is beyond my expectation. How did this miracle happen?

Teacher 1 : Well, the entire credit should go to the students. They were so brilliant. It was a pleasure to take their classes, and they worked very hard. After all, they were the best students of the school.

Principal: (Smilingly) Please allow me to share a secret. They were not the best students, they were picked up randomly as what all was done was a part of a psychology experiment done at our school.

Teacher 2 : How come the ordinary students put up such an extra-ordinary performance.

Principal: That's precisely what I want to know from you.

Teacher 3: Well, Mr. Principal, did it not happen because we being the best teachers gave our best ?

Principal: I think, time has come when I must share with you the other part of the experiment. It is that you too were not the best teachers of the school and your names were also picked up randomly.

So, neither the students were the best nor the teachers, but a belief based on false information created the magic.

Look at this story shared by Dr. Nirmal Choraria, CEO, Nirmal Children and General Hospital, Surat:

The Lion's Club conducted an exercise in a village school. A room of the school was converted into an open shop where stationary and books were placed for sale without a sales man. The students were told that the club had full belief in the honesty of the students and therefore no sales man was appointed. The students were supposed to read the price tag of each article and place the required money in a sealed cash box. The shop was run for one month. After one month when stocks and cash were checked, a big surprise was there. The cash in the box did not fall short, it indeed exceeded the total sale.

Attitude is the function of your beliefs.

Let us have one more story.

In a school, a young teacher was assigned to the roughest class of boys. The class was so tough that in past many teachers failed to discipline it. One day, this new teacher accidently saw a listing of the boys' IQ and could not believe it. These boys were brilliant. So that's how the teacher began treating them as brilliant and capable human beings with incredible potential. You could do this sum, Can't you? You could solve this problem. Can't you? The result was that the students proved the teacher right by passing with very good marks.

Yet. Here is the clincher: the teacher had not actually seen the boys' IQ scores. The teacher had misread the paper, it was their locker numbers the teacher had seen. Yet because the teacher thought the numbers reflected their IQ scores and treated the boys as such, the teacher dramatically changed the way those boys lived. The boys responded because they had been sold an image of themselves as intelligent people who had great potential.

These stories reveal the powerful impact of belief in our life. Indeed, belief system is one of the four most important components of success system which are: Belief System, Question System, Character and Self esteem.

Belief System

Amazing is the power of belief. If somebody believes in you then your self esteem goes up. Parents who do not believe in their children destroy self esteem of their children and make them neurotic. If you believe a person, then you transform his/her life. This transformation occurs through boosting of self esteem. Praise is a wonder tool. It boosts self esteem. When you help others in boosting their self esteem, your self esteem automatically goes up. You get what you give but to give you must have.

Events of life do not influence us, but our beliefs about the meanings of those events do. Events or experiences have no meanings in themselves. We attach meanings to them. Belief is the guiding force that tells us what will lead to pain or pleasure. Whenever anything happens, our brain asks us two questions: 1. Will it mean pain or pleasure? 2. What should I do to avoid pain/gain pleasure? The answers to these questions depend on belief.

All human actions are results of their beliefs. Whatever we do is due to our conscious or unconscious beliefs about what will lead to pain or pleasure. Beliefs not only affect emotions and actions but they influence entire body chemistry. Beliefs affect our immune system. The accepted beliefs work like unquestioned commands to our nervous system. Beliefs can expand or destroy the possibilities of our present and future.

Beliefs become true to the extent you believe in them

What is a Belief?

Basically, belief is a feeling of certainty about anything. The basic building block of belief is an idea. The difference between an idea and belief is that the latter has great amount of certainty. Certainty depends on our reference experiences. This information tells us that we can turn any idea into a belief by collecting and organizing enough reference experiences. We can collect reference experiences from various sources like our own self, others, books, movies, and even our imagination. These experiences need not be accurate or true as our brain cannot differentiate between true and false. An optimist will see his behaviour as being more effective than it actually was. Yet this unrealistic evaluation of his own performance is the secret of his future success.

Wrong beliefs destroy our life. Three wrong beliefs that lead to learned helplessness are:

1. Permanence (problem is permanent)
2. Pervasiveness(one problem controls the whole life)
3. Personal (the problem is personal)

Why People Focus More on Negative Aspects?

Research shows that 50 per cent of our belief system is formed at the age of 2 years, 60 per cent at 6 years, 80 per cent at 8 years and almost 90 per cent at the age of 14 years. This belief system determines what we think about our own self and our capabilities throughout our life. Since up to age of 14 years we were immature and felt innsecured about many things, the judgments we make about ourselves, others and our situations were inaccurate and so were our beliefs. While we grow further, become adult and beyond, our belief system continues to remain unchanged, and those false/irrational beliefs still dictate our feelings and actions. The past false beliefs still decide the beliefs we hold today about ourselves and our capabilities. Since past beliefs were mostly about our limitations at that time, that is why people focus more on their limitations than on assets now. It is absolutely essential to change a wrong belief. As long as you believe something, your brain works on automatic pilot, filtering any input from the environment, and searching for references to validate your belief whether it is right or wrong.

How to Change a Belief?

We can change any belief by the following steps:

1. Associate massive pain to the old belief and tremendous pleasure to the idea that has to become a new belief.
2. Create doubt. Question the old belief enough
3. Turn the new belief into conviction. Beliefs have 3 levels: A. Opinion (reference experiences few and emotional intensity low). B. Belief (reference experiences more than that of opinion, and emotional intensity high). C. Conviction (reference experiences are many and well organized, and emotional intensity is so high that the person will never question the reference experiences). We can turn a belief into conviction by the following steps:

Step 1: Reinforce the basic belief by adding new and more powerful reference experiences

Step 2: Find or create a triggering event by asking, "What will it cost me if I don't change ?" "Unless I believe this, what massive pain I will suffer?"

Ask questions that create emotional intensity. Make painful experiences feel real by viewing films, visiting affected people, reading books, etc.

Step 3: Take action: Each action you take raises the level of emotional intensity and conviction. Decide first for small improvements. Since small improvements are believable, they are therefore achievable.

You always choose what you believe. Each one of your beliefs has been a choice.

Remember pain is the most powerful tool for changing your beliefs. Focus on consequences of all your beliefs. List your beliefs about yourself, life, work, people, everything. Identify both empowering and dis-empowering beliefs. Strengthen empowering beliefs to the level of convictions, and eliminate the dis-empowering beliefs.

Question System

To understand the power of this system, consider the following conversations and the conclusions drawn from them:

Conversation 1

Mohan: I am shocked to know that Sohan my former associate, demonstrated a technique before the audience which was developed by me. He took all the credit for it and did not even make a reference about me. How dare he? How could he do this to me?

Ram: What do you respect about Sohan?

Mohan: Nothing.

Ram: What could you respect about Sohan if you wanted to?

Mohan: Well, at least he is not sitting idle. He is using and disseminating the knowledge he earned from me.

Conclusions

1. Mohan was asking wrong questions, his focus was on weakness of Sohan

2. When he changed the question, his focus changed from weakness in Sohan to goodness in Sohan.

3. Questions can change our state immediately.

Faith is unquestionable belief.

Conversation 2

Arjuun: Krishna. Are you feeling as frustrated as I am about this project?

Krishna: What great impact this project will create in lives of several people?

Arjun: Well, they will only learn that we must fight the evil forces.

Krishna: What great impact this information will create in lives of several people?

Arjun: They must fight even if the forces are their own relatives.

Krishna: What great impact this project will create in lives of several people?

Arjun: Attachment must be destroyed. We must lead our lives in a detached manner.

Krishna: What is great about this project ?

Arjun: Well, demonstration of importance of detachment even while using an activity like war which appears to be completely an attached process.

Krishna: Are you feeling as frustrated about this project now as before?

Arjun: (Smilingly) Not really.

Conclusions: 1. Questions can help you obtain what you were deleting. 2. Questions can change your state immediately.

Questions have the power to affect our beliefs. All human progress has been due to the ability to ask better questions. Questions change focus and how we feel. Questions change the resources available to us, and questions help us acquire what we had been deleting. Since early childhood till death, one activity that human brain continues to perform is asking questions. Thinking is indeed a process of asking and answering questions. Unfortunately most of us unknowingly ask wrong questions most of the time. Consequently, we create problems with ourselves and others in home and in business. Whenever any thing happens, human brain immediately asks two questions:

1. Will this give me pain or pleasure?
2. How can I avoid pain and gain pleasure?

The process of asking more questions continues and our perceptions of who we are and what we are capable of doing and what we are willing to do to achieve our dreams are influenced by the kind of questions we ask. We must learn to consciously control the questions we ask. Questions are the starting point in the process of action as shown below:

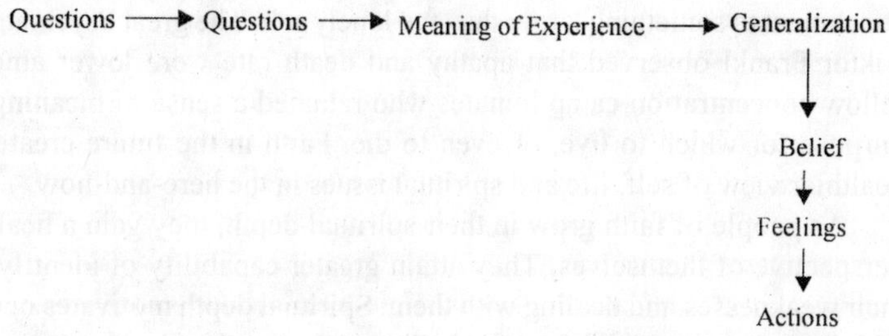

Let us learn about some wrong questions that people ask in different situations, and the right questions that they should ask to get out of the bad situation.

Character

What is character? Your character is the degree to which you live your life consistent with The Natural Principles. Character is the foundational and catalytic ingredient of success. According to Covey, character is indeed the primary greatness and personality is the secondary one. Can people with high character have a poor personality and vice-versa? The answer could be yes or no. Character is the primary greatness. It enables us to lead a principle-based life. Spirituality and character-centredness are closely related to each other. It is a pity that after second world war, our attention shifted totally from character to personality. As a modern successful man you may have lots of money, women, friends, comforts, travels, good job, good future, freedom to do what you want, but this all will not give you real significance until you know where your life is leading, why you are doing what you are doing? You are like getting on road and driving along fine, but not knowing why you chose that particular road, and where it is leading?

Character is the tap root of inner strength. Spirituality brings life to the root. Life is energized by your character. Your power and success flow out of your character. Character-centredness gives the real satisfaction. It creates certain perceptions and attitudes which give real happiness and fulfillment. Poet Norwid has beautifully stated: "To be happy, you should have three things: something to live on, something to live for, and something to die for. The lack of one of these will result in drama, and the lack of two in tragedy."

The fact remains that the search for meaning motivates human beings at one time or another. According to Seligman, "meaning" demands an attachment to something larger than the lonely self. The great Psychiatrist, Viktor Frankl observed that apathy and death rate were lower among fellow concentration camp inmates who retained a sense of meaning- a purpose for which to live, or even to die. Faith in the future creates a healthier view of self, life and spiritual issues in the here-and-now.

As people of faith grow in their spiritual depth, they gain a healthy perspective of themselves. They attain greater capability of identifying their weaknesses and dealing with them. Spiritual depth motivates one to a higher cause in the life and feeds the roots of authentic success.

It is essential that we concentrate on "being" not "having" It means that we must begin from inside and develop character. Instead of focusing too much only on outward performance, we must also focus on our inner being- character. The over-focus only on personality has led to lack of internal motivation and duality- projecting one life and living another. We must live from the inside out.

While developing numerous character qualities, we must realize that all desirable character qualities belong to the concept of authenticity. We must be the same on the inside as we are on the outside. This means being a person of integrity. We must align our inner private life and outer public life with the same principles. It is from here that real energy flows. Make a commitment to be consistent- inside and outside. The focus of this consistency must be based on our value system.

Since you are incharge of your attitudes, you are the master of your attitudes

---

A value is your perception of where you are going in life. Values may change but principles do not. Principles are always true in every circumstance. Although everyone is value-driven, the question here is: are the values based on right, universal principles or not? We must know our values. Values can be identified by answering the following questions:

1. How do you spend your discretionary time?
2. How do you spend your discretionary money?
3. Who are your heroes?
4. When you are alone, what do you think about most?

We must also identify things that are non-negotiable in our life-principles. What principles affect our work, personal life, family, finance, and spirituality? We have to promote values based on universal principles.

We must establish truth in our lives. Unfortunately, we are mostly diluting truth in our lives as we find truth too strong a medicine to digest undiluted. Look what truths we are telling these days:

"Enjoy sex whenever and wherever you wish, but wear a condom" Instead of telling the hard truth, we are substituting it with moral ambiguity. Are we not playing with universal principles? We must be bold enough to tell the society that we should not have sex whenever we wish and whomsoever we wish because it is wrong as it is against the universal principles. Because we have spent many thousand years as a race of rational human beings in discovering a truth that is compatible with universal principle of evolution, and this truth alone can evolve us from animality to divinity.

To establish truth in our lives we must feed our minds with true knowledge through good literature and translate this knowledge into practical living. Knowledge until translated into action is of not much use. Therefore, we must transform knowledge into wisdom by putting knowledge into action as was done by Mahatma Gandhi. We have to grow on daily basis by becoming more aware of opportunities that life gives us in form of adversities, mistakes and failures.

To proceed systematically in this direction, we should separate our life into three areas: personal, family and business, and put our values to work in all these areas. We must strive to develop servant leadership which means build up other people in all possible ways.

A servant leader becomes excited about making others more successful than himself/.herself. Ask yourself: how you can become a servant leader in your personal life? How can you be a source of encouragement even to small people like house keepers, attendants, waiters or even people you call on phone? Your servant leadership in your family may include various activities including devoting time to be with your family members, understanding them, showing respect to their opinions etc. In the area of business, servant leadership may mean developing your employees in a holistic manner, meeting their particular needs and at the same time helping them move towards ultimate success. We must put various servant leadership activities in our weekly schedule and evaluate our efforts on daily basis. At the end of each day, we must ask following questions related to our stated values:

1. Did I schedule my principles and philosophy into my daily schedule?
2. Did I keep my schedule as I planned?
3. How did I spend my idle time?

4. How did I spend my spare money?
5. What did I daydream?
6. Did my values inside match my values outside?

You may establish a support group whose members will regularly ask how you are doing. We must share the truth but not in an offensive manner. We have to be a friend, a servant to meet others' needs and watch them grow. Instead of dealing a conflict in a fight or flight mode, we must learn to be assertive. We must learn to communicate personally, positively, practically and patiently. While communicating, most people will push buttons in you, but you have to learn to be patient during the process of communication. Remember that patience is the most important value based on right principles, that should never be ignored in communication.

A man's character is his guardian divinity
-Heraclitus

Cultivate Spirituality

To cultivate spirituality, pray regularly in a correct manner. Seek forgiveness from God for your failings, thank God for all you have, and simply talk to the God throughout the day just as you would to a friend. Meditate on principles that God is all around us, human beings are basically good and God within us will bring us full joy. You can also meditate on great thoughts that will positively influence your life style, help you grow and build character into your life. Meditate as many times as possible but certainly before going to bed and leaving bed in the morning.

Faith is believing that positive things will come out of wherever you are in life. Faith is only as good as the object in which it is placed. Ask: is this faith historically credible? Do I see evidence of changed lives because of this faith? Does this faith adequately address the core issues in my life- meaning, forgiveness, power, direction, values, etc. The effectiveness of your faith is in direct proportion to your sense of the reality of a living God. Remember that faith is like a muscle- the more you use it, the bigger and stronger it grows. We must learn to express our faith when it comes to resolving any kind of conflict- physical, mental, spiritual, emotional or financial. Build a relationship with God the way you build relationship with any close personal friend. So, build a relationship with God and base your life on character (on "being") so that you become more and more a person of success and significance.

For your holistic development, take following action steps:

1. How do you differ in your character (the real you) and your personality (your external projection) in the following areas:

Area	Character (inner self)	Personality (outer self)
Personal life		
Family life		
Business life		
Social life		

2. How can you create alignment in one of these areas this week? Develop and implement action plan (example- fill your hollowness by building your roots into truth by reading great new books, reflecting on majesty of creation, listing all things you are thankful and meditating on truth several times each day)
3. Which of the three spiritual development skills do you need to focus on at this time? What 15-minutes-a-day practice you can implement to begin?

People with low self esteem deal with their sense of inadequacy with actions of either superiority or inferiority. Superiority complex is as bad as inferiority complex. Both these complexes are the two ends of a rod called low self esteem.

Self Esteem

Every child comes to the world with almost no self concept. Every single concept of who you are is indeed learned through growing up. The child can go in any direction depending upon what happens to him/her after he/she is born. The child comes to this world as a pure sensation with extremely high need for love and touch. The child develops a sense of self by the way he/she is responded by the parents. The messages we send to children influence them the way they see themselves as well as our relationship with them.

Self concept is a combination of all ideas, thoughts, pictures, and experiences that have come to us. Self concept controls our performance as belief is determined by self concept.

Self esteem has been confused with self concept, self worth and similar other terms. Our self-concept means our knowledge, assumptions, and feelings about ourselves. Self-concept is central to most of the mental processes. While self image represents the picture component of belief system, self esteem is the emotional or the feeling component. The self image is what your mind focuses on and your self esteem is how you feel due to this specific image. How do you feel about yourself. is self-esteem. It is your perception of how you are doing in the world. Self-esteem is changeable. Self-worth is what you are born with. As one of the creations of the universe you are worthwhile and have value, which cannot be taken from you. You can't lose it, but you can lose sight of it. You can forget your value.

Self-esteem refers to the feelings of picture of ourselves that each of us carries around in our heads. This image or picture is constructed through our experiences and is strongly influenced by the messages that others send. The way we interact with children on a daily basis influences the positive picture that they construct of themselves. Let them know through our language and our behavior that they are capable and worthwhile and they will begin to believe it. The image component of "who do you think you are" is most important because it is the only component which is under your control. The feeling component is automatic. People fail because of failure-oriented self image not because of lack of abilities. The relationships between self concept, self esteem and success can be depicted as follows:

SUCCESS

↑

ATTITUDE

↑

EXPECTATIONS

↑

BELIEF

↑

SELF CONCEPT

(Around 300 miniconcepts: how lovable I am, how knowledgeable I am, how do I dress etc)

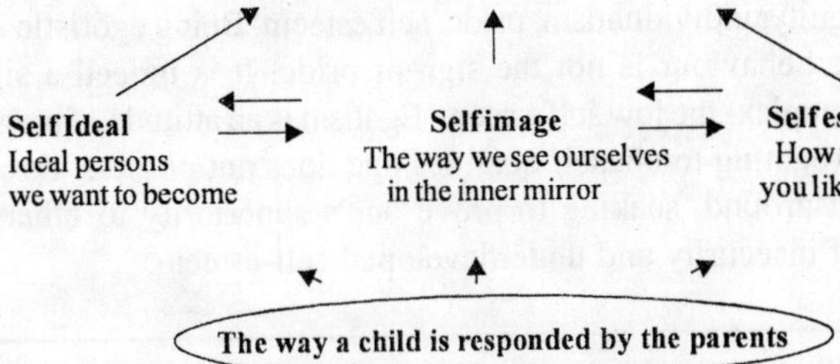

Healthy or high self-esteem is characterized by :

1. Tolerance and respect for others
2. Accepting responsibility for one's actions
3. Having integrity
4. Taking pride in their accomplishments
5. Self-motivated
6. Willing to take risks
7. Capable of handling criticism
8. Loving and lovable
9. Seek the challenge and stimulation of worthwhile and demanding goal
10. Take command and control of their lives

Self Ssteem & Egotism

Egotism, arrogance, conceit, narcissism, violence are actually defensive reactions due to the lack of authentic self-esteem. Individuals with defensive or low self-esteem typically focus on trying to prove themselves or impress others. They tend to use others for their own gain. They have arrogance and contempt towards others. They generally lack confidence in themselves. They have doubts about their worth and acceptability, and hence are reluctant to take risks or expose themselves to failure. They frequently blame others for their shortcomings rather than take responsibility for their actions.

Low self-esteem is closely related to violence, alcoholism, drug abuse, eating disorders, school dropouts, teenage pregnancy, suicide and low academic achievement. Some people feel that we should not have ego. Can we live without ego? Is ego bad? What do we mean by the term "ego"? A newly born baby has ego. We All Have Ego Since Our Birth. Ego is the mark of Image of God within us. That is why you want to be treated with respect. You want to know that you are important. You want freedom, dignity, individualism, pride, self esteem. Being egotistic is bad but egotistic behaviour is not the sign of pride. It is indeed a sign of inferiority complex- the low self esteem. Egotism is an attitude of bragging, boasting, arrogating to oneself qualities one does not possess, throwing one's weight around, seeking to prove one's superiority to others -all evidences of insecurity and underdeveloped self-esteem.

Low self esteem is the root cause of most psychological problems.

Elements of Self Esteem

Self-esteem is difficult to define because of its multiple dimensions. "Self-esteem" is not merely "feeling good" only having positive feelings about oneself. It has both psychological and sociological facets. It includes : cognitive, affective, and behavioral elements.

Cognitive :
Thinks about discrepancy between ones ideal self, and the perceived self
Affective :
Feelings or emotions that one has when considering that discrepancy.
Behavioral :
Assertiveness, resilience, being decisive and respectful of others.

Self-esteem can fluctuate from time to time. Self-esteem is strongly connected to a sense of competence and worthiness. Worthiness (psychological aspect) is not simply feeling good about oneself It includes whether or not a person lives up to certain fundamental human values (finding meanings that foster human growth and making commitments to them in a way that leads to a sense of integrity and satisfaction). Competence (behavioral or sociological aspect) is the conviction that one is generally capable of producing desired results, having confidence in the efficacy of our mind and our ability to think, as well as to make appropriate choices and decisions. For high self esteem, both worthiness and competence are required. Worthiness prevents competence from becoming arrogance. Competence prevents worthiness from becoming egotistic by requiring good feelings to be earned, not given.

Self Love and Self Esteem

The fact is that we cannot love others unless we love our ownself. That is why the spiritual teaching, "Love your neighbour as yourself" is found in all major religions. In the great Indian spiritual text, "Ashtawakra Gita",this great teaching has been described in so many different words. Surprisingly, many persons including some spiritual masters have missed the central point of this teaching. To follow, "Love your neighbour as yourself" who do you begin with? Who do you love and value first? Is it your neighbor or yourself? Most people think it begins with the neighbor. They focus on the neighbor so exclusively that they neglect themselves. They give and give to others until they give out and then sink into hopelessness and helplessness.

Many of us were taught to focus on the neighbor and not on ourselves. As children we are told not to brag or be selfish. As teenagers, wanting to be accepted, we minimize our accomplishments to avoid appearing conceited. As adults we develop a false humility to avoid looking prideful. We may come to not like ourselves and believe that we don't deserve anything good. These false notions damage our self-esteem and we almost forget even about our self worth.

The reality is that loving your neighbor as yourself begins with you. You must love and value yourself if you are to love others. You have to respect yourself and acknowledge your own self-worth. You must take care of yourself so that you *can* love and help your neighbour. Does this make you selfish? No. It makes you responsible.

The most widespread disease in the world today is not cancer or heart disease or AIDS but low self esteem caused by low self image.

Self Esteem and Human Relationship

It is impossible to like or love others more than we like or love ourselves. How much we genuinely like and respect ourselves forms both the outer and inner limits of our relationships with other people. Others will like and respect you to the degree you like and respect yourself.

How much we like ourselves is the critical determinant of the quality of human relations. Most important thing in the life is to learn to like and respect ourselves as a valuable person. Everything we do to raise our own self esteem and to like ourselves even more and to value ourselves and see ourselves as worthwhile and important, will make us like others, and see them as worthwhile and important, and value them. Live to the credo, "Learning to love ourselves and learning to love others" This is self actualization.

Don't neglect others by neglecting yourself. Love yourself so that you can love your neighbor. Don't lose you self-worth. Each day make sure that you take care of yourself so that you *will* be able to take care of your neighbor. When we love ourselves only then we love others. When we give love to others, we get it back many folds. Have kindness and compassion for yourself so that you can have these for others.

People who do not accept themselves as valuable and worthwhile feel frustrations and insecurities in their interactions with others.

Self Esteem & Self Absorption

Doesn't a focus on self-esteem encourage excessive and inappropriate self-absorption? Self-esteem demands focuses on the practices of living consciously, of self-acceptance, of self-responsibility, of self-assertiveness of purposefulness, and of integrity. Self-esteem demands a high reality-orientation; it is grounded in a reverent respect for facts and truth. Excessive and inappropriate self-absorption is symptomatic of poor self-esteem, not high self-esteem.

Can't one have too much self-esteem? No, not if one is talking about reality-based self-esteem rather than grandiosity. It is no more possible to have too much self-esteem than it is to have too much physical or mental health. Look at some other similar confusions tabulated below:

People Confuse Between

A	*B*
Pride	Shame
Self esteem	Narcissisms
Self respect	Vanity
Dignity	Conceit
Individuality	Selfishness

A and B are opposites of each other

Low A = High B=High Self-centredness = **Low happiness**
High A= Low B= Low self- centredness = **High Happiness**

Hunger for self esteem will never go away (self esteem is our relationship to God). Unsatisfied hunger for self esteem leads to its fulfillment through neurotic behaviour and criminal ways.

In today's modern world, we cannot afford to neglect personality. We must therefore develop both: personality as well as character. What is the position of self esteem ? Is self esteem a part of character or personality? Well, self esteem is the bridge that connects personality and character. It is the bridge that connects humanity and divinity. It is the central force which maintains a balance between an individual, society and God.

Your belief about yourself forms your self image. Your self image determines the level of your self esteem. Level of self esteem determines everything in your life. Accept yourself unconditionally. Self acceptance is the foundation of all personal growth because it provides the courage and determination to achieve whatever you want.

Self Esteem and Spirituality

We were created in the image of God. God created everything in the world to serve us, giving us dominion over everything and entrusting us with responsibility and accountability for what we do with creation.

Each human being has an important mission to accomplish that no one else can fulfill. This is the spiritual dimension of self-esteem. Our place in the world is special and we have to figure out how we can contribute with the special gifts or talents God has given us. We must feel good about ourselves and what we are doing. Self-esteem is like a bank account . God makes the initial deposit by creating us in His image. We make deposits into the account by emulating Him when we are compassionate, slow to anger, or pursuers of truth.

California Task Force Definition of self esteem: "Appreciating my own worth and importance, having the character to be accountable to myself, and to act responsibly to others"

Success is synonymous with self esteem

The fastest way to build self esteem is: make the person feel that he/she is responsible for his/her life. We are 100 per cent responsible for our life after our childhood, no matter what kind of childhood we had.

People see in you what you see in yourself.

Changing Your Self – Concept and Building Self Esteem

Step One - *Do an accurate self-assessment. List your positive and negative traits.*

The people who emphasize their bad points and failings need to focus on their assets and positive traits. List your strengths and weaknesses in several areas: appearance, relationships, personality, morals, work (school), art, sports, daily tasks, mental functioning, and sex. Then underline all the negative characteristics. The first task is to re-write each negative statement. This is to be certain that each criticism is stated accurately; for instance, take out all the emotionally laden words. Make the statements factual, not judgmental.

In addition to self-put down words also eliminate over-generalizing words, such as never, always, and completely; these are seldom accurate. In fact, it is beneficial to look for instances or circumstances in which you would not have the negative trait

Step Two - *List the ways you could improve. What are the ways to build self-esteem? Develop self-accepting attitudes.*

Step Three - *Write a list of your more important positive traits. Repeat them frequently with feelings.*

Step Four - *Challenge the internal critic. Then use healthier ways of achieving the critic's purposes.*

Examples of how to **challenge the critic** by saying more reasonable, self-tolerant things to your internal critic:

- "You are putting me down like my parents did, and I'm still accepting this stuff like an unthinking child. I'm not going to take it any more. So, shut up."
- "You say, 'If I had studied, I would have done OK,' but that does not tell about my intellectual ability and finding out just how smart I really am. Let's see how well I can do when I really try."
- "I will feel much better by doing my work and avoiding stinging insults from you. So, shut up!"
- "You think I'd like myself if I were perfect. It's unreal. I'll do it well enough...and still enjoy myself."
- "You are telling me 'I can't do it' so I won't try and get all upset. But I want to carefully make my own decisions about what to do with my life."

Strangely the fears we acquire get translated into verbal messages that keep repeating to ourselves all the time.

To stop the critic's hurtful messages, you can also use thought stopping . As soon as you recognize the critic's voice, yell (silently inside),

"Shut up!" or "Get out of here!" or "This is the crap my mother told me!" or "No more put-downs!" Another way is to think of all the ways low self-esteem hurts you in the long run, e.g. refusing to try things or to meet people, feeling scared and inferior, and unable to express affection, etc., etc. Then say to the critic, "Go away! Look at what you cause me to do...." When you have shut up the critic, replace the negative thoughts with positive ones: "I am a unique and worthwhile person. I have many good traits... I'm in control and doing well."

A very powerful technique for silencing the negative messages of the inner critic is "Five Power Technique" (see last chapter). Further, use self-help methods to achieve the same useful purposes that the unhealthy internal critic is trying to serve so that you won't need the critic. Take following steps:

- Decide what is right to do for rationally choosing your values and learn to live by them.
- Control your behavior and find healthy motives.
- See yourself objectively
- Handle guilt or frustration or self-depreciation
- Reduce the fear of failure. Remember that making mistakes doesn't mean you are worthless. We make decisions based on our views, needs, knowledge and hopes at that moment. What we do is lawful—what seems best at the time.
- Cope with a fear of rejection and learn to handle criticism or to assess the true likelihood and consequences of rejection. Remember good things sometimes result from a failure.
- Deal with anger. Use assertiveness. All of us have to ask for the things we want and politely demand that everyone be dealt with fairly.

Realize that you can feel competent and moral without a nasty, lying and brutalizing critic inside you.

Step Five - *Recognize the internal critic and realize what pain the critic helps you avoid*

The inner voice keeps talking to us all the time. This voice is mostly negative. If you accept this negative voice, you lose your self esteem. The person with low self-esteem may be over-attentive, giving and solicitous, believing that no one will like him/her unless he/she is super nice, or he/she may be hostile and offensive, rejecting the other person first. We must carefully listen to this voice and recognize the critical message. We have to find out what pain this message can help avoid.

Step Six - *Have the serenity to accept the things that can't be changed: Understand and accept your permanent weaknesses; accept the past*

Step Seven - *Learn a variety of self esteem building methods through books, workshops, group activities, and techniques detailed in the last chapter.*

Define yourself as a worthwhile person. Have unconditional self acceptance. You and your activities are different. You are not your activities. Do not evaluate yourself at all. Evaluate your activities not your self. Separate yourself from your performance. Being cannot be measured as doing. Consider yourself as a worthwhile person whether or not you perform well, and whether or not people accept you. Do not give yourself generalized ratings. Conditional self acceptance gives feelings of worthlessness, which leads to self pity.

The Two Mahamantras

All the knowledge contained in the literature can be easily put into action by simply following the two mahamantras. They are:

1. I like myself
2. I am responsible.

Chant these mantras every moment so that they are deeply drilled into your subconscious mind. Follow the mind programming techniques. The subconscious mind, once programmed properly, will automatically take command of your life. You can reprogramme. You can erase the old negative, counterproductive, work – against- you programming and replace it with a healthy, new, positive and productive programming. And it is easy. Erase and replace. All you have to do is learn how to talk to yourself and use proper techniques. You have to make use of your freedom to choose your thoughts, the words that you speak to yourself, and the actions you take.

2
Attitudes for Superior Human Relationship

Humanistic Psychology tells us that around 85 per cent happiness in life comes from good human relationship and only 15 per cent from achievement and success. Superior human relationship is therefore, the most important thing in our life. We interact with others in different ways. We love some people-we don't love some other people; we like some people-we don't like some other people; we respect some people-we don't respect some other people. Our attitudes of love, liking and respect determine our behaviour with others. There are still only 3 basic ways in which human relations problems can be solved:

1. Change the situation: If you do not like your boss, wife, husband, or neighbor, then leave them.
2. Change the person: If the person is bugging you, does things you don't like, has an unpleasant personality, is irritating in some way, then change him/her.
3. Change yourself: You can learn to adapt to the situation or to the person.

Of these, the most effective and easy way is to change oneself. The only person on this earth we can completely change is our own self. We cannot change the fact that people will act in a certain way. We cannot change the inevitable. The only thing that we can do is to play on the one string we have and that is our attitude. Life is 10 per cent what happens to us and 90 per cent how we react to it. And so it is with you to decide how to respond. We can be in charge of our attitudes." Attitude is the foundation for all good human relationships.

What is most important: love, liking or respect? Most people would say : love, but it is not true. It is respect that is most important in human relationship. You love those who have character, you like those who have personality, but your relationship will not be harmonious with others until you respect them. Will you like to have relationship with people who love or like you but insult you? The central theme of human relationship is therefore respect, not love or liking as most people seem to believe.

The Five Basic Attitudes

Attitude is thoughts + feelings + action. These ingredients are related and by changing any one of them, the other two can be easily changed. Thoughts can be easily changed by thoughts, actions can be easily changed by actions, but feelings cannot be easily changed by feelings. The easiest way to change your feelings is change your thoughts or action. What are you doing when you are seeing good things in others? You are changing your feelings for that person by first changing your thoughts for that person- you are adopting a sure, certain and easiest process of changing your feelings. Once the feelings are changed, the required behaviour comes almost naturally. Further, when you focus on good things in others, your actions also start changing which further enhances the process of changing the feelings. The following 5 attitudes are very important for good human relationships:

1. Attitude of understanding

You can either have attitude of understanding (AOU) or attitude of misunderstanding (AOM). We mostly live with the attitude of misunderstanding (AOM). AOM leads to negative feelings which in turn cause negative behaviour. The moment we get AOM, we begin judging others and start rejecting them. Judging is quickly followed by criticism and blaming. . We judge others to defend ourselves, criticize others to feel better and blame others to escape responsibility When you judge, you cut off understanding and shut down the process of learning to love. In judging others, you reflect your lack of self acceptance.

AOM deters us from reaching the true facts. We fail to understand the cause of misbehaviour of the other person . Consequently, our relationship with others starts spoiling. Since almost 85 per cent happiness comes from human relationship, we become unhappy due to poor, dry or cross relationship with our colleagues, subordinates, officers, wife/ husband, children, parents and others.

People mostly have attitude of misunderstanding (AOM) because they – judge, criticize, and blame others. You can never have good interpersonal relationship as long as you hold AOM for the other person.

Make others feel that you are trying to understand them. Communicate an attitude of understanding. Understand why people acted the way they did. And this understanding will alter your feelings of irritation, aggravation, and frustration. The important barriers to understanding are: Justification, self-concern, rationalizing one's own feelings, and refusal to change. AOM also leads to another dangerous attitude, "Attitude of person and non-person"

How to develop an attitude of understanding ?

Understanding is an attitude. You cannot control situations, circumstances and people. But you can develop understanding .With an attitude of understanding , your relationship with other people becomes harmonious. Here are twelve suggestions for developing AOU.

A. Be sure you WANT to understand people. It's easier not to understand the other person or simply dislike a person. As long as you want to be dominated by your own negative feelings, you will never learn to understand others.

B. *Look for the good in others.* For good human relationship, we must have an attitude of respect or attitude of seeing good things in others. Having respect and seeing good things in others are non-different. You don't have to cultivate respect for goodness, it comes automatically. The most fundamental attitude of human relationship is always seeing good things in all people (even your subordinate or child). The attitude of seeing good things in others is the master key of excellent human relationship. According to the laws

---

Every human being yearns for a positive self-image. If a child senses he is a disappointment to those who should love him unconditionally, in desperation, he might seek approval elsewhere, often with negative and destructive peer groups, for example.

---

of psychology, a person can be considered psychologically normal if he can : 1) Always see good things in all people in all circumstances, and 2) deal with people of different age, caste, taste, nationality, beliefs, etc with the same ease. Lord Krishna was such a perfect personality who would always see goodness in all circumstances and people including his enemies. How does this attitude of seeing good things in others work? In Shrimadbhagwatam, it is mentioned that if you focus on any trait or feeling, it will enhance. Accordingly, when you focus on good things in others even when the person is abusing you, his goodness will start growing. When you focus on good things in others, when you focus on good times others gave you, when you focus on help others rendered you, your attitude of understanding others begins to grow and your tolerance for others starts building. Consequently, your relationship with others remains protected from damage.

This attitude of seeing good things in others should be adopted at all times irrespective of what the person is currently behaving or have behaved in the past. If you will stick to this one attitude at all times, you will soon find others seeing only good things in you, and their behaviour shifting from acrimonious to harmonious. Always focus on positive characteristics in the other person. Make it a habit to see good things in others. If you have only positive thoughts of others then you will find it easier to develop AOU.

C. Accept the differences in others. Judging is the root of all problems in human relationship. Judging promptly leads to criticism and blaming. The ways that people are different might be viewed as their faults or weaknesses. We tend to unconsciously judge others. We judge whether or not they are doing something we like or dislike, whether they are right or wrong. If they do not measure up according to your judgment, you stop tolerating them and become irritated. The challenge of an AOU is to have faith in people and believe in them. Strangely, we treat people as imperfect yet expect perfect love from the so called imperfect people. We tend to cast people in a mold of perfection. When the person falls short of our expectations, we become irritated and start criticizing and blaming the person.

D. Never expect people to be perfect. Have faith in people, believe in them, love them, like them, enjoy them – but accept them the way they are! They come with a lot of good and a little bad.

E. Be tolerant of others. All people are different from you. They are not going to act out exactly the way you think it should be done.

F. Learn to love the unlovable. People become rude, sarcastic, arrogant, and self-centered because someone has hurt these people. Someone had made them feel unimportant and unwanted. These are the people who really need our understanding.

G. Get all the facts. If you really knew all inner compulsions, needs, experience, and problems of others, you would not be irritated with another person.

H. Place yourself in the other person's situation. You can "imagine" how another person feels. It gives a bond of feeling and compassion for others.

I. Hate the act, not the actor. Restrict your dislike to "the thing" rather the person.

J. Control the attitudes. Always there is usually nothing in the other person's actions that irritates you. It is your thoughts that cause the negative feelings – the misunderstanding. Learn to control your "thoughts" about others and you will automatically control your feelings.

K. Develop a mental image of understanding. Picture yourself as an understanding, patient, and kind individual. Model your picture, if you wish, after an actual person whom you consider as having those characteristics. Hold that picture in your mind. Start acting out the image.

L. *Use positive affirmations*. Go to alpha level and use proper affirmations of yourself as an understanding person. The technique to reach alpha level is described in the last chapter.

To overcome anger and aggression, choose empathetic understanding over assuming the worst intentions; choose unconditional positive caring over insensitivity; choose the happiness doctrine over the fairness doctrine; choose accepting the unchangeable aspects of reality over hostility—"its the way of things," take constructive energetic actions to help get rid of the steam inside, and remember, there is inherent justice for harmful behaviors and most of all, remember, every moment of anger is one less moment of happiness.

---

2. Attitude of Person-Non-Person

You think of others generally as "persons" or "non-persons". Since all humans have humanity, we should never treat some people as person and others as non-person. Most of the people think that they can hide this attitude but it is impossible to hide any attitude towards others. The ability to see humanity and individuality in others (as "person") is the basic attitude that is required to relate to people in a warm, friendly manner. People will respond to you positively only if you have developed this characteristic. You either have it for all human beings or your attitude tends to become more and more cynical, critical, and indifferent.

To have excellent interpersonal relationships, all you have to do is to relate to others' positive characteristics instead of their negative characteristics. People have both. But if you are always looking for the good things in people, your relationship will be positive and others will react positively to you.

3. Attitude of forgiving

The infliction of suffering by one person on another is a common problem of interpersonal relationship. Forgiving means an attitude of understanding. An important cause of mental distress is the inability to forgive. Life becomes much more harmonious by developing an attitude of forgiving. At one time or another we have all been hurt in our relationships. The reaction to the hurt is to sometimes say, "I will never forgive." Consider this statement, "When you don't forgive, who suffers?" What happens when you don't forgive? Look at the following:

(a) Often you will think about the hurt.
(b) Events of the day will remind you about the hurt.
(c) Once reminded, you start thinking about how bad it was? How unfair ? How you didn't deserve it? You are filled with anger and resentment, or sadness and loss.
(d) You say again, "I will never forgive."

At this point who is feeling bad? Who is miserable? The answer is "You!" Your lack of forgiveness is only hurting you. You end up miserable. Not forgiving and holding a resentment is like having a wound which you check everyday to see if it is healing.

What would happen if you were to forgive? Who would get better? Again the answer is "You!" Always remember that, "Forgiveness is always for you." You don't forgive for the other person. You forgive so you can get better.

Why is forgiveness so difficult? The main reasons are:

1. It is considered as a sign of weakness. We don't want to be weak, so we don't forgive.
2. It can seem like an approval of what happened. We may worry that forgiving might be an invitation to be mistreated again.
3. Not forgiving appears to give a sense of power and control through holding a grudge.

These considerations are baseless. Remember, forgiveness recaptures the energy that you were giving away in sadness, anger, and revenge. Forgiveness also empowers you. It puts you back in charge of you. Forgiveness is a sign of strength. When you forgive someone, you enable that person to contact his/her conscience and change his/her behaviour towards you. Holding on to the pain makes you bitter while forgiving makes you better. Make the better choice. Be a forgiving person.

4. ***Attitude of first meeting the needs of others***

> "To the degree that you give
> others first what they need, they
> will give you what you need."

Determine the needs of others. Be sensitive to determine the needs of the people. First find out what the other person needs, then only the other person will respond to your needs. A wrong attitude which people adopt is "Give me what I need, then I'll give you what you need." This is a wrong attitude which creates problems in human relationships.

5. *Attitude of helping others feel good about themselves*

People always react/respond to you - positively, negatively or passively. Life is pleasurable, if those reactions to you are positive. Remember that people respond favorably to you to the degree you make them feel important and they benefit from your attitudes/actions. Help others feel good about themselves. They should like themselves better when they are talking to you.

3

Principles and Laws Governing Superior Human Relationship

Human beings are highly evolved animals. They are still evolving, but they are most self – destructive beings. They have a deep hunger to feel good about themselves. To make others feel good about themselves, follow these 5 principles :

Principle 1. Let the other persons criticise and advise you.

Most people like to give their opinions, criticize, and advise. Acccpt and use the useful criticism and advise.

Write answers to the following questions:

1. Describe how people react when you ask for their opinions. Do they seem to enjoy it – react favorably to you? How do you feel when you are asked to advise to others?
2. Think and write how can you take criticism and advice without becoming irritated, upset, defensive?
3. Describe people you know who are good at practicing this rule? How do you feel toward them?

Principle 2 - Help the other person succeed

We need people for survival and success. No one can achieve success without help of others. Do not look at the other person as an obstacle to success. Try to make other person's idea work even if it is different from yours. There are always more than one correct way to do a thing properly.

Write answers to following questions:

1. In what ways do you benefit by helping the other person become successful?
2. Name some people you can help to become successful in their endeavours.
3. Name some people you could help whom you do not like? How would it benefit you as a person to do this?

Principle no. 3 – Never Ignore Others (never Pout, Sulk, Brood, or Carry Grudges.)

Write answers to the following questions:

1. Are you carrying a grudge now? Against whom?
2. How do you lose by sulking, brooding, or ignoring others?
3. How do you feel when someone ignores you?
4. How do you feel about people who sulk, brood, or carry grudges?
5. In what instances are sulking and brooding most apt to occur? What are the results?
6. How can sulking, brooding, and carrying grudges be overcome?

Principle 4 - Learn to Tolerate Others Weakness.

People need each other to make up for what they lack. They need you because of their weakness, not because of their strengths. Do you need a doctor when you are well? They need help when something is wrong.

Write answers to following questions:

1. The very thing that you criticize in the other person is the reason that person needs you. What are some of the most common criticism of boss? Husbands? Wife? Children? Friends? Co-workers? Students? Teachers?
2. What are some of the weakness of those you know? How can you help?
3. How do you feel about others who are tolerant of the weakness in others?

Principle 5 – Take Discourtesies, Accusations, and Injustice Calmly, Even the Ones you don't deserve.

You can not control the abusive actions / unjust accusations of others, but you can control your reactions to them.

Write answers to the following questions:

1. In what situations have you been subjected to an unjust, rude, or accusing person?
2. What do you lose by fighting back, arguing, or being hostile?
3. How can you teach yourself to act calmly?
4. "You burn three times as much energy when you are aroused emotionally, and are negative, than when acting calmly and positively." How would you use this principle in your day to day life?

How to Show Respect ?

— Listen respectfully. Show them that you care about their

opinions, and that while you may not always agree with them, their ideas have value.

— Always respect their dignity, their need for space or privacy,
— Never belittle them, or laugh at them.
— Go for respectful discipline. By maintaining your dignity, by not getting personal, by not hitting or name-calling, you communicate the incredibly important twin messages of love and respect.

Law of Indirect Effect

An important law of human relationship is the *Law of Indirect Effect.* This law tells us that happiness comes only when you make somebody happy. If you want to impress someone, first get impressed by that person. That person will get impressed by you to the degree you get impressed by that person. How we make others feel about themselves influences the way we are going to feel about our own self. When you put down others, you feel terribly bad about your own self.

Seven Factors that Make you Likeable

We must always strive to make others feel good about themselves so that we could feel good about our own self. What makes others feel good? There are seven factors that make others feel good. These are:

1. Acceptance: Interpersonal psychology informs us that degree of acceptance is the degree to which a person feels important. Thus acceptance means feeling important. When we meet somebody what is the first thing that we look for in the other person? It is whether the other person shows acceptance for us or not. Acceptance is the deepest subconscious craving in human mind. It begins right in the childhood when a two-year old cannot look at things around for more than 2 minutes without looking into the eyes of the elder/care taker close to the child. The child looks into the eyes of the elder to look for acceptance. This craving continues as long as we live. Acceptance should be total and unconditional. We must accept other human beings irrespective of their age, dress, caste, religion, nationality, status or stature. We must especially show acceptance of those who are different from us.

The best way to show acceptance is smile. A single smile coveys what a thousand words convey. A smile says, "I consider you as a worthwhile person and accept you irrespective of who you are and what you did". It is important to remember that acceptance must be conveyed to others.

2. Approval: It builds self esteem (SE) of the person approved. Praise others for the good job they have done so that their SE goes up. Remember that people repeat actions for which they are praised and stop those actions for which they are not praised. Praise is indeed a miraculous agent that can bring permanent change in behaviour of people. Praise should be done carefully. To be effective, praise should be:

(a) Specific and not general
(b) Intermittent
(c) For the act and not the person
(d) Immediate
(e) Genuine
(f) Done after using statements that convey to the other person that you understand him/her and his/her situation or work

3. *Appreciation*: Use words like "please" and "thank you" to express your gratitude. Appreciation builds SE.

4. *Admiration*: Praise traits like sincerity, honesty, punctuality, and generosity.

5. *Attention*: The more you pay attention to a person, the more you convey to him/her that he/she is valuable. The best way to give attention is to listen actively. Active listening enhances SE of the speaker.

6. *Never criticize*: It lowers the SE of the person and damages human relationship.

7. *Never argue*: When you argue with a person, you indicate to him that he is wrong, his values are wrong and he is worthless.

Developing your Interpersonal Style

The characteristic way in which you think, feel and interact with other people is your interpersonal style. To get a feel for your own style, try to answer the following questions with your initial reactions and write them down.

1. Needs and Wants
(A) How do I let others know my interpersonal needs: directly or indirectly?
(B) Do I resent being challenged?
(C) Do I resent these questions?
(D) Do I like to be reassured?
(E) Do I like to be left alone?
(F) Do I like being assertive and responsible?
(G) Do I want others to take responsibility for me?

2. Caring
(A) Do others know that I care? Is it obvious in my behaviour?

(B) Do I sometimes wonder if I care at all?
(C) Do I take others for granted? If not always, when?
(D) Who really cares for me? Can I list them?
(E) Just how do I show care?
(F) How is care shown to me?

3. Competence
(A) Am I a warm person?
(B) Can I communicate my understanding to others?
(C) Can I communicate my respect to others? If yes, how do I do it?
(D) Am I willing to talk openly about myself?
(E) Can I challenge others and invite them to explore their behaviour without being accusatory or punitive?
(F) When I meet strangers, am IS awkward, embarrassed, resentful, enthusiastic, poised or confident?

4. Emotions
(A) What do I do about my emotions when in public places?
(B) Do I try to hide them or some of them?
(C) Is it easy for others to judge how I feel?
(D) Am I moody?
(E) Am I comfortable when I am with someone who is expressing deep emotion?
(F) How do I react when others keep their emotions to themselves?

5. Intimacy
(A) With whom do I have intimate relationships?
(B) How far do I let intimacy go without stopping it?
(C) What does intimacy mean to me?
(D) Do I recognize different ways in which intimacy can be expressed?
(E) What kind of people attract me?
(F) What kind of intimacy do I find 1. Most rewarding, 2. Most interesting?

6. Rejection and Alienation
(A) Is loneliness ever a problem for me?
(B) Do others see me as a lonely person?
(C) What do I do when I see others who appear lonely?
(D) What circumstances or experiences do I find threatening in my relationship with others?
(E) Do I ever ignore or reject others?

(F) How do I respond to people who want to relate to me?

7. Interpersonal Influence
(A) Do I try to manipulate others when dealing with them?
(B) Do people try to manipulate me?
(C) Do I tell people exactly what I want from them?
(D) Am I usually dominant or submissive in my relationship with others?

8. Mutuality
(A) Do I allow for give and take in my relationship with others?
(B) Am I usually authoritarian or parental in my relationship?
(C) Am I democratic, laissez-faire or do I compromise when reaching agreement with others?
(D) Do I encourage dialogue?
(E) Do my relationships involve mutual responsibility?

9. Work Relationships
(A) How do I get along in my various work relationships?
(B) Do I treat people at work as people or as roles ?
(C) Do I assert myself with my superiors?
(D) Am I understanding with my subordinates?
(E) Am I a loner at work?
(F) Am I over-personal at work?

10. Values
(A) Which of the previous headings would I identify as my main interpersonal values?
(B) What am I willing to risk with others?
(C) In what areas am I not willing to risk?
(D) Am I tolerant of others who have different opinions to my own?
(E) What are my prejudices?
(F) How rigid or flexible am I in my relationships with others?
(G) Do I share my values and beliefs with others?

The main purpose of these questions is to start you thinking about your own personal style. Reflect on your answers and make a note of any new insights or patterns you may become aware of.

The Platinum Key

You are Sat- Chit- Anand. You are here to enjoy the supreme pleasure. Anand is easiest to get. You cannot get anand without respecting others.

We are all non-different spiritually and acceptance is the deepest craving in human nature. That is why showing respect for others thoughts, feelings and behaviour is so important. To show respect, focus on virtues of others. This focus on positive in others automatically changes the meaning of experience which gives birth to belief. Belief as you are aware causes feelings which in turn determine behaviour. Since you cannot respect others without respecting your own self, you have to constantly ask yourself 3 golden questions depicted in form of the platinum key below:

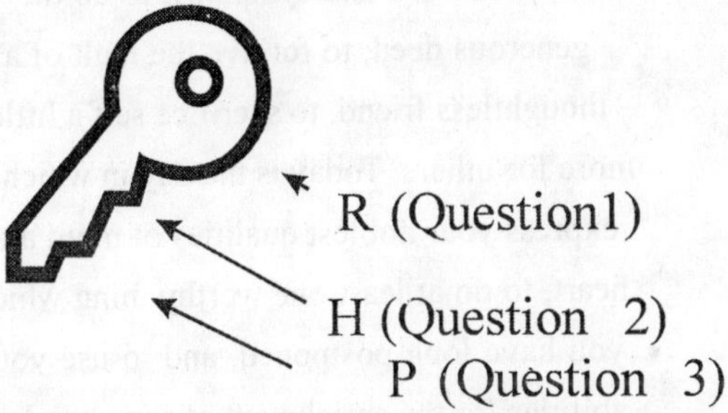

Question 1 : What for do I respect this person? If you don't get the answer, reframe the question: What for can I respect this person, if I wanted to?

Question 2 : What for do I respect myself? If you don't get the answer, reframe the question: What for can I respect myself, if I wanted to?

Question 3 : What for am I proud of myself ? If you don't get the answer, reframe the question: What for can I be proud of myself, if I wanted to?

"There are many fine things which you mean to do someday, under what you think will be more favorable circumstances. But the only time that is surely yours is the present, hence this is the time to speak the word of appreciation and sympathy, to do the generous deed, to forgive the fault of a thoughtless friend, to sacrifice self a little more for others. Today is the day in which to express your noblest qualities of mind and heart, to do at least one worthy thing which you have long postponed, and to use your abilities for the enrichment of someone less fortunate. Today you can make your life....significant and worthwhile. The present is yours to do with it as you will"

4

Emotions

Negative Emotions

All unhappiness, crimes and diseases are rooted in negative emotions. None of the 54 negative emotions is caused from outside. All negative emotions are already inside us. Every negative emotion is our reaction to the situation, and not contained in the situation. The three major negative emotions are fear, anger and guilt.

Fear

Fear plays an essential role in nearly all our psychological problems. Whenever trauma knots get triggered by our thoughts or by life events, fear arises. For it was fear of fully experiencing the original traumas that caused them originally to be tied in knots. Stress is fear. Fear shows itself in a multiplicity of ways. Those who were not loved will often sabotage their close relationships because of fear of being loved. Those who couldn't ask their parents for love will fear doing so with their current partners.

Those who were trained to be tough will be afraid of signs of weakness (weakness according to their definition). Those who learned to be afraid of anger will often have fearful rationales for their avoidance of anger. Phobias, anxieties and depression are symptoms that often have significant roots in fear. Whatever trauma knots you have not resolved will cause you fear (i.e., stress).

Often we deny the fear, switching instantaneously to anger, addiction, depression, or other favorite dodges. It is often an important first step just to recognize the fear as fear. The process of change can then start, for one can examine the situation more rationally to see if fear is warranted. Perhaps something different next time can be experienced instead of getting locked in the fear. Much fear is fear acquired as a child, which frequently may be discarded once it is in full conscious awareness. If it cannot be discarded, then examining the relevant trauma knots may be required.

Emotionally healthy adults (with respect to fear) have following characteristics:

1. They are not fearful or anxious for other than brief periods of time.

2. They will experience fear (or anger) if physically threatened. (This is the natural fight/ flight response.)

3. They are able to confront and change their fear-causing beliefs to happier beliefs. Thus, they do not get stuck in stress.

4. They are often capable of appropriate action, despite high levels of fear.

Few of us achieve the above, yet wouldn't you be happier if you could? There are several so-called emotions that are inherently stuck. Feel them and you stay in them. They remain around forever, unless the real truths beneath them are felt. Some inherently stuck feelings are: guilt, jealousy, depression, humiliation, shame and degradation. Feeling them for any longer than it is necessary to recognize them is not productive. Be on the lookout behind these stuck feelings for other unwanted feelings (such as childhood hurt, love, fear, rage or grief) which, if felt, could help change the immobility

Most of our emotional expressions are skewed. The reason is that 97 per cent of us learned in our growing-up years to stuff one or more of our emotions (causing trauma knots). Stuffed emotions are remembered by our bodies and our unconscious minds, and they act like internal irritants. They keep causing us anxiety and keep leading us into addictive situations in which we can discharge the irritating energy in a skewed fashion. A skewed discharge reduces our anxiety, although temporarily. A discharge of most of the important emotions of the original trauma knot, on the other hand, usually eliminates the knot.

Anger

There are 54 negative emotions like doubt, envy, fear, jealousy, guilt etc., and nearly all the 54 negative emotions boil down to ANGER directed inwardly or outwardly. Anger causes a number of problems including cancer, depression, blood pressure anomalies etc.

Anger is a signal. The significance of anger is to act as a signal that something in our lives needs to be changed. It is not a tool to control others or a weapon to blast family and friends, although that is the most common use for anger. The justification for its destructive use (for parents and children) is that other people are to be blamed for one's own problems.

When we blame others, we are absolved of all anger management responsibility. Listen to children talk about why they got angry and hit another child. It will almost always be because the other person "made them" do it because they took their toy or hit them first or said something mean. Blame the other person and they are required to change, not you. You didn't do anything wrong, right? Wrong! The only thing we have absolute, 100 per cent control over is ourselves.

Anger and Belief

Anger and other related emotions cannot arise unless the following four irrational beliefs exist:

1. Awfulizing
2. Can't-stand it
3. shoulding/musting
4. Undeservingness or damnation

Anger will not be created without attaching emotional idea to the term "awful". Thus awfulizing is the basis of irrationality. Awfulizing means something beyond actual unpleasantness of the action. This awfulness which you add, means that action has more than badness and it must not exist. The rational ideas, "very bad", "ugly", "disagreeable", "disappointed" or "frustrated", after adding "awfulness" now mean that this action has more than badness. It means that Ms A treated me 100 per cent badly or more than 100 per cent badly which in reality can never happen.

A (Activating expeience) → B (Belief system) → C (Emotional consequence)

Although C is triggered by A, C does not directly & fully result from A. It is the evaluation done at B which determines C. To manage anger, you have to manage belief. To manage belief, you have to analyze belief. To analyze belief, first analyze C. To analyze C, find out whether you are feeling anger, anxiety or depression. Irrational beliefs about others cause anger, irrational beliefs about self lead to anxiety, and irrational beliefs about conditions lead to depression.

Let us take an example to understand the relationships between origin of anger, anxiety and depression, and the irrational beliefs.

I am living in Mumbai in a rented house. The rent is high and I am economically pressured. One day, I accidently meet Gita, a young lady I knew since my childhood. We were neighbours in a small village. Gita had the same problem in Mumbai as I had- high house rent. I suggested her to share the accommodation with me and pay half the rent. Gita agreed provided I got a new bed and got my room painted. She promised to move into my flat on 15th May. I had 10 days for the preparations, but no money, so I borrowed Rs. 5000 from a friend. I readied the accommodation on 13th May. On 15th May, she phones at 10:00 AM, "Pathak, thanks for being so helpful, but I am sorry, I won't be sharing the accommodation with you, as I got a cheaper and better room close to my workplace".

What do you guess I would feel? Anger, anxiety or depression? What irrational beliefs must exist before I feel these feelings? Look at the following table:

Irrational Belief	*Type of Irrational Belief*	*Outcome*
1. Awfulizing	How awful that she treated me like this	Anger
	How awful that I cannot manage	Anxiety
	How awful that things have turned out so badly for me	Depression
2. Can't stand it	I can't stand her irresponsible behaviour	Anger
	I am not able to cope up with the inconvenience	Anxiety
	I can't stand things turned out this way	Depression
3. Shoulding	She should not have acted in this bad manner	Anger
	I should have ability to cope up	Anxiety
	Things should not have happened this way to me	Depression
4. Damnation	Because she behaved badly, she is a rotten person and deserves punishment	Anger
	I don't cope as well as I must. I am inferior and deserve punishment	Anxiety
	Nothing ever works out the way I want. Life is always unfair to me.	Depression

Anger, anxiety or depression cannot appear in absence of the four irrational beliefs. Why these beliefs are irrational? The analysis in respect of anger will be as follows:

1. How awful that she treated me like this? The situation was not

really awful. It would have been so had she arrived, shared the accommodation, but refused to pay half the rent. She at least cared to inform me that she would not be coming for the valid reasons. So, she did not cheat me. The financial burden I got into can be reduced if not compensated. The awfulness is not in her behaviour but in my beliefs.

2. I can't stand her irresponsible behaviour? Her behaviour was not irresponsible. The situation is not awful, and I am not going to die due to her behaviour. I can stand her behaviour.
3. She should not have acted in this bad manner to me. Was her manner rally bad? Why should she spend more money on rent and go for other inconveniences because of me? People will not behave the way I would like them to. How I would have behaved, had I been in her situation?
4. Because she behaved badly, she is a rotten person and deserves punishment. People and their acts are not same. We can never judge people by their actions. In the first place should we judge anybody? People are people, neither good nor bad. A person will act at a particular moment in a manner that he/she considered most appropriate. She does not deserve a punishment simply because she did not share the accommodation with me.

The above analysis reveals that the four beliefs that give rise to anger are irrational. Instead of getting controlled by them, we must control them at the earliest. The anger comes as a signal to inform us that our beliefs are going to be irrational unless steps are taken to challenge and control them. Management of anger means management of irrational beliefs. Dr. Albert Ellis and associates have proved that anger control can be achieved by changing the irrational beliefs.

The basic premise of the anger management for families should include:

1. Anger is a natural human emotion. It is O.K. for children and parents to feel angry. It is not O.K. to use it to hurt your self or others. Knowing how to control anger is not natural and must be taught by significant adults in our life.

2. Children must learn how to control self before they can control anger. Self control can be learned by simple children's activities (i.e., play). These activities must be developmentally appropriate and fit the age of the child.

3. In order to help children cope with their anger, adults must become aware of how anger affects their life. They also must be a model of appropriate anger management.

4. Adults must intervene when anger becomes explosive and use appropriate methods to cope with angry children.

A common myth of anger management in our society is that anger is bad and therefore it must be eliminated. Take for example the parent who tells the child to go to her room when she gets angry or the parent who doesn't allow anger feelings to be expressed in the home. This is due to the parent's feeling of discomfort with anger and not the child. And it most probably stems from the parent's own childhood experiences with anger with his parents.

The reality is that anger cannot be eliminated no matter how you try. If you succeed in suppressing it, it will only come out some other way. Push it in one side and it comes out another. A more common example is the parent who comes home from a particularly tough day at work and yells at the children. Although the children might have been misbehaving, the reality is that the parent is reacting from the earlier days events more than the immediate situation.

Can you remember a time when you were angry? How about a time when you were a child and you were angry? What did your parents or adults do when you were angry? Did they tell you to go to your room? Did they punish you for being angry? Did they talk to you about the problem without shaming or blaming you for your anger?

Parents have a tough time dealing with anger in children simply because they did not learn how to deal with anger as children. Our parents did not know how to deal, and so, we don't know how to deal. Or, what worked for our parents doesn't seem to work in today's society.

In order to help our children know how to manage anger we must get in touch with what it was like to be an angry child. Take a few moments to remember what it was actually like, for you, as a child, to be angry. Did you feel your anger physically? Headaches, stomach aches, cold flashes, hot flashes, dry mouth, tears, numbness, tingling fingers? These are all symptoms of anger. How did you express your anger? Yelling, sarcasm, cynicism, rapid speech, overeating, arguing, hitting, revengeful fantasies, isolation and withdrawal, stealing? These are all ways people express their anger.

Children do not naturally know how to deal with anger. Anger is a natural emotion but anger controls must be taught and modeled to children. And if parents did not learn them as children, they must learn them now.

Here are four steps to manage your anger and your child's anger:

1. Identify the underlying cause. Don't over-focus on the symptoms. Look at what is causing the situation. What stressors are occurring in

your life? Who is involved in the situation? What other feelings are you experiencing? Are you overly tired, hungry, scared, lonely, bored, or nervous? Much of our anger stems from other sources and is almost always tied into other stressors. Anger is mostly displaced.

2. Decide how to behave. This is best done ahead of time. Anger cuts off our rational thinking skills. Take a time-out to cool down. Use "I" message and not "You" messages to decrease defensiveness. Do something physical, such as walking, jogging, or playing. Count to ten or backwards from one hundred in the heating situation.

3. Talk directly with the person involved. Pick a good time to talk to the other person. Look at the person you are talking to. Use a calm and natural voice. Use "I" messages. Alternate listening with talking. Reflect the viewpoint or feelings of the other person to build cooperation. Don't interrupt. If you are too angry, practice with a friend before communicating. Be persistent. If you do not get what you want or need the first time, wait and try again later.

4. Get help. If steps 1, 2, and 3 do not produce the results you want, find someone to help you negotiate, manage, or mediate the angry situation.

Anger Management Kit

1. How am I feeling right now? The first step in resolving our anger problem is to **identify** it as anger! The purpose of this step is to make our anger more specific. No one can manage anger that is vague and covered up. The following table lists some feelings. These are some of the names that we give to our feelings of anger! There is no cure for any of them :

___ Anxious	___ Worthless	___ Hostile	___ Depressed
___ Mean/evil	___ Revengeful	___ Bitchy	___ Bitter
___ Rebellious	___ Paranoid	___ Victimized	___ Numb
___ Sarcastic	___ Resentful	___ Frustrated	___ Destructive

2. What happened to make you angry? Focus on the specific incident which triggered your anger.

3. Who am I angry at? Our anger usually will involve five (5) general areas.

(1) Our anger at others, (2) Others anger at us, (3) Our anger at self, (4) Residual anger from the past, or (5) Abstract anger.

4. How did the situation make me feel besides angry? Pin-point your feelings underlying your anger (Example : His criticisms of me makes me feel unappreciated and good for nothing.)

5. What about this angers me the most? Peel your anger down to the next layer.

For example, you have established the fact that in the above situation it made you feel powerless, unappreciated or good for nothing. Now take a closer look at these feelings underlying your anger. What is it about being made to feel powerless that angers you the most? You might find upon deeper analysis that:

- "there is nothing that I can do about it."
- "I feel so stupid!"
- "I feel guilty for allowing it to happen."
- "I feel inadequate to cope with this situation."

6. Now, what about this angers me the MOST? Penetrate your anger at its deepest level. Focus on the real issue underlying all of the prior layers and levels of your emotional distress. Come to the fundamental issue which underlies all the others, and which must be identified and relieved. For example you discovered : "I feel so worthless!" The final step in managing our anger will consist of replacing this feeling or worthlessness with self respect.

Four proven techniques of anger management

1. Identify the mistaken attitudes and convictions that predispose to being excessively angry.Once these mistakes have been corrected, we will be less likely to fly off the handle than we were in the past.

2. Identify those factors from childhood that prevent from expressing anger appropriately (fear, denial, ignorance and so on). These impediments to the effective and appropriate management of anger towards others can be removed so that suppressed anger will not compound itself inside.

3. Learn the appropriate modes of expressing our "legitimate" anger at others so that we can begin to cope more effectively with anger provoking situations as they arise. Further, when we are anxious or depressed in our relationships, we are often experiencing the consequences of our suppressed anger. We have suppressed our anger so deeply that we succeeded in concealing it from even our own selves. Consequently, all we are left with is the residual evidence of it (anxiety / depression). When we are depressed, very often we are also angry at our self without realizing it. Learning to appropriately manage our anger at ourselves is the antidote to much of alcoholism and drug abuse.

4. Bind up the wounds left by the potentially devastating emotional

impact of anger. "Anger wounds" left in are against those who have wronged us. Forgive others

Besides these techniques, some other techniques like desensitization, paradoxical intention technique, referenting etc. are very effective. These are described in the last chapter.

Guilt

Guilt is worst of all negative emotions. Guilt has been the major psychological problem of 20th Century. Guilt is the major cause of all broken marriages and other psychological distortions. We begin to receive guilt as a child. A child, the victim of destructive criticism, growing without/ with inadequate love cannot understand why he/she is being continuously criticized. The child therefore gets convinced that he/she has done something wrong and therefore mom / daddy condemn me and don't give me love. This is how the child begins to feel guilty.

A person suffering from guilt engages in destructive criticism of self and others: "I am late", " I am incapable", "I am not good enough for this", etc., and he/she finally engages in criticizing others. Such a person can be easily manipulated by guilt. The guilt throwers and guilt catchers attract each other and guilt gets perpetuated. Such a person is continually blaming others and making others feel guilty.

We all remember the injustice done to us by our parents. As a child we looked at our parents as God, and as adult we never realize that parents after all are human beings with feet of clay. As an adult it is traumatic for us to remember that one or both the parents did not love us. We push out this traumatic thought, and this causes undue stress and strain in our conscious and subconscious minds.

To eliminate guilt, we must forgive our parents 100 per cent for everything they did to cause unhappiness to us. The moment a thought of blaming parents arises, cancel it and say I forgive them 100 per cent. Talk to your parents and tell them that you forgive them 100 per cent.

There are four strategies to eliminate guilt:

1. Eliminate destructive criticism and never allow any body to say negative things about you. Never have any negative feelings about your ownself, and never say anything negative to yourself that you don't want to happen.
2. Refuse to be manipulated by guilt thrown by others. Whenever you find that people are trying to make you feel guilty, smile and say in a calm voice, " You are trying to make me feel guilty. Are you?" If the person tries again, interrupt again and repeat what

you said earlier. Break the pattern. Never allow others to make you feel guilty. Remember people use guilt as a habit unconsciously on a regular basis.

3. Refuse to use guilt on others. Whenever you feel tempted to blame others, remind yourself that no one is guilty and you alone are responsible for your own life. Never blame others otherwise you will yourself get trapped by guilt.
4. Follow the law of forgiveness: Forgiveness is a way of releasing ourselves from the pain we have experienced at the hands of others. It is a release from judgment, including our judgment of ourselves.

Forgiveness

Forgiveness is not Condemnation. Forgiveness does not mean you agree with what the other person did to you. It does not mean you can change what happened or erase what they did. What's done is done. All you can do is release yourself.

Forgiveness is indeed not for others, it's for You. Forgiveness is not something you do for someone else, but to free yourself from the continuation of pain and anger. It is a gift to your peace of mind, your self esteem, your relationships with others, your future.

Ability to forgive completely is the hallmark of a truly healthy personality. To hold grudges is the sign of diseased personality. Never allow this negative garbage to accumulate in your mind. The three categories of people who need to be forgiven are:

(a) Parents
(b) People other than parents
(c) Yourself

Research findings have clearly revealed that an average adult is still walking around with deep rooted feelings of bitterness and anger towards one or both parents. You will never become an adult in yourself and never develop adult relationship with your parents, and develop ability to interact with them as human beings and friends until you forgive your parents totally. The glorious day in your life will come when you have sincerely forgiven your parents totally, and have started seeing them as human beings, and to relate them as human beings and friends. You have to forgive persons other than parents especially those who have caused you pain. This must be done because we alone are fully responsible for our own life.

Forgive yourself 100 per cent for all the mistakes you have done.

Accept yourself and feel that you are a human being, and go ahead. Accept responsibility but don't blame yourself. Acceptance of responsibility is directly proportional to control, freedom and positive emotions.

New studies clearly show that anger and resentment double the risk of myocardial heart attacks in women with previous coronary problems. Other studies indicate that cancer and other deadly illnesses are also caused by anger and resentment. So be willing, for your sake, to begin to process out these deadly emotions as soon as possible.

Being forgiving is a courageous act on your part. It has nothing to do with whether the other person can admit they are wrong. You are forgiving to liberate yourself no matter what the other person decides to do.

Find a new way to think about the person who wronged you. What was his or her life like growing up? What was his or her life like at the time of the offense? What were this person's good points up to the time of the hurt? Notice you may not be able to see much good within until you have processed out your anger and/or grief or fear.

Understand that forgiveness does not condone or approve or forget the harmful acts; forgiveness does not allow yourself to be abused. We forgive the doer, not the doing. Remembering this helps us to break harmful cycles of behavior. Realize that you are the only person responsible for your own feelings and for healing the hurt that is going on inside of you.

Understand that love is what you ultimately want for yourself from yourself. Regardless of what the other person does, see the person with love and goodness. Forgiveness is a way of releasing ourselves from the pain we have experienced at the hands of others. Be willing to do and learn whatever it takes to forgive. Commit to do processes, to read courageous stories of forgiveness, to write in journals, to see a therapist, to do trainings, or to do whatever it takes to heal the wounds involved. Remember these wounds may be deeply tied to past hurts going back to your interactions with your parents. Resolve to follow them through for your total healing. Remember that the true happiness and joy will come from true forgiveness. Decide to forgive. Even if this decision is half-hearted at first, it will lessen your hurt and anger immediately.

We must apologize if we have committed a mistake. To apologize is the hardest thing for some people. They think that apologizing is a sign of weakness while it is a fact that only strong can apologize and not the weak. Clear your slate by apologizing.

10 Ways To Forgive Others

1. Understand that forgiving does not mean giving permission for the behavior to be repeated. It does not mean saying that what was done was acceptable. Forgiveness is needed for behaviors that were not acceptable and that you should not allow to be repeated.

2. Recognize who is being hurt by your non-forgiveness. Does the other person burn with your anger, feel the knot in your stomach, experience the cycling and recycling of your thoughts as you re-experience the events in your mind? Do they stay awake as you rehearse in your mind what you would like to say or do to 'punish' them? No, the pain is all yours.

3. Do not require to know 'why' as a prerequisite to forgiveness. Knowing why the behavior happened is unlikely to lessen the pain, because the pain came at a time when you did not know why. Occasionally there are times when knowing why makes forgiveness unncessary, but they are rare. Don't count on it and don't count on even the perpetrator knowing why.

4. Make a list of what you need to forgive. What was actually done that caused your pain? Note what you felt, what was done.

5. Acknowledge your part. Were you honest about your hurt or did you hide the fact that the behavior hurt you? Did you seek peace by reassuring the perpetrator that it was all right? Did you stay when you could or should have left? If so, then you, too, have some responsibility. Here you start to move away from being a victim.

6. Make a list of what you gained from the relationship, whatever form of relationship it was. Looking back you may be focusing on the negatives, the hurts. Yet if they were repeated, you must have stayed to allow the repetition. You did not remove yourself. Why? There must have been some positives if you chose to stay around. What were they?

7. Write a letter to the person (no need to mail it). Acknowledge what you gained from the relationship, and express forgiveness for the hurts. Allow yourself to express all your feelings fully. Do not focus only on the hurts.

8. Create a ceremony in which you get rid of your lists and the letter, so symbolizing the ending of the link between you. You may choose to visualize placing them on a raft and watching it drift gently away down a river. You may prefer to burn them and scatter the ashes. You may invent some other form of ritualized separation.

9. Visualize the person you are forgiving being blessed by your forgiveness and, as a result, being freed from continuing the behavior that hurt you.

10. Now that you have freed yourself from the painful links and released the pain, feel yourself growing lighter and more joyous. Now you are free to move on with your life without that burden of bitterness. Do not look back in anger.

Worry

Worry is an important epidemic in the psychological world. Worry is a sustained form of fear caused by indecision. We always learn worrying from the parents.

It's not what happens to us but our response to what happens to us- that hurts us

We always worry about something which would never happen.. Worry is a negative goal setting. We are imagining and thinking exactly what we don't want to happen. The laws of attraction and expectation make worry a monster. The best antidote to worry is deliberate and systematic action.

What to do?

1. Write on a paper, what you are worrying about? Define clearly.
2. Ask what is the worst outcome of the situation possible and write down all the possible worst outcomes clearly.
3. Resolve to accept the worst outcomes and say," I will live with it. It will not kill me."
4. Swing into action and begin improving upon the worst that might happen. Take positive steps.

Emotions give us messages, which must be clearly understood so that proper solutions are searched and applied. The following table depicts messages and solutions of some important emotions.

Emotion	*Message*	*Remedy*
Fear : apprehension, low concern, intense worry, anxiety, freight, terror	Anticipation that something wrong is going to happen. Make preparations soon.	Review feelings. Clarify what you want. Change your way of feeling. Change approach to solution.
Anger : mild irritation to rage	The important rule/standard that you hold true for your life has been violated by other person or you.	Realize that you have completely misinterpreted the situation. Change your perception: may be the person did not know your rules/standards. Find out within yourself why the other person does not know what is most important for you. Ask: how can I communicate information about my rule/standard? Change your perception: you did not communicate your need properly. Tell the person straight what do you want. Realize your rules may be wrong. Ask yourself: "In the long run, is it true that this person cares for me?" What can I learn from this?.
Hurt : sense of loss, loss of trust	Your expectation has not been met	Realize that you have really lost nothing. Lose the false perception that other person is trying to hurt you.Realize that other person does not realize impact of his action on your life. Tell yourself that you are judging the situation too early & harshly. Communicate your feelings of loss properly to other person.
Guilt: Painful emotion to an experience	You have violated one of your highest standards. Do something so that you don't violate it again in future. Don't surrender to guilt by experiencing learned helplessness	Acknowledge that you violated a critical standard. Commit yourself to make sure that this behaviour never happens again in future. Rehearse in your mind how you

		could deal with guilt-producing situation.
Frustration: putting efforts but not getting rewards, surrounded by road blocks	You believe that you could be doing better than you currently are. Be more flexible.	This emotion is your friend so brainstorm to find new ways to get results. Find how to deal with the situation. Find a role model. Find how you will deal with this situation in best possible manner in future.
Inadequacy: Feeling of unworthiness, when we feel we cannot do something we should be able to do. Mostly, we have an unfair rule to determine whether we are inadequate or not	You don't presently have a level of skill for the task at hand.. You need more information, understanding, strategies, tools & confidence.	Ask yourself:"Is this really an appropriate emotion to have to feel in this situation.?" "Am I inadequate or do I have to change my perception?" Find a way to do something better than you have done before. Remind yourself that you are not perfect and that you don't need to be. Commit to constant & never-ending commitment in the area. Find a role model. Realize you are not inadequate. You may be untrained/unskilled in a area.

"Create your own reality."

Eliminate Negative Emotions

To eliminate negative emotions, consider them like a tree. You have to kill this tree. There are two ways to do this.

1. Stop nutrients to the tree roots
2. Cut the tree down the trunk

The two nutrients to the roots are :

(a) Justification.

(b) Identification

We can only experience negative emotion to the degree to which we can justify our right to the negative emotion. We feel we are entitled to anger, hate etc. As long as we justify a negative emotion, we cannot eliminate the concerned negative emotion.

We have to remember that we can only experience a negative emotion to the degree to which we identify ourselves with the situation and take personally. To stop negative emotions, we must stop justification and identification.

The tree of negative emotion has a trunk of blame. Every negative emotion originates from the trunk of blaming somebody. We have to cut the tree down the trunk which means we have to stop blaming. Stop blaming others. To do this use the Law of Substitution. already described in the first chapter.

According to this law, conscious mind can use only one slot at a time, and you can short circuit the negative emotion by saying, "I am responsible". Say it immediately 5 times. The more we say "I am responsible", the more we assert complete control over our conscious mind. As long as we are saying "I am responsible", it is impossible for the negative emotion to get rooted and grow in our conscious mind.

5
Communication

Limitations in Human Communication

Human beings are the biggest problems for human beings. The most important cause of human problems is faulty communication. The process of talking and listening is far more complicated than realized. Human limitations in communication are enormous. The talker is rarely able to communicate fully his thoughts and feelings and the listener is rarely able to understand fully what the talker intended to communicate. Words are inefficient vehicle for thoughts and feelings while non-verbal language is poorly understood by most human beings.

There is an external event and we run that event through our internal processing. The events come through visual (including the sights we see or the way someone looks at us), auditory (including sounds, the words we hear and the way that people say those words to us (unless you specifically want variety in form), kinesthetic (external feelings which include the touch of someone or something, the pressure, and texture), olfactory (smell) and gustatory (taste).

We make an Internal Representation (I/R) of every event. That I/R of the event combines with a physiology and creates a state. "State" refers to the internal emotional state of the individual — a happy state, a sad state, a motivated state, and so on. Our I/R includes our internal pictures, sounds and dialogue, and our feelings (for example, whether we feel motivated, challenged, pleased, excited, and so on). A given state is the result of the combination of an internal representation and a physiology.

Why and How we Delete, Distort and Generalize the Information?

Normally, the conscious mind can only handle 7 (plus or minus 2) items of information at any given time. Of course, many people can't even handle this number. How about you? Try this: Can you name more than 7 products in a given product category, say cigarettes? Most people will be able to name 2, may be 3 products in a category of low interest and usually no more than 9 in a category of high interest. There is a reason for this. If we didn't actively delete information all the time, we'd end

---

> A powerful agent is the right word. Whenever we come upon one of those intensely right words..., the resulting effect is physical as well as spiritual, and electrically prompt.
>
> Mark Twain

---

up with too much information coming in. That's why we filter the information. When two people have the same stimulus, they don't have the same response because they delete, distort, and generalize the information from the outside.

Deletion

We selectively pay attention to certain aspects of our experience and not others. We then overlook or omit others. Without deletion, we would be faced with much too much information to handle with our conscious mind.

Distortion

We make shifts in our experience of sensory data by making misrepresentations of reality. A man walking along the road sees what he believes to be a snake and yells "SNAKE." However, upon arriving at that place he is relieved as he discovers that what he sees is really only a piece of rope. Distortion also helps us in the process of motivating ourselves. The process of motivation occurs when we actually distort the material that has come into us that has been changed by one of our filtering systems.

Generalization

We draw global conclusions based on one or two experiences. At its best, generalization is one of the ways that we learn, by taking the information we have and drawing broad conclusions about the meaning of the effect of those conclusions.

We delete, distort and generalize the information that comes in from our senses based on one of five filters: meta- programs, values, belief system, memories and decisions.

Meta-Programs:

The first of these filters is Meta Programs. Knowing someone's Meta

Programs can actually help you clearly and closely predict people's states, and therefore predict their actions. Meta Programs are not good or bad, they are just the way someone handles information.

Values:

The next filter is values. They are essentially an evaluation filter. They are how we decide whether our actions are good or bad, or right or wrong. And they are how we decide about how we feel about our actions. Values are attractions or repulsion's in life.

In the beginning was the word...

- John 1:1

They are essentially a deep, unconscious belief system about what's important and what's good or bad to us. Values change with context too. Since values are context related, they may also be state related, although values are definitely less related to state than are beliefs.

Beliefs:

Beliefs are generalizations about how the world is. One of the important elements in modeling is to find a person's beliefs about the particular behavior we are trying to model. Beliefs are the presuppositions that we have about the way the world is that either create or deny personal power to us. Beliefs are essentially our on/off switch for our ability to do anything in the world.

In the process of working with someone's beliefs, it's important to find out what beliefs they have that cause them to do what they do. The disabling beliefs do not allow people to do what they want to do.

Memories:

The fourth element is our memories. As we get older, our reactions in the present become reactions to past memories, and that the present plays a very small part in our behaviour.

Decisions:

The fifth element, and related to memories, is decisions that we've made in the past. Decisions may create beliefs, or may just affect our perceptions through time. The problem with many decisions is that they were made either unconsciously or at a very early age, and are forgotten.

These filters determine our internal representation of an event that is occurring right now. It is our internal representation that puts us in a certain state, and creates a certain physiology. The state in which we find ourselves, will determine our behavior. Remember that in this model the map, the I/R, is not the territory. Our every experience is something that we literally makeup inside our heads. We do not experience reality directly, since we are always deleting, distorting, and generalizing. Essentially, what we do experience is our experience of the territory and not the territory itself. Since both speaker and listener have their own filters, the chances of what the speaker really wanted to communicate get tremendously reduced.

Believability- the Core of Communication

In interpersonal communication what really count is not usually taught. But the key ingredient to effective communication is the BELIEVABILITY. Most of us would agree that in business, as in all of life, the believability of the presenter is critical to the success of presentation. The believability of a person is critical to any interpersonal success. No matter what is said, it is not going to make much difference in the mind of the listener unless a person is credible and believed. There can be no action where there is no belief and agreement. *Interpersonal communication skill is the ability to continuously build credibility and believability into everything we communicate.*

Speaking is not the Most Important Aspect

In a study of communication at the University of Pennsylvania in 1970 the researchers determined that in communication, 7 per cent of what we communicate is the result of the words that we say, or the content of our communication. 38 per cent of our communication to others is a result of our verbal behavior, which includes tone of voice, timbre, tempo, and volume. 55 per cent of our communication to others is a result of our nonverbal communication, our body posture, breathing, skin color and our movement. The match between our verbal and non-verbal communication indicates the level of congruency. Most of us spend 70 per cent of the day communicating, 45 per cent of that time listening. We all want to be listened to (but spouses talk only 10-20 minutes per day). It is insulting to be ignored or neglected. You feel badly ignored and neglected when you are not listened to. Indeed, the biggest crisis in the world is listening crisis. Listening is a complex task. Listening can be done at twice the rate of talking, so use the extra time to review what was said and to wonder what wasn't said.

Speaking is only a fraction of total communication. What most people don't know is that 93 per cent of all communication is done non-verbally at subconscious level. Our body language and the tonality of our voice send subliminal messages that are picked in the subconscious of others. The non-verbal communication is totally a reflection of our attitude that we hold for the other person.

> The average person's vocabulary consists of 2000 to 10,000 words only. In English language, we have half a million words, that means we regularly use only half of one to two per cent of the language.
>
> -Anthony Robbins

Non-Verbal Communication

Importance of Non-Verbal Communication

Non -verbal communication permeates the speech and is inseparable from the total communication process. Non verbal messages make up as much as 70 to 90 per cent of the transfer of meaning and emotion in face to face interaction.

Non- verbal messages are influenced by your feelings about your listeners, your subject and yourself. Since much non-verbal communication is unconscious, it is more sincere. One can improve interpersonal relationships by learning to receive the unspoken and often unplanned messages of other people and by becoming aware of one's own unspoken language.

Non -verbal communication is a complex process involving people, words, tone of voice and body movements. It permeates the speech and is inseparable from the total communication process. Non verbal messages make up as much as 70 to 90 percent of the transfer of meaning and emotion in face to face interaction. Albert Mehrabian found that the total impact of a message is about 7 per cent verbal (words only) and 38 per cent vocal (including tone of voice, inflection and other sounds) and 55 per cent non-verbal.

Appropriate and effective non-verbal communication makes the total communication process effective and successful. Proper eye contacts, planned gestures and facial expressions, flexible posture and controlled body movements combined with appropriate clothing and appearance can reinforce the meaning you are expressing through words. The absence of any of these may leave the communication ineffective.

Types of Non-Verbal Communication

There are 3 major types of non- verbal communication :

1. Sign Language
2. Action Language
3. Object Language

Sign Language

Includes all forms of codification in which words, numbers and punctuation signs have been supplemented by gestures. Example : Language of the deaf.

Action Language

Includes all body movements that are not exclusively used as signals. Example : Acts such as walking and drinking.

Object Language

Includes all intentional and non - intentional display of material things such as machines, art objects, architectural structures, human body and the clothing.

We communicate much through personal appearance, which is achieved through both action language, including posture and movements and object language as expressed by clothing, jewelry, handbags and make up. We express meanings through eye contact, facial expressions, actions and gestures in response to our companions, and everything else we do, in addition to the use of words.

The following 5 behavioural characteristics and traits are to be considered for effective interpersonal communication:

1. Eye communication
2. Posture/Movement
3. Gestures/Facial expressions
4. Dress/Appearance
5. The natural self

Eye Communication

Eye communication is the most important skill in your personal impact toolbox. Your eyes are the only part of your central nervous system that directly connect with another person. Good eye communication is not mere eye contact but it is more than a fleeting glance.

In individual communications the normal eye communication should be from 5 to 15 seconds. To individuals in a group it should be 4 to 5 seconds. Make sure that you maintain a confident eye pattern, when you are under pressure.

Improve your eye communication

- Intimacy, Intimidation and Involvement
- Five seconds for more effectiveness
- Beware of eye dart
- Beware of Slow-blink
- Angle of eye incidence

Intimacy, Intimidation and Involvement

The three "Is" of eye communication are intimacy, intimidation and involvement. Intimacy and intimidation means looking at another person for a long period- from 10 seconds to a minute or more. But over 90 per cent of personal communications especially in business setting calls for involvement. Make sure that duration of eye contact is used properly.

Five seconds for more effectiveness

When we talk to another person and are excited, enthusiastic and confident, we usually look at them for five seconds before looking away. That is what is natural in a one to one communication. That's also what you should strive for in all situations-whether speaking to one person or one thousand. This five second period is what listeners are comfortable with in the majority of their communication.

Beware of Eye Darts

Under pressure we tend to glance at anything but the listener. This conveys a nervousness that undermines our credibility. By not looking directly at the person we are talking to, we make our listener uncomfortable.

Beware of Slow-Blink

'Slow-blink' is keeping your eyelids closed for up to 2 to 3 seconds. It conveys the message 'I really don't want to be here." It is a bad signal given to the other person.

Angle of Eye Incidence

If you are addressing a large group and your angle of eye incidence between each individual is small, you may extend eye communication period of 5 seconds. This is because when you look at one person, dozens of people around that person will think you are looking at them.

Application to business

You use your eyes for communication 90 per cent of the time in business excluding the telephone. Concentrate on how you look at colleagues, customers, superiors, etc. Envision how you look when you are upset or pleased. Notice the eye patterns of others during job interviews and performance appraisals. Use the new awareness in creating more effective and confident eye patterns of your own.

Eye Communication Skill Development Exercises

- Where do you look?
- Reinforce the five second habit
- Increase sensitivity
- Relieve intimidation

Where do you look?

In your next fifteen conversations, determine where you generally look when you talk to others. Note that you do not look directly in both eyes. You may look at either a person's left eye or right eye, but it is impossible to look at both at the same time. In one to one conversations eyes tend to move around the face, but there is a predominant place most of us tend to rest. Find where your spot is -the right eye, bridge of nose? left eye? or directly between the eyes. Any resting place near the eye is acceptable. Anywhere else is not acceptable.

Once you have found your pattern, increase your awareness and sensitize yourself to the complexities of eye communication. Then try to look somewhere else, and feel the dissonance. This will help desensitize you to the feelings of awkwardness when you might not want to look directly at someone, but should for effectiveness.

Reinforce the five second habit

When you are in a meeting or giving a speech, ask a friend to count how long you look at specific individuals. Consciously keep five second eye communication with individuals in the group to whom you are communicating.

Increase your sensitivity

Talk to a partner for a minute. Ask the partner to look away from you after 15 seconds as you continue talking. For the rest of the exercise have your partner look anywhere else but while he or she is still listening. How does this feel? Reverse this process, and then discuss the relevance of eye communication in verbal conversations. Notice how often good eye contact is lacking at certain social functions. Practice better eye contact in these informal situations and notice what a difference it makes to a conversation.

Relieve intimidation

If you feel uncomfortable with an individual that you must talk to (such as meeting with your superior or the chief executive of your company), try looking at the persons forehead. To experiment with this, get in a conversation with a partner sitting 4 or 5 feet away. Look at the middle of his or her forehead, just above the eyes. That person will think that you have good eye communication with him/her. But you will not feel like you are in touch at all. This will help reduce the emotional connection so it is almost as if you are talking to a wall. Reverse the process so that your partner can experience the same phenomenon.

Observe others and notice how different an individual's eye communication patterns make you feel about them. Ask your friends how they feel about your cyc communication. Ask your friend or associate to analyze your eye contact in various communication circumstances.

Where and How do You Look?

Answer the following:

1. Do you know where you look when you are talking to another person?
2. Are you aware where you look when you are listening to another person?
3. Do you have a feel for how long to maintain eye communication in a one to one communication?
4. Do you know how long to maintain eye communication with specific individuals when presenting to large group?
5. Are you aware where you look when you look away from a person?
6. Do you know what eye dart is and whether or not you have it?
7. Do you know what's low-blink' is and why it occurs?
8. Do you realize that eye communication is the most important behavioural skill in interpersonal communications?

Posture/Movement

Human animal

'*Stand tall*. The difference between towering and cowering is totally a matter of inner posture. It's got nothing to do with height, it costs nothing but impacts a lot.

Most people do not stand tall. They keep their inner posture dwarf which causes both internal and external damages to their body. The general tendency is to 'slump' in both upper and lower body posture. One has to learn to stand tall and move naturally and easily. When communicating it is more effective to be fluid rather than locked into rigid positions. This applies to gestures, but particularly leg and foot movements.

How to Improve Your Posture and Movement?

- Stand tall
- Watch your body
- Use the 'Ready position'
- Move
- Your own style

Stand tall

Poor upper body posture often reflects low self esteem. Not always, but other people always see it that way until they have enough other information to change this opinion. Many times upper body posture comes from an outdated habit pattern. Many tall men walk around hunched over because they grew fast as teenagers and didn't want to stand out. Others simply never considered posture to be important and allowed the slouching and slumping 'teenage' period to extend into adulthood.

Watch your lower body

The second part of the posture that often gets neglected is the lower body. When you are talking to others you may decrease your effectiveness because the way you stand. You can divert your communication energy away from your listeners through inappropriate body language. One of the most common adverse posture pattern is 'going back on one hip'. If you tend to go back on one hip you are subconsciously saying 'I don't want to be here' and literally distance from others. Other variations are rocking from side to side, going back and forth on your heels and toes, or pacing.

Use the ready position

What you can do to combat these negative habits is to take the ready position. The ready position means basically weight forward. Communication rides on a 'horse' of energy. When you are speaking-when you are confident and want to get your message across- you have your energy forward. The 'ready position' is slightly leaning forward so you could bounce up and down on the balls of your feet, with your knees slightly flexed. It is similar to practicing for competition in athletics where you are ready to move in any direction. When your weight is forward, it is impossible to go back on one hip or rock back and forth on your heels. Get in the habit of the ready position in both formal and informal communication situations.

Move

Communication and energy are inseparable. Use all of your natural energy in a positive fashion. When you are speaking to others, move around. Come out from behind the lectern if you are in the formal situation. This will remove the physical barrier between yourself and the audience. In a group meeting, you have space to move a bit-your feet as well as hand or arms. In a seated situation you might think of standing when you are 'on' or leaning forward to give yourself more impact. Movement adds to your energy, reflects confidence and adds variety to your communication. Don't overdo it, but do move with your own natural energy level. Although high energy level people have an advantage, greater personal impact is available to all who stay conscious of using what they have.

Your own style

Be sure to adapt posture and movement concepts to your personal style. There is no absolute right or wrong way to stand or move. But these concepts especially 'stand erect' and 'keep your energy forward' add to your communicability. Think of them as your ready position and then work to fit them to your personal style.

Posture and Movement Skill Development Exsercises

- See yourself
- Walk away from the wall
- Do the 'Two Step'
- Stand at meetings

See yourself

Posture and movement is one skill set that you can readily observe. Mirrors or through assistance of observation of others will help. Notice what the upper body communicates?-standing tall? hunching down? some where in between? If you cross your legs and lean against walls when you are standing informally, you will notice that it often appears sloppy rather than casual. Try variations of 'ready position' to see how it looks.

Walk away from the wall

The upper body posture in erect position exudes confidence. It is suggested that you stand against a wall with your heels and shoulders touching the wall. Then straighten your spine so that a small of your back is also touching the wall. Walk away from the wall, (shake a little so that you are not rigid), and then walk a few steps. Notice how you feel tall, and project more confidence. If you practice this regularly you can improve your posture dramatically.

Do the two step

The next time you are talking to a group, have some one count the number of steps you take (if you move at all). Then think of the "Two step". Often we take tentative half steps, because we want to move, but feel inhibited. That degree of movement is better than none, but it still reflects exactly what we feel-tentativeness. If you do two step, taking at least two steps towards someone, you will force yourself with apparent purpose. When you combine it with good eye communication, you will be talking and presenting yourself in a confident, direct fashion.

Stand at meetings

Experiment with posture and movement. At your next meeting, stand when you have something important to say. This will give your message more emphasis. When you go to one-to-one meeting to sell a product/ an idea, consider making a stand up presentation. You can have fun trying new ways to use posture and movement for maximum effect, and gain some impact in the process.

How do you Hold Yourself ?

Answer the following:

1. Do you lean back on one hip when you are talking in a small group?
2. Do you cross your legs when you are standing and chatting informally?
3. Is your upper body portion erect? Are your shoulders in straight line or do they curve inwards towards your chest?
4. When you speak formally, do you plant yourself behind a lecturn or table?

5. Do you communicate impatience by tapping your foot or a pencil when you are listening?
6. Do you know if you have any nervous or inhibiting gesture when addressing a group?
7. Do you move around when talking informally?

Gestures/Facial expressions

'We don't know our presidents. We imagine them. We watch them intermittently and from afar, inferring from only a relatively few gestures and reactions what kind of people they are and whether they should be incharge. Much depends on our intuition and their ability at a handful of opportune moments to project qualities we admire and respect'

Learn to be relaxed and natural while you speak. To be effective at interpersonal communication you should have your hands and your arms relaxed and natural at your sides when you are at rest. You should gesture naturally when animated and enthusiastic. You should learn to smile when you are comfortable.

Improve your Gestures and Facial Expressions

Communication reflects energy. Those born with extra energy have an advantage. However, we all can be aware of and increase our energy levels. These are most apparent in our gestures and facial expressions.

To communicate effectively, you need to be as open as possible in your face and gestures. The following ways would improve your gestures and facial expressions:

- Find out your habits
- Find your nervous gestures
- You can't over - exaggerate
- Smile-which third are you in
- Remember the personality factor
- Smiles have muscles
- Phony smiles won't work

Find out your habits

Find how you look to others when you are under pressure. Get this into conscious level. You can make this discovery through feed back from others. You have to know what you are doing that is natural before you can be natural. You need to be able to recognize your habits at a level of conscious incompetence.

Find your nervous gestures

We all have nervous gestures, a place we tend to go with our hands when we are speaking and don't have anything to hold onto. Find out what your primary gesture is, and then do anything but that gesture. Don't try to gesture at certain words or phrase-it doesn't work well. Just concentrate on not doing your nervous gesture. Ultimately your hands should fall to your sides when you are not emphasizing an idea or point. When you do want, the emphasis that comes from natural enthusiasm will occur naturally. But it can't occur if your hands are locked in a nervous gesture.

You can't over - exaggerate

Surprisingly very, very few people exaggerate their gestures or facial expressions. This is such a dramatic finding, that it is almost possible to say that you cannot over exaggerate. Push yourself. Try to exaggerate your positive gestures. You would be surprised how normal they actually look. Don't worry about over doing it.

Smile- Which third you are in ?

We all think that we smile much of the time. In reality others observe us having very strong predisposition to either smiling or not smiling. Studies have shown that proximately one-third of people in business have naturally open and smiling faces. The middle third tend to have neutral faces which can readily go from smile to a serious and intense look. The lower third have faces that are serious and intense, whether they think they are smiling are not.

Find out which third you are in. Ask others to help you. If you are in the easily smiling third, you have distinct advantage in your communication with others. People will perceive you as open and friendly, and will be more open to your ideas. If you are in the neutral third (easily moving from smiling face to a serious one), you have flexibility. But if you are in the lower one-third you have to work on this area of communication. You may be smiling on the inside, but your face will reflect doom and gloom on the outside. This is exactly what you communicate. Perception is reality in the eyes of the beholder.

Remember the personality factor

Your gestures particularly your facial expressions will tend to show you to be open and close, or closed and distant to those with whom you are communicating. To have friends, show yourself friendly to others. People will buy your ideas and be persuaded more readily if they like you.

People like those who are more open. It pays to cultivate the personality factor. Serious people such as technocrats, analysts, programmers, engineers, academicians etc. are usually more effective in writing. Interpersonal communication means connecting with another person on an emotional level, not just an intellectual level.

Smiles have muscles

A smile has a magical effect. It is physically caused by muscles and they can be exercised. The best way to practice smiling is not by moving your lips into a smile as much as it is raising your cheek bones. Consider the upper part of your cheeks as apples and just lift your apples to smile. Put muscle into your smile.

Phony smiles don't work

People look at your face and if a good smile dominates your face, they feel good about you. Become aware of how you smile and practice and exercise the ' smile muscle'. Phony smiles don't work. Not only do they not last- they send wrong signals about you. While training your facial muscles, remember that a true smile comes from within. Train your muscles so that they are ready to use at the right time. Have the right attitude so that true smile automatically springs out from your heart.

Gestures and Facial Expressions Skill Development Exercises

- Play with a partner
- Count your nervous gestures
- Watch television with no sound
- Test your smile

Play with a partner

Stand six to eight feet from another person who will be your observer. Talk about how your hands and arms are resting at your sides. Then continue talking about gestures in general and how they feel when they are natural, gesturing as you do so. Then exaggerate your gestures, even moving little bit it if you feel like it, and describe your partner how awkward and foolish you must be feeling. Make sure your gestures are exaggerated and they definitely go above your waist and out to the side. Then ask your partner for feedback. You probably will be surprised that your partner does not feel that you over -exaggerated as much you feel like you did. Reverse the process and let your partner do the gesturing and you give the feedback. Practice this several times until you get a good feel of how energetic you can actually be without being perceived as exaggerated.

Count your nervous gestures

The next time you speak in front of a group, have someone count the number of times you display your nervous gesture. This can be at a meeting or in a formal or informal speaking situation. If you have a particular nervous gesture, tell your partner to count the number of times you actually do during that presentation. This will sensitize you to how serious your problem is, and will also be a good way to start your program of behaviour modification to do anything but your distracting gesture.

Watch television with no sound

One day look at television from comedies and talk shows to the news-but turn the sound off. If you do that just five or ten minutes a day you will be amazed at how much is communicated by those you observe. Their interpersonal communications, beleivability, confidence and credibility as individuals is largely conveyed through their gestures and facial expressions.

Test your smile

This can be done with the help of a partner. Tell your partner to look at you and give him/her a big phony smile. Then wipe your face clean and convey what is a normal, easy and friendly smile. Ask your partner how did he or she feel during both the occasions. Now change the roles. Discover that the natural smile makes human face more friendly and easily approachable.

Are you Aware How You Look to Others?

Answer the following:

1. Do you smile under pressure, or does your face become a stone face?
2. When you talk on the phone, do you find yourself smiling or frowning?
3. Do you have an inhibiting gesture- an awkward place where your hands tend to go when speaking under pressure?
4. Do you ever raise your hand or arm above waist level when making a presentation to a group?

5. Do you lean forward and gesture when you are seated, just as you do when you are making a presentation?
6. Do you communicate impatience by drumming your fingers on the table when you are listening?
7. Do your fingers twitch if you try to keep them at your sides when you are speaking to a group?

Dress/Appearance

We form immediate and vivid impressions of people during the first five seconds we see them. Experts estimate that it takes another five minutes to add fifty per cent more impression, to the impression we made in the first five seconds.

Since ninety percent of our persona is covered by clothing, we need to be aware of what our clothes are communicating.

Improve Your Dress and Appearance

The following steps can improve your dress and appearance:

- Be appropriate
- Dress at the conscious level
- It's bigger than you think

Be appropriate

There is not so much a right or wrong way to dress or groom, as an appropriate way. This means appropriate first of all as to how comfortable you feel. This is more important than what others feel. If you feel uncomfortable, you will not communicate very effectively. Your appearance should be appropriate to the company you are in, your geographical setting, the time of day, social situation and circumstances.

Dress at the conscious level

Since we are creatures of habits, most of us dress on past habits. Take a careful and conscious look at how you dress and groom. The colour of the dress you wear should be matching you and the occasion. You cannot wear the T shirt and jeans to an interview. You cannot wear a suit when you are going for a picnic. All it depends on the occasion.

It's bigger than you think

The effect of your initial appearance on others is far greater than you think. It is not a superficial thing, but communicates extensively to others how you feel about yourself. It also shows what you sometimes do just to get attention.

Dress and appearance skill development exercises

- The first five seconds
- Pick five people
- Others will not tell you
- Pick a new outfit
- Research
- Ask how you look

The first five seconds

When you next meet a person for the first time, consciously keep a mental picture of how you felt about that person after the first impression. Then analyze how much came from dress, from expression, from how the hair was styled, from eye contact, jewelry, etc. What made a positive impression and what made a distracting impression? What was neutral? Do this exercise daily.

Pick Five people

Write the names of five people you know well. Think of how you would design their dress and appearance differently. Pick it apart in detail- the clothes, shirts, skirts, colours, patterns, make-up, hair, jewelry, glasses, etc. It works best if you write out the changes so you will become consciously aware of the differences each of these elements make.

Others will not tell you

Now that you have analyzed five other people, do the same for yourself. Analyze in detail what you do and what you should change. Realize that almost nobody will volunteer to tell you. What needs changing? Dress and appearance is one of the most self conscious and personally sensitive issues in interpersonal communications, so few people will tell us what they really think and feel. You can help them provide feedback by just asking. It can help verify your own analysis.

Pick a new outfit

Every day look at something in a new way. Choose one area like your dress, shoes and grooming/ appearance habit. Change it. Combine it with something to give a new look. Pick an appropriate but different outfit the next time you are shopping. Dressing differently daily will sensitize you to how you feel in your dress and appearance, and will also make you aware of how others feel about your appearance. You will also discover what works well.

Research

Read literature (books, magazines and newspaper articles) on the subject. Although they are filled with subjective opinions, they will help increase your awareness. Then you can fit your own personal style and taste into the general principles.

Ask, "How you look?"

The simplest way to get immediate feedback is to ask others. Although people will be sensitive, be continuously open and forthright. Ask, 'how does this look ?' 'How does that look? You will gain a valuable perspective on your self. Don't be shy. Others will soon realize you are serious and give you their honest opinions. Once this happens your dress and appearance will become more and more effective.

Do you Dress for Work by Habit or by Design?

Answer the following:

1. Do you look better with your hair parted where it is now, or parted on the other side, or frizzed, premed, crew-cut, sprayed or tinted?
2. Do your glasses inhibit good eye communication?
3. Do you look different with glasses or contact lenses? Is there a difference in effectiveness?
4. Are clothes in your closet organized out of habit, or by design?
5. Do people notice your dress outfit?
6. Are people distracted by your outfit?
7. Do you ever dress to shock people, or for effect, or for any reason other than to cover your body?
8. Are you always aware of your grooming?
   (Are your nails trimmed and clean? Are your clothes always clean and pressed ?)

The Natural Self

It is to be authentic: to be yourself in all communication circumstances, understanding and using your natural strengths, and building communication weakness into strengths.

Improve your natural self

Think of the most forceful speaker you know. Think of the most impressive leader you know. Are they copy of each of each other? We are all different from each other. Each one of us has our own strengths and weaknesses. We all have resources to draw on-natural strengths that are already there, as well as aspects that can be turned into strengths.

To improve your natural self:

- Acknowledge your strengths and your weak areas
- Convert your weaknesses into strengths
- Learn like a juggler
- Communicating well is a lifetime process

Acknowledge your strengths and limitations

First acknowledge your natural strengths and be thankful you don't have to learn them from scratch. You may have an easy natural smile, where others may have to work at lightening themselves up in their interpersonal communications. On the other hand, you may find it difficult to gesture naturally, where others might have been born more effusive. Acknowledge those strengths and work to improve and capitalize on them.

Convert your weakness into strengths

Next, work on the limitations, one at a time, until they become strengths. Take your weakest area first and concentrate on improving it every day for a week. Eye communication may be difficult skill for you to master. Put your conscious mental energy into developing eye communication each day for a week or two. Then move to another skill. Continue that process until you have gone through all nine skills.

Learn like a juggler

If you ever learned to juggle, you probably learned to start with one ball first just to get the rhythm, then add another to practice with both hands working together. Finally, you practiced adding a third ball until you could juggle. Becoming an expert in interpersonal communications is much like juggling. You master one skill at a time, and add to them once they become a habit.

Communicating well is a life time process

No one is a completely effective communicator. We always find new unwanted habits that pop up, as well old undesirable habits that creep back. We also find new strengths that occur as we mature and as we experiment with various behavioural skills.

Often synergy occurs where a new found habit will work to improve an old habit or two habits work together to form an effective new behaviour. For example, movement and extended eye communication can breed confidence that allows somebody to maintain excellent eye communication with an individual and even allow perhaps a reaching out and touching the arm of the listener.

Who are you in Other's Eyes?

Answer the following:

1. Are you more comfortable speaking to a small group of people, in front of a large audience, in high pressure one-on-one sales situation....or none of the above?
2. Do you know what behavioural changes you experience during high stress communications?
3. Do you know the three strongest communication skill areas?
4. What about your three weakest communication areas?
5. Can you list your strengths and weaknesses?

Art of talking

Voice/Vocal Variety

Learn to use your voice as a rich, resonant instrument, especially when you are communicating with others on phone or in group setting. Your voice has to command their attention and not act as a barrier.

Improve Your Voice and Vocal Variety

Your voice is the primary vehicle to carry your message. It is like transportation- you can have an old bullock cart that rattles along or a smooth running, finely tuned automobile. Both will get you to your destination, but the quality of the ride will vary greatly. The following tips can improve your voice and vocal variety:

- Your voice transmits energy
- Your vocal tone and quality can count for 84 per cent of your message
- The sound of one word
- The four aspects of voice

- Use vocal variety
- Don't read speeches

Your Voice Transmits Energy

We usually get into habit patterns in which the sound of our voice does not directly convey the excitement and enthusiasm we feel. Such habit patterns are difficult to change but it is not impossible to do so. Record your voice to become aware about how much, or how little, energy you transmit to others.

The Sound of one Word

Subtleties of voice are far greater than we think. We can read an enormous amount into the vocal tone of people on the telephone during the first few seconds. Call someone you know well and listen as they say 'Hello'. You can almost tell their exact mood by that single word.

The Four Aspects of Voice

The four components that make up your vocal expression are relaxation, breathing, projection and resonance. Each can be altered through exercises to expand your vocal effectiveness. All work together to give your voice their unique characteristics.

Use vocal Variety

Vocal variety is a great way to keep people interested and involved. One should be aware of monotone and therefore get into the habit of putting variety into your voice.

Don't Read Speeches

One of the greatest culprit of monotone delivery is reading aloud. Writing, reading and speaking are different communication media. Use notes and outlines of main ideas when you speak. This will allow you to let your mind spontaneously select words. It will also force your voice to be active, animated and natural because you are continuously thinking, adapting and altering your content.

Voice and Vocal Variety Skill Development Exercises

- Emphasize the right word
- The voice of the company
- Good and bad voices

- Record yourself
- Voice exercises

Emphasize the right word

Take the sentence 'Now is the time for change'. Read it emphasizing a different word each time. Notice the difference in the meaning, depending on the word you emphasize. Emphasis is critically important. Experiment emphasizing the appropriate word in your every day conversation.

The voice of the company

Call five companies at random from the phone book and rate them by the vocal tone and quality of the way they answer the phone. How does your organization rate on initial image. And how do you personally rate when you answer your telephone?

The words you consistently select will shape your destiny.
-Anthony Robbins

Good and bad voices

List five people you know with attractive and pleasant vocal deliveries. List five people you know who have poor vocal deliveries. Analyze why they are good or bad.

Record yourself

The best exercise to develop your vocal skill is to record yourself. Do it as often as possible. The most important improvement mechanism for your vocal delivery is getting audio feedback.

Voice exercises

- Learn to tone and relax your head and neck
- Tone and relax your shoulders
- Tone and relax using shoulder rolls
- Tone and relax your face
- Tone and relax your lips
- Increase your resonance
- Learn to project your voice
- Control and vary your pitch
- Practice your pacing

Checklist : Is Your Voice an Asset ?

1. Does your voice project to others or do you simply speak?
2. Do you know if you have a high nasal or low resonant voice, or some where in between?
3. Are you aware when your voice goes into a monotone, and for what reasons?
4. Has anyone ever complemented you on your nice voice? (If so, why? If not, why not?)
5. Does your telephone voice differ from your speaking voice?
6. Are you aware of what impact your voice has over the phone?
7. Do you know how to put a "smile" in your voice?
8. When you hear a person answer a phone for an organization do you think about what kind of image is conveyed?
9. Do you know what impact the tone of your voice has compared to the content of your message?

Language/Non- Words

Use appropriate and clear language for your listeners, with planned pause and no non-words. Language is made of both words and non-words. People communicate most effectively when they are able to select the right words. This requires a rich vocabulary that can be used responsively and appropriately as the situation demands.

Improve Your Use of Language

One would not talk to a child the same way as to a group of physicists. Non-words are barriers to communication. Umm's, OK's, you know's, well's, and's, etc., are not only sloppy, but distracting when repeated as a habit. Pauses are an integral part of language. An effective communicator uses natural pauses between sentences. Outstanding communicators pause for dramatic effect as well. The following are the ways to improve your use of language:

- Direct language
- Vocabulary increases with use
- Beware of jargon
- The pause-A most important tool
- Replacing non-words with pause

Direct language

State and ask for what you want and mean. It makes a difference by replacing 'I'll try', with 'I will' or 'We can't' with 'We can'. Replace, "I'll try and get an answer for you" with "I will check and get back to you before 4 pm"

Vocabulary Increases with use

Children increase their vocabulary through formal study at school. Adults don't have the same motivation because we are not being directly graded. But our education level, clarity and effectiveness in communications is graded daily by the choice of words we use. Anyone can increase his/her vocabulary through the active incorporation of new words.

Beware of jargon

Jargon is an excellent communication short hand for people who share the same language. Even English words will sound like a foreign language if your listener doesn't understand your language.

The Pause- A Most Important Tool

You can pause naturally for three to four seconds, even in the middle of the sentence. The problem is we are not used to doing it. When we do it, a three or four second pause seems like twenty seconds in our own minds. Practice pausing and getting feedback to learn how natural you sound when you pause. Push pausing to the limit during practice and you will do it more naturally in real conversations.

Replacing Non-words with Pauses

Some people call them 'word whiskers' -those unnecessary, unwanted, and superfluous which are barrier to communication. Don't use umm's, ahh's, er's, and's, weel's, OK's, you know's, and any other unnecessary 'pause filters'. Record yourself and/ or solicit feedback to recognize your non-words, and then consciously concentrate to eliminate them.

Language Skill Development Exercises

- Use one new word a day
- Use a dictionary
- Watch your jargon
- Talk in pauses

- Get rid of your non-words

Use one New Word a Day

Force yourself to use one new word every day in your conversation. Find a half a dozen times where you can use that word. Try words such as: dissemble, jocular, fulsome, empirical, robust, espouse, etc. The words do not have to be long or intellectual-just different. Make your own list and work at it daily.

Use a Dictionary

Put a dictionary at your desk in your office and at home. Use it! Most of us rarely use a dictionary unless and until it becomes a habit. Just looking up each new word you read or hear will go a long way to increase your vocabulary. A larger vocabulary gives you the ability to draw on the right word or phrase, when appropriate. It does not mean you use big words to show off. It simply means that you are able to use the clearest, most colourful and most apt word in the right situation.

Watch Your Jargon

We all have some jargons in our lives. List ten jargon phrases common to you. Make yourself aware where you use them. It's fine to use them with people who understand what they mean, but very alienating or confusing to others.

Talk in Pauses

Talk into a tape recorder and consciously leave three second pauses. Leave those pauses between each sentence at first. Then leave a three or four second pause in the middle of the sentence. Exaggerate the pauses so they feel very long to you when you are recording them. Then play back to listen to how naturally they sound.

Get Rid of Your Non-words

The most distracting area in language is non-words-those 'umm's and ah's. We don't need to use the non-words. There are two ways to effectively get rid of these through simple behaviour modification:

Ask an associate or friend to say your name every time you use your habitual non-word. For example, if you use 'umm', every time you say 'umm' in a conversation, ask your partner to simply state your name. They should do this without saying anything else. Your name is simply a feedback tool. Very quickly you will become sensitized to your use of that non-word. Your mind will stop you before you say it and you will leave a pause as replacement.

Record yourself at every opportunity to sensitize yourself to your non-word. Listening to it over and over will soon remind you to leave a pause instead of the irritating and distracting non-word that you use.

Checklist: Do You Use Non-Words ?

1. Do you know how long you pause when you are speaking formally?
2. Does your occupation require you to use 'jargon'?
3. Do you use slang, code words or jargons in your normal conversation without realizing it?
4. Can you recall the last time you looked up a new word in the dictionary?
5. Do you know the appropriate length of a pause?
6. Do you use pauses automatically?
7. Are you able to pause for a dramatic effect?
8. Do you know what the most common' non-word' is?

Listener Involvement

Realize that an information can be effectively communicated in writing. People can read five times faster than you can talk. When you speak, you must maintain the active interest and involvement of each person with whom you are communicating. When you speak and engage a listener with only content aimed primarily at the intellectual level, you are operating in a very narrow range. You are appealing mostly to the linear processing of the left brain. For information that is facts and figures this would be adequate. For other kinds of information this would not suffice.

In interpersonal communication, when you speak, you reveal ideas and opinions. You are trying to move people to action or persuade them to agree. If you miss involving your listener's right brain, you are missing much of your potential for impact.

Improving Listener Involvement Skills

Listeners, whether one person in a conversation or a thousand people in an audience, are bombarded by stimuli every instant. You need to engage all of their senses and all of their minds. The more involved a listener is, the more you can convince and persuade that person of your message.

Swirls

A swirl is an instant of total involvement on the mind of a listener. A swirl can be a laugh, a mental 'ah-hah', being asked to do an exercise, having to think of a question, deciding whether or not to volunteer and so on. Many swirls can be created through humor and humanization.

There are basically nine listener involving techniques. These can be adapted to large groups or to individual communication. These techniques center around the following three areas:

- Your style
- Your interaction with the listener
- The actual content of what you say

These three areas can be further divided as:

Style

Drama
Eye communication
Movement
Visuals

Interaction

Questions
Demonstrations
Samples/Gimmicks

Content

Interest
Humor

STYLE

Drama

Create a strong opening by announcing a serious problem, telling a moving story, or asking a rhetorical question to get each person thinking. You can also make a startling statement.

Include a dramatic element such as a long pause to emphasize a key statement, vocal tone and pitch changes, or higher intensity emotions such as anger, joy, sadness or excitement.

Add visual and kinesthetic elements such as colour, smell, temperature and other sensations to vividly recreate a story or experience for your listeners.

End your communication with a dramatic or inspirational quote, or a firm call to action.

Eye communication

Survey your listeners when you start speaking before beginning extended eye communication with an individual.

Keep your listeners involved and engaged by maintaining 3 to 6 seconds eye contact. Do this with as many listeners as possible. Don't forget 'orphans' at the far edges of a room or along your side of a conference table during meetings. Gauge the reaction of your listeners throughout your presentation. Do they agree?Are they bored?Do they have questions?

Movement

Change the dynamics of your presentation with purposeful movement. Whenever possible, move around. Never back away from your listeners. Move towards them-especially at the beginning and the end of your communication.

Visuals

Add variety by using visuals. Give your listeners something to look at in addition to you. Use different types of visual aids in a formal presentation. For instance, use overheads, flipcharts and power point. Rehearse in advance so the transitions are smooth and non-distracting. Get on-the-spot listener participation by writing listener concerns on a flip chart or filling in an overhead transparency as you go.

INTERACTION

Questions

There are three types of questions you can use in group setting. Each allows you to obtain a deeper level of involvement. Rhetorical questions will keep your listeners active and thinking. This is especially valuable when you don't have time or it is not appropriate to actually discuss an issue. Ask for a show of hands to get listeners more involved and to quickly gauge their reactions. Ask for a volunteer. Even though only one person will speak or act, you can feel the adrenalin rush through the others as they consider whether they might be the volunteer.

The two other types of questions are closed questions and open-ended questions. While answers to closed questions come in "yes" or "no", answering open-ended questions requires description of the situation, thoughts and feelings.

Demonstrations

Plan ahead for every step or procedure and be sure to accurately time the demonstration before you use it.

Have a volunteer from the group to help you in your demonstration.

Samples/Gimmicks

Have fun with your listeners. Get them involved, but always stay in control of the session. Keep things appropriate for your profession as well as for your listeners. If you are promoting a product, consider using samples of it to 'reward' volunteer participants. Use creativity. Gimmicks can be used effectively in most business settings.

CONTENT

Interest

Before you speak, review what you plan to say by asking'How will I benefit my listeners?' Remember short attention spans. Use eye contact to gauge interest. Use examples, drama, humor, visuals and movement to engage your listeners.

Maintain a high level of personal interest. If you make the same presentation repeatedly, consider changing examples, getting listeners involved in different places, or changing the order of your presentation to maintain your enthusiasm.

HUMOUR

Begin with a friendly, warm comment. A personal remark will start the ball rolling and relax things. Make your humour appropriate to your listeners and relevant to your point of view. Be a professional while allowing your 'humanness' to appear. Develop a sense of humor and use it. You might tell stories, refer to current events, include one-liners, poke fun at yourself or even play off listeners' comments.

Listener Involvement Skill Development Exercises

- Learn from the TV Masters
- Use the conversational Gambit- Answer a question with a question
- Do it daily

Learn from the TV Masters

Look at the TV talk show hosts and notice how they continuously involve their listeners and their guests. They move around, ask questions, engage individuals with eye communication, use gimmicks and props, visuals, humor, etc. As a professional, you have to use the same skills.

Use the Conversational Gambit-Answer a Question with a Question

A spontaneity exercise called 'hot potato' can be effective. This is where you answer a question with another question. Although it is an exercise in spontaneity as well as a sales technique for 'discovery', the same exercise can be used to involve any listener in any setting. First focus on what you want to know about the person with whom you are talking, and then ask him/her a question about that subject. Most people will just answer and stop. Use their answer to trigger another question, geared towards the subject area of interest that you want to pursue. Often this will get the other person engaged in also asking you questions which leads to a very involved interaction. Respond to any question asked, but while you are talking, think of the next question that you want to ask. Your mind can think at the same time you are talking, and you move a conversation where ever you want to go.

The 'hot potato' can be used anywhere. It is very effective to use at dinner parties and other formal settings. A memorable Dale Carnegie story is when he sat next to a wealthy matron at a dinner party and spent the entire night asking her questions about her life. At the end of the evening she said' What an interesting conversationalist you are, Mr. Carnegie'. He had never talked about himself at all.

Do it daily

Take each of the nine listener involving techniques and apply one each day in your business life. When you finish the cycle of nine, start again so every day you are consciously aware of making an effort to involve people.It won't be long before it becomes a positive habit.

Checklist: When Your Listener Looks Bored, Do You Get Upset, or Do You Change Your Strategy and Involve Him?

1. Do you know the three different forms of questions?
2. Do you physically move around when you are in a speaking situation?
3. Are you aware of the need to engage your audience's right brain?

4. If you are presenting a lot of information, do you obtain regular feedback signals by involving your audience?
5. Do you know the two most important elements of your content to involve a listener when you are talking?

Humor

Humor is one of the most important skills for effective interpersonal communication. It creates a bond between yourself and your listeners which enables them to enjoy listening to you more. Some persons are naturally personable and likable. Others have to work at it. Humor is a learnable skill and we can all learn to use this important tool more effectively. Following tips can improve your use of humor:

- Don't tell jokes
- Do tell stories and anecdotes
- Humanization is humor
- Remember "The Personality Factor"
- Your smile is what people see
- People learn best through humour

Don't Tell Jokes

Approximately one in every one hundred persons is a good teller of jokes, but ten times that number think that they can tell jokes well. Unless you really are effective at pacing, delivery and style, don't try telling jokes in formal situations.

Do Tell Stories and Anecdotes

We are funny, humorous and human when we open ourselves to be vulnerable- to be part of the human comedy. There is much to be gained in interpersonal communications in telling humorous stories, anecdotes, or reactions.

Humanization is Humor

In most interpersonal communications, comedy is not really what we offer. Rather, we want to connect on the personal level with our listeners. That connection is most often made on a level of 'likeability'. This quality comes through factors such as being: personal, open, friendly, caring, interested, personable, emotional, concerned, pleasant, comfortable, confident, unselfish, feeling and fun.

Remember the 'Personality Factor'

Many people often vote for political leaders on the basis of likeability. In day to day life, people 'vote' on whether they agree with you or support your position on the basis of 'The Personality Factor'. This factor is most characterized by the level of humor or humanization you project.

Your Smile is What People See

When you talk, people look at your face. The predominant feature on your face is your smile. This important feature of our physiognomy shows quickly whether we are excited, enthused, angry, serious or somewhere in between. Our sense of our humor is largely perceived non-verbally through a smile. It is important to know your natural 'smileability'.

People Learn Best through Humour

Some of the most effective swirls come from moments of lightness or involvement. Those emotional moments are the best time to get your message through. You reach both the right brain and the left brain when you use humor and humanization.

Humour Skill Development Exercises

- Determine what makes you laugh
- Make someone laugh
- Think funny
- Gain awareness through feedback
- Watch others
- Keep a humor journal

Determine What Makes you Laugh

Find out more about your sense of humor. Do you have a dry wit? Do you like to tell stories? Do you have a infectious laugh ? Do you exhibit an easy smile? Everybody is different. Yet, most of us love to laugh and have fun. Find out what your 'humor profile' is. Ask others to rate your sense of humor on a scale of one to ten.

Make Someone Laugh

People can consciously use humor. In a few seconds, one person can make another person or a group laugh, smile, chuckle or relax. By putting humour as a conscious goal, everything that passes through one's mind will automatically look for the connection that relates to the human comedy.

Think funny

People who laugh easily tend to filter their world through a sense of humour. They look for the bright side rather than the dark side. They can turn a crisis into opportunity. Think 'funny' on a conscious level. Take your subject seriously but don't take yourself seriously. You will be surprised at how this conscious effort will enable you to be more spontaneous, open and fun.

Gain Awareness Through Feedback

Record yourself on audio tape at every formal presentation you give. Make a conscious effort to use humor and see how it works. Count the laughs, chuckles, smiles that you are able to generate from your audience.

Watch others

We all know people who enjoy being around. We want to be with them because they are fun, light and lively. Observe how they involve others. You will find that these people continuously create 'swirls' in their interpersonal communications. Experiment with some of their habits and adapt them to your style.

Keep a Humor Journal

In your journal or diary, keep a page of quotes, quips, anecdotes, stories and 'funny things' that happen in your daily life. Consciously keep it for a week, marking down ten 'light' items in your life each day. If you don't have ten, work harder at humor. Life is full of joy.

Checklist: Do You Use Humour in Your Communications ?

1. Are you funny? Do you laugh at yourself?
2. Do you know the estimated percentage of people who know how to tell jokes well?
3. Do you tell more than two jokes a week?
4. Do people tend to laugh when they are around you?
5. Do you know what makes you laugh?

Talk Sweetly- the Ancient Indian Wisdom

Importance of sweet behaviour in human relationship was recognized long back in Eastern religious thinking. In his discourses, venerable &

adorable saint Shri Asharam ji Bapu emphasizes on use of sweet words in a proper manner. He looks at human relationship from a spiritual angle. According to him, the Supreme Soul is the store house of supreme pleasure and supreme peace. The more closer your relationship will be with Him, the more pleasure and peace will grow in you. Wherever you will go, pleasure and peace will remain with you. People of this world will also get peace from your association. His thoughts on talking are summarized below:

1. Understand that a language filled with sweetness and goodness gives others and attracts delight. The language filled with sweetness and goodness nurtures virtues, gives pure power to mind and cleans intelligence. The God's blessings come through such a language, and it helps ourself, others and everyone. It protects truth and the truth becomes magnificent in such a language.

2. Never utter a word that may hurt and harm others. Bitter and unhelpful language cannot save truth and the form of part of truth living in such a language becomes very ugly and dangerous, which is not liked and accepted by anybody. A person with a dirty tongue has a dirty mind. One should not be rude in talking. One should not utter words that may embarrass some body. A dry speech that agitates somebody takes the speaker to the planet of sinners. Therefore one should not speak like that. Arrows in form of words come out of mouth and the person pierced by them remains in grief day in and day out. Hence, words that may agitate some one should not be uttered. A forest pierced with arrows and cut by axe grows again but the dangerous wound caused by arms of bitter words never heals.

Different kinds of arrows even if they have pierced deep into the body can be taken out by the surgeon, but it is difficult to extract out arrow of word because it has plunged deeper into the heart.

Such alienating words that induce agitation in the other person and take the speaker to hell, should never be spoken. A wise person should remain calm even when an uncultured person is showering on him arrows of bitter words. A person who remains cheerful even when the other person is angry with him, gets all virtues of the angry fellow. A person who controls anger, the emotion that is unpleasant because it is cursed in the world and it produces excitement; does not allow any vice or weakness in his intellect; always remains cheerful; and does not focus on weaknesses of others, gets virtues of the person who has enmity towards him. Even demi-Gods remain eager to meet a mahatma, who does not utter rough or sweet or anything even against a person who has spoken bitter words for him, always remains static in equanimity, and never wishes ill for the other person.

3. A talk conversed properly becomes sweet and likeable. It feels good when you call mother's brother as "Mama" but it feels bad when you call him "brother-in-law of father".

4. A matter talked about at a wrong time causes opposite influence. Even a right information given at a wrong time becomes unpleasant. In his behaviour and conversation, Lord Shri Ramachandra used to be very careful about timeliness of talking. He would not speak in an argumentative way or criticize. That is why there used to be no instance of anybody getting hurt by him. He would support even the right matter at the right opportunity in a tactful manner. That is why no one used to oppose his talks and his talks never used to harm anybody.

5. The key to success is to respect others and remain humble while talking. Shri Ram's talking never agitated anybody. A person who agitates others every time while talking goes to the sinners' planet. Imagine the influence of a talk before uttering a word so that you don't have to repent later.

6. While talking with family members, it must be certainly realized that the person to whom we are talking to is not a machine or robot or iron statue, he/she is a human being with a heart. Every human heart needs affection, sympathy, love and respect. Therefore behaving respectfully with the elders, lovingly with persons of your age, and compassionately and sympathetically with juniors will have a magical effect.

7. To snatch somebody's shop-house or money–property is not a bigger crime. The bigger crime is to break his heart. Do not break his heart because in the heart resides the lord of heart himself. Enmity will not grow in the family, if during conversation, mutual affection is remembered and then suggestions are given.

8. A small difference in the way of talking causes immense effect on cleverness to do a job. If you want to get a work done from somebody then say to him," Would you kindly do this if it is convenient to you? "During the course of conversation, importance be given to the other person not to our own self. A talk made in the proper manner has the influence and anything talked about in a thoughtless manner brings the opposite result.

9. A person can work amicably with others only when he does not impose his vanity on others. A leader like this takes the blame on himself of the mistake committed by his subordinates and if there is any achievement, he gives all the credit for this to others.

10. The sign of good leadership is to have sympathy for the personal and family problems of the colleagues and help them as much as feasible. To praise a person who does good work and guide him wherever he commits mistake is also a sign of clever leadership.

11. Only those who remain cheerful have the tact of getting work done by others. Only those can remain cheerful, who meditate and remain in company of saints. Others work according to the wishes of cheerful people.

12. Give up this thought that your friends-colleagues, wife-children or servants-juniors will get spoiled without your reprimanding, threatening and adopting dubious methods. The truth is that by using fear, yelling and unfair means, you alienate them and distance them for ever.

13. Words spoken by us in a taunting manner produce grief in others and harm is caused to us also.

14. Behave in a friendly manner with sympathy and humility for all. In this world, you will come across more number of people whose difficulties and pains are more than you can imagine. Understand this fact and instead of behaving disrespectfully and with malice, behave very lovingly with others.

15. Use of rough language is so disastrous that it pierces through a human heart. A language used with awareness has good judgment in it. Any bad word that may be fatal or hurt other's feelings, should not be uttered. Cleverness in life is achieved through coordination of well judged sweetness, likeability and truthfulness in the language.

16. To give you a pure smile is more than giving you a treasure of diamonds.

17. The four sins of talking are: lie, cursing, backbiting and harshness. The four vices of speech are: (1) To say, "You are ordering". (2) Shouting. (3) Speak obscene words. (4) Speak roughly. The five virtues of good speech are that it is helpful, friendly, calm, sweet and lovely.

18. The dry food cannot satisfy a person, same way a charity given without sweet words does not lead to happiness. A person using sweet language controls the whole world despite taking away articles of other people. A person should speak assuring words even to that person he wishes to punish. This way he gets his requirements met and nobody gets annoyed with him.

19. Speak to all with humility using sweet language. Never backbite or blame any body.

Only those comments of a person be communicated to others that enhances good feelings and love, destroy or reduce enmity or bad feeling, if it is there. Speak to a person in distress in a sympathetic manner. Do not laugh at him.

Effective Talking

We learned to speak but not communicate and that has led to so much unnecessary personal and social misery. For effective talking, use following steps:

1. Explain your conversational intent and invite consent. Learn to treat other person's participation in conversation as a gift and not an obligation. To get cooperation from your conversation partner and to reduce possible misunderstandings, invite him/her to join you in the specific kind of conversation you want to have. Begin special conversations with a preface, *"I would like to talk with you for a few minutes about [subject matter]. When would be a good time?"* Become more aware of and honest about your intentions. Give up intentions to injure, demean or punish.

2. Express yourself more clearly and completely. Use a wide range of "I-statements." Express more of the five basic dimensions of your experience: Here is an example :

1. What are you seeing, hearing or otherwise sensing?.
"When I saw the dishes in the sink..."
2. What emotions are you feeling?
"...I felt irritated and impatient..."
3. What interpretations or wants *of yours* that support those feelings?
"...because I want to start cooking dinner right away..."
4. What action, information or commitment you want to request now?
"...and I want to ask you to help me do the dishes right now..."
5. What positive results will receiving that action, information or commitment lead to in the future?
"...so that dinner will be ready by the time Jayesh and Meeta get here."

The more dimensions of your experience you share with "I statements," the easier it will be for your listener to reconstruct your experience *accurately* and understand what you are feeling

3. Translate your (and other people's) complaints and criticisms into specific requests, and explain your requests. Ask for what you want by using specific, action-oriented, positive language rather than by using generalizations, or "somebody should." Help your listeners comply by explaining your requests with a "so that...", "it would help me to... if you would..." or "in order to...." Also, when you are receiving criticism and complaints from others, translate and restate the complaints as action requests.

4. *Ask questions more "open-endedly" and more creatively.* Our usual "yes/no" questions tend to shut people up rather than opening them up. In order to encourage your listener/talker to share more of their thoughts and feelings, ask "open-ended" rather than "yes/no" questions. Open-ended questions allow for a wide range of responses. For example, asking "How did you like that food/movie /speech/doctor/etc.?" will evoke a more detailed response than "Did you like it?" (which could be answered with a simple "yes" or "no "). Questions be asked more creatively. When we ask questions we are using a powerful language tool to *focus conversational attention* and *guide our interaction with others.* But many of the questions we have learned to ask are totally fruitless and self-defeating (such as, parents to a pregnant teen, *"Why???!!! Why have you done this to us???!!!").* In general it will be more fruitful to ask "how" questions about the future rather than "why" questions about the past.

5. *Express more appreciation.* Life is full of problems (opportunities) and breakdowns. It gets very easy to see in life only what is broken and needs fixing Therefore, we must express more appreciation, delight, affirmation, encouragement and gratitude. Further, satisfying relationships require us to notice and respond to what is delightful, excellent and enjoyable. We must appreciate a work well done. It is appreciation that makes a relationship strong enough to accommodate differences and disagreements. Healthy relationships need a core of mutual appreciation.

6. Make better communication an important part of your everyday life. Practice communication skills in a wide variety of situations, until like driving or bicycling, they become "second nature." See each conversation as an opportunity to grow in skill and awareness, each encounter as an opportunity to express more appreciation, and each argument as an opportunity to translate your complaints into requests. Further, pay attention to the speed and pitch as well as tone of your voice and also ensure that the nonverbal communication does the value addition to your verbal communication.

Listening and talking more consciously and cooperatively is highly rewarding. Just as guitar playing and basketball take great effort and bring great satisfaction, so does communicating more skillfully

Listening

Listening is a great healing force. People recover from loss or pain when they are allowed to talk about the pain/loss when they wanted to, and when their all feelings are accepted.

People usually do not have patience to listen because they don't like being around people in pain. When others are hurt, we are hurt. We really want to make others feel better and try to make others "hurry through the pain" but it does not help. We should develop patience to listen and accept what we hear to convey the fact that we care and are willing to share in the suffering.

To help a sufferer, arrange for a time when the two of you can be alone. Do not waste time on trivia after the first few minutes. "Well how are you?" is an excellent bridging phrase. Don't interpret the silence unless you can improve on it. Don't be in a hurry. Say something like, "It's hard for you to talk about it…just take your time" or it's not easy to talk about this. I'll stick with you". Reminisce about the "good times" and continue to refer to the missing person by name. *Don't force or suppress expression. Instead, encourage and enable it by asking open ended questions, and giving empathetic responses* without false or premature reassurance. Reassurance offered too soon can stop conversation.

Besides being a great healing force, listening has other important aspects. Our society places much more attention on the spoken side of the communication equation, but think about who influences you, are they good talkers or good listeners?

As we come to understand ourselves and our relationships with others better, we rediscover that "communication is not just saying words; it is creating true understanding." Active listening is an important skill in that process

Importance of listening can be summarized as follows:

1. It makes others feel important
2. It communicates understanding.
3. It is the basis of all good human relationships.
4. People form impression about you based on the way you listen to them.
5. It builds trust.
6. It builds self-esteem of both listener and talker.
7. Listening builds self-discipline in the listener.
8. It enables talker to understand his/her thoughts and feelings more clearly.

9. It enables talker to make proper decisions.
10. It enables talker to accept the reality.
11. It heals psychosomatic and mental problems.

Ten requirements of a talker:

- When I ask you to listen to me, just listen..

  You crush my feelings when you tell me why I shouldn't feel that way,

  You fail me when you feel you have to do something to solve my problem.
- Do not talk or do anything, just listen me.
- Advice is cheap. Please do not give it to me.
- I'm not helpless, may be discouraged and faltering.
- When you do something for me that I can and need to do for myself, you contribute to my fear and inadequacy.
- Irrational feelings make sense when I understand what's behind them. Allow me to understand that.
- Accept the simple fact, that I do feel what I feel, no matter how irrational, When you do this then I can quit trying to convince you and can get about the business of understanding what's behind this irrational feeling, and when that's clear, the answers are obvious and I don't need advice.
- Please listen and if you want to talk, wait a minute for your turn, and I'll listen to you

The 12 common barriers to careful listening

1. Constantly *comparing* yourself to the speaker (Who is smarter? Who's had it rougher? This is too hard for me).
2. Trying to *mind read* what the talker really thinks (Suppose he really likes his wife? He probably thinks I'm stupid for saying that).
3. *Planning* what argument or story to give next.
4. *Filtering* so that one hears only certain topics or doesn't hear critical remarks.
5. *Judging* a statement to be "crazy," "boring," "stupid," "immature," "hostile," etc.
6. Going off on one's own *daydreams*.
7. *Reading one's own biography.* Remembering your own personal experiences instead of listening to the talker.

8. Busily drafting your prescription or *advice* long before the talker has finished telling his/her woes.
9. Considering every conversation an intellectual *debate* with the goal of putting down the opponent.
10. Believing you are *always right* so no need to listen.
11. Quickly *changing the topic* or laughing it off if the topic gets serious.
12. *Placating* the other person ("You're right...Of course...I agree...Really!") by automatically agreeing with everything.

Because of these barriers, we typically retain for a few minutes only 65 per cent of what is said to us (recall 2 months later is 25 per cent). Effective listening is really a combination of so many techniques. It includes gestures, personality traits, posture, movement of eyes, head, mouth, etc., all of these expressing the keen desire to listen.

The ability to become a good listener depends upon just one thing, and this is your attitude. To be a good listener, you must want to listen. Develop genuine desire to listen. You do not realize what a great impact you create on people by the way you listen to them. *Indeed you convey whether you like or dislike people by the way you listen to them.* You tell people what you think of them by the way you listen to them. Your good listening makes you respectable, lovable and likable

It is not easy to listen actively all the time. Our concentration lasts only 15-20 minutes. All of us get distracted at times. But the good listener gets back on track and asks clarifying questions when things aren't clear. Above all we must guard against prejudices, closed-minded opinions, defenses, and fears of being wrong which prevent us from hearing what is said. Furthermore, we must check what we hear against our knowledge of the situation and human nature. We should ask:

1. How is the talker feeling and thinking about him/herself?
2. How does he/she see the world?

Finally, we must "listen to" the facial expression and body language as well as the words.

Communicating that we are listening: This has following important components:

(a) Non—verbal and verbal attending
(b) Art of questioning
(c) Focus
(d) Reflections
(e) Summarizing

(a) Non-verbal attending:

- eye contact
- body language
- use of silence

Verbal attending: minimal encouragers

(b) The art of questioning

- Open questions: How? What ? Could ? Would ?
- Closed questions: Is? Are? Do? Did?
- Why questions: sometimes open, sometimes closed

(c) Focus—be aware that the conversation may take on a variety of focuses:

Speaker focus	Topic focus
Other (s) focus	Listener focus

(d) Reflections:

- Reinforce and support the speaker
- Clarify the meaning of communications
- Reflect factual content
- Reflect feeling content
- Under-reflected vs. distorted reflections
- Leave reflections tentative

(e) Summarizing:

- Recapitulation for easier remembering
- Better understanding
- Showing relationship of main points
- Beginning discussion (remembering where we left off)
- Summarizing in mid-discussion
- Drawing together main points
- Ending a discussion, a sense of what happened

General Techniques to Improve Conversation

- Pausing
- Asking

- Paraphrasing

Pausing

Pause before replying. A short pause (3-5 seconds) helps you accomplish three goals : 1.You avoid running the risk of interrupting if the other person is just catching his or her breath before continuing. 2. You show the other person that you are giving careful consideration to his or her words by not jumping in with your own comments at the earliest opportunity. 3. You actually hear the other person better and understand with greater clarity.

Asking

Ask questions for clarification. Never assume that you understand what the person is saying or trying to say. When you assume, it means: ass-you-me that is making an ass out of you and me. Instead, ask, "How do you mean, exactly?" When you ask, "How do you mean?" the other person cannot stop himself or herself from answering more extensively. You can then follow up with other open-ended questions and keep the conversation rolling along. Some examples of open-ended questions (OEQ) and closed questions (CQ):

1. OEQ: What does your daughter feel about him leaving?
CQ: Is your daughter feeling angry about him leaving?
2. OEQ: What you did when he left last night?
CQ: Did you go after him when he left?
3. OEQ: What made you feel so angry?
CQ: Did you feel angry?

Paraphrasing

Paraphrase the speaker's words in your own words. After you've nodded and smiled, you can then say, "Let me see if I've got this right. What you're saying is..."

By paraphrasing the speaker's words, you demonstrate that you are genuinely paying attention and making every effort to understand his or her thoughts or feelings. When you practice effective listening, other people will begin to find you fascinating. They will want to be around you. They will feel relaxed and happy in your presence.

Empathetic Listening

Empathetic or empathic listening is the key to success in human relationships. Empathic listening means really listening to get inside another person's mind and heart. It is listening with empathy or trying to see the world through someone else's eyes. Here you do not take a position yourself on what the person is talking about but you give the feedback of the essence of what he or she said to you. Read carefully the following conversation between a daughter and a mother. Figure out how empathic response differs from other responses:

Daughter: "Our family rule that I cannot go to Dandia (a religious dancing festival) until I am older is disturbing me to death. My all friends are going and they talk about their experiences, but I am out. Jayesh asks me for a dancing partnership but I tell him I am not old enough. He is going to ask me again on Friday and if I say no, he is going to stop asking me. Other friends will also stop talking to me. Everyone is talking about it."

Mother:

1. Don't worry! No body is going to leave you (Evaluating or judging response)
2. Don't worry about what others say or think ! (Advising response)
3. Tell me what they are saying about you (Probing response)
4. When they talk about you like this, they admire your stand. What you are feeling is normal insecurity (Interpreting response)

These four responses are inappropriate because they are based on mother's values, needs and her point of view. These responses are not aimed at understanding the other person but at making the other person understand you.

An understanding or empathic response would be :

"You feel very much disturbed inside. You understand the family rule but you also feel disturbed when everyone can go to Dandia and you have to say no. Is that it?"

Here you attempted to reflect back what your daughter feels and says so that she feels you really understand. Your daughter will now respond:

."Yes that's what I mean. But the thing I am really afraid of is that I won't know how to act around boys when I do start going. Everyone else is learning and I am not."

Over 3000 words are related to emotions, of these 1051 describe positive emotions while 2086 describe negative emotions. No wonder people feel bad more than they feel good.

- Anthony Robbins

Again an understanding or empathic response would be :
"You feel somewhat scared that when the time comes, you won't know what to do"

She will either say yes and will go deeper into her feelings or she will say " Well not exactly. What I really mean is...." And she will try to give you a clearer picture of what she is feeling or facing.

When mother gives an understanding response, both mother and daughter gain greater understanding of what daughter is really thinking and feeling. The mother has made it safe for the daughter to open up and share. The mother has made it comfortable for the daughter to engage her own inner abilities to help deal with the concern.

Empathy is two-fold:

1. Understanding the talker's expressed feelings
2. Reflecting this understanding tentatively back to the talker without any judgment.

Empathic listening is not always reflecting back in words what someone is saying and feeling. The heart of empathy is *to understand* how people see the situation and *how they feel* about it and the essence of *what they are trying to say*. It's not mimicking or summarizing or even attempting to reflect back in all cases. In some situations, you need not say anything, the facial expression is enough. The point is that empathic listening is not merely a technique but is a sincere desire to truly understand a person. *This desire is ultimately based on respect.*

Empathic responses usually involve the following sentences:
" Correct me if I am wrong. but I sense that................"
" I am trying to see it from your point of view, and what I sense is ...."
"What I hear you saying is ...."
"You feel that..............."
"I sense you mean.........."
"If I heard you correctly, probably you mean ...."
"How do you mean it?"

Empathetic listening is paying attention to another person with empathy [emotional identification, compassion, feeling, insight]. It can be through "active listening" (you repeat back to the person what you think she or he said to make certain you understand) and by asking how the talker feels about the situation or perhaps to make a statement about how you believe the talker feels.

For example, a boy might say, "My dog got hit by a car this morning." An active listening response might be, "Your dog got hit by a car?" or "Was it hurt?" Another response might be, "I can see this has upset you. Do you want to talk about it?" More examples of empathic listening (feeling words are in bold, the content summary is underlined):

"You seem very **upset** with me *about my being late.*"

"Are you saying that you are often **confused** because you didn't *think that I told you clearly what I want.*"

"On the one hand you feel **very sad** *about her leaving*, but on the other you also feel **very relieved.**

"You seem to be saying that you feel **guilty** *about what you just said to me.*"

Empathy and Sympathy

Empathy is not sympathy. Whereas sympathy is "feeling for someone," empathy is "feeling as someone." To give empathy, you don't have to experience what the other person is feeling. In fact, if you do feel it, you are not empathizing. Look at it this way, when you are fully involved in a good book, you don't feel your toothache. This is empathy. Our attention is entirely on the book.

Importance of empathetic listening

It renders following benefits:

- It shows you care and that you understood the other person. Thus, people will enjoy talking to you and will open up more.
- If you have misunderstood, the talker can immediately correct your impressions. You learn more about people.
- It usually directs the conversation towards important emotional topics.
- It lets the talker know that you (the listener) accept him/her and will welcome more intimate, personal topics. It invites him/her to tell his/her story and vent his/her feelings.
- Since it is safe to talk about "deep" subjects, the talker can express feelings and self-explore, carefully considering all his/her deep-seated emotions, the reasons for those feelings and his/her options. Thus, it is therapeutic.
- It reduces our irritation with others because we understand. To understand is to forgive.

- It may even reduce our prejudice or negative assumptions about others because we realize we now have a means of finding out what another person is really like. Furthermore, we discover everyone is "understandable."
- It fosters more meaningful, more helpful, closer friendships.

If One Day

If one day you feel like crying......call me.
I don't promise that I will make you laugh,
But I can cry with you.
If one day you want to run away,
Don't be afraid to call me.
I don't promise to ask you to stop...
But I can run with you.
If one day you don't want to listen to anyone....call me.
I promise to be there for you.
And I promise to be very quiet.

If we were supposed to talk more than we listen, we would have two mouths and one ear

-Mark Twain

Demonstration of empathy

Empathy can be demonstrated by:

1. Listening accurately
2. Noticing verbal and non-verbal signals
3. Reflecting content expressed by talker
4. Reflecting feelings expressed by talker
5. Timing the responses
6. Making appropriate responses
7. Checking meanings
8. Paraphrasing
9. Asking open-ended questions
10. Focusing (helping to be specific)
11. Summarizing

Dr. Marisue Pickering identifies four characteristics of empathetic listeners:

1. Desire to be other-directed, rather than to project one's own feelings and ideas onto the other.
2. Desire to be non-defensive, rather than to protect the self. When the self is being protected, it is difficult to focus on another person.

3. Desire to imagine the roles, perspectives, or experiences of the other, rather than assuming they are the same as one's own.
4. Desire to listen as a receiver, not as a critic, and desire to understand the other person rather than to achieve either agreement from or change in that person.

STEPS TO EMPATHETIC LISTENING PROCESS

Step 1—Identify talker's emotions. Use his /her "body language," statements, and your own feelings as ways of identifying his/her feelings.

(a) Is the emotion positive or negative?
(b) What is the general type of emotion? Negative emotions: anxiety/confusion, guilt, anger, or depression. Positive emotions: love, joy, relaxed, happy, or excited
(c) Intensity of the feeling? (0 to 100) Which of the following is it? Extremely strong, strong, moderate, mild, extremely mild
(d) Find an appropriate *word or phrase* to describe the feeling

It is better to choose a feeling expression that is too mild rather than too strong. To describe moderate anger, say: "you're **feeling resentful**..." and to express mild anger, say,"You're feeling **a little annoyed with**..."

If conflicting feelings have been expressed, state both ("On the one hand you feel (feeling) because (content), on the other hand you feel..."). If speaker is talking "nonstop," frequently break in to state your empathetic summary. Say something like, "Let me see if I'm following you so far..."

Step 2—Mentally summarize content (talker's main points).

State your summary in *words the talker would use or agree with*. If you state your summary in words that come from your frame of reference (or position) instead of talker*'s frame of reference*, then the talker may not accept that you understand their point of view. Consequently, he/she may *begin to argue or stop constructive* exploration of the problem. *You must normally get their approval that you understand their position.*

Example: NOT: "You're saying that you were really selfish about how you spent their money." INSTEAD: "You're saying that you spent the money on purchases that you thought were important."

Step 3-State your empathetic response to the talker

Formula: "You feel (feeling), because (summary of content/causes)."

Example: "You feel **hurt** because you think he was inconsiderate."

Step 4—Use talker's feedback to correct your response if necessary.

Positive feedback- talker keeps exploring the problem: If the talker says that you understood and/or continues to explore the problem in a constructive manner, then you can be assured that your empathetic response was "on target." The talker believes that you understand her/his feelings and content so far.

Negative feedback-the talker STOPS exploring the problem: If talker corrects you, but continues, that is OK too. However, if he/she argues with you about your interpretation of their position or stops exploring the problem constructively, then it is crucial that *you assume that you did not state the talker's point-of-view adequately.* The talker *is always right about what his/her feelings and thoughts are.* If you believe the talker is being dishonest, you can still say, "I hear you saying that you feel..." (If you think the talker is not being open or truthful, tell him/her what you think later when it is your turn to state your position).

> One of the most effective ways to learn how to listen empathically is to simply change the way you see your role-to see yourself as a faithful translator.
>
> \- Stephen Covey

The Violent Communication

"Words, Tones, and Gestures Cause Deepest Wounds"

You do not require any license to use these innocent weapons. In terms of violence, a good and a bad communicator can behave as tabulated below:

All human beings have human - feelings, positive feelings and needs, yet they hurt others and their own self by talking and listening in a violent manner. The miscommunication and lack of communication are the cause of all miseries of human beings.

Human beings, more of males are surprisingly so much deficient in communicating their feelings that one wonders what good they have by having the abilities to feel, express, understand and change their feelings. Human brain is still in the process of evolution. It is perhaps at its lowest when it comes to identifying, contacting and expressing feelings accurately. Since human relationship depends basically on feelings, no wonder that most humans do not enjoy good interpersonal or intra-personal relationship, in absence of their ability to identify their feelings, contact the feelings, find the needs that gave rise to those feelings and communicate their feelings and needs in a manner that would be taken as a request and not threat or demand.

Hinsak Vartalaap Model

Unfortunately, we seem to be conditioned to cause violence through speaking by starting from the very first step (observing) in a wrong manner. This hurts others. We mostly begin by judging or by observing contaminated with evaluation (judging) and end with threatening, forcing,

Bad communicator	*Good communicator*
Speaks from head	Speaks from heart
Does not express feelings and needs	Expresses feelings and needs
Punishes expressions of feelings & needs	No. Expresses feelings and needs No.
Judges, blames & criticizes	Acknowledges that he/she has no control over others.
Expects others to do what he/she wants because he/she expects others to prove their love to him/her	
Feels angry thinking that cause of his anger is other person	Thinks that cause of his/her anger is his/her unmet needs/wants/wishes, and not the other person
Thinks that the other person's misbehaviour is an attack on him/her and he/she should defend herself/himself	Thinks that the other person's misbehaviour is a tragic expression of the other person's unmet needs
Takes attacking statements of other person as his/her insult	Takes other person's attacking statement as an expression of the other person's need to be listened to. He/she even guesses the other person's feelings and needs.
Pushes, breaks, criticizes, shouts and blames the other person, thinking that the other person has attacked him/her personally and angered him/her.	No. He listens and guesses the other persons feelings and needs which are being expressed so tragically.
Feels fear in the attacking statements of other person and reacts to the verbal attack.	No. He/she hears tragic expression of the other person's feelings & needs in the other person's attacking statement
Thinks that other person is making a verbal attack on me to prove that I am wrong. Therefore, I must defend myself	Thinks that other person is making a verbal attack so that the person's feelings are recognized, and the needs listened to.
Says straight "No" to other person's request	States his/her needs that are preventing him/her from fulfilling other person's request.
Says, " Don't do this"	Says,"Please do this, if you like to"
Considers bad behaviour of others as the cause of his/her hurt feelings	Sees unmet feelings and needs in the bad behaviour of other person. Knows that cause of his/her hurt feelings is not the bad behaviour of other person. No. He/she knows that only person
Thinks that he/she can change/control others	son he/she can change/control is himself/herself

criticizing, controlling, blaming, arguing, etc. These violent reactions hurt others and finally our own self.

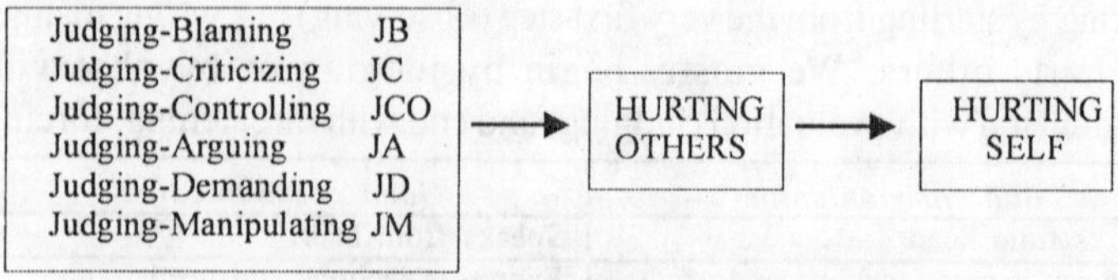

HVM (Hinsak Vartalaap Model)

We use HVM unknowingly. Instead of identifying and contacting our own feelings we expect others to know our feelings. Further, the moment we lose contact with our feelings and needs we develop a emotional glaucoma that blinds us from knowing the feelings and needs of others. Notice that this happens because expressions of F (feelings) and N (needs) are missing in the HVM. When we speak without expression of our own F and N, it puts the listener in a very difficult situation, who helplessly decides to speak less, just carry out whatever is required and distance from the speaker who causes nothing but pain. No emotional closeness can occurwhen HVM is used. Unfortunately, HVM is unmindfully and commonly used in most communications.

The Non-Violent Communication

We observe (listen or see or read) and get feelings in relation to what we observe. These feelings come out of our basic needs. We speak or act on the basis of our feelings.AVM requires that we observe accurately, identify and contact our feelings and search out the needs that produced those feelings, and then speak in a requesting mode stating that the request being made would be mutually beneficial to both the partners in respect of self, society and God.

AVM (AHINSAK VARTALAAP MODEL)

Use of AVM in Homes

When we make request without O (observation), F (feelings) and N (needs), our request becomes an order, threat or demand, which no human being likes to take, that is why HMV produces the results just opposite to what the speaker expects. Consequently, communication becomes restricted. No wonder, spouses at global average hardly communicate with each other for 15-20 minutes in 24 hours.

Let us look at the limited communication that takes place between the husband and wife in the Indian scenario:.

The day begins and ends but countable exchanges :

1. Good morning. How are you?
Fine? And you?
Fine.

2. Shall I get you some tea?
OK, thanks.
You like the tea?
Yes.

3. Where is the newspaper?
It's on the table.

4. Bathroom is ready?
Yes.
My dress?
I have put in the bedroom.

5. What is in the breakfast?
Some toast and a glass of milk.

6. My lunch box ready?
Yes.

7. Okay. Leaving.
Okay.

8. Shall I get you some tea?
Not now.

9. Tomorrow we need to ....
Tell me tomorrow morning.

10. Sunnny has a little fever
Did you give medicine?

11. Shall I fix your dinner?

Not now. Let me be through....

12. Can we talk something important now?
Tell me what you want. I don't want to miss
this interesting serial.

13. Are you feeling sleepy?
No........................

Do you find observation, feeling, need and request expressed sincerely in these transactions? Instead of these dry exchanges, emotionally rich experiences can be created through the use of AVM. Let us look at the following exchanges and notice how dry statement is turned into emotionally close expression by including OFNR into the routine statements.

Example 1
Routine

Talker: I love you.
Listener: I love you too.

AVM

Talker: I love you.

Listener: Thanks. I feel that you like me. It fulfills my need of security. Please do express your love for me whenever you feel like, so that our relationship is enriched, and we become good role models for our children.

Example 2
Routine

Husband: Could I play TV a bit louder?
Wife: Yes!

AVM

Husband: Could I play TV a bit louder?

Wife: You would like to play TV a bit louder because you feel keenly interested in some programme and your need is to capture all details of the programme. Would you like me to join you in watching this programme?

Example 3
Routine

Wife : We have to have some feeling talks.

Husband: Yes! Tell me what do you want ?

AVM

Wife : We have to have some feeling talks.

Husband: I hear you saying that we should have feeling talks. It seems to me that you are feeling some loneliness because of your need to feel secured in our relationship. Would you like me to tell you when we are going to have this sharing of your feelings?

Words form the thread on which we string our experiences.

-Aldous Huxley

Example 4

Routine

Husband: Today Sam was praising you

Wife: What did he say?

Husband : He said that despite your illness, you are serving humanity by traveling distant places.

AVM

Husband: Today, when I heard Sam saying that Mrs. Pathak is handicapped yet she is a deeply committed to service of mankind, I felt proud and joy because his comment fulfilled my need of letting people know your valuable contributions, and also about the good relationship we enjoy.

Wife: You felt proud and joy on hearing my praise from Sam because this indicated recognition of my efforts to serve the society, as well as how good a husband you are and good relationship that we enjoy? I guess, you would like me to continue supporting you in this manner to ensure continuance of our loving relationship, as well as serving the community for a longer period?

Any communication can be turned ahinsak (non-violent) provided it contains : 1. Speaker's observation without judgment, 2. Speaker's feelings, 3. Speaker's needs and 4. Speaker's request. The following steps recommended by Marshall Rosenberg are effective:

Step 1—Observations: Descriptions of what is seen or heard without added interpretations; for example, instead of "She's having a temper tantrum," say "She is lying on the floor crying and kicking."

Step 2—Feelings: Our emotions rather than our story or thoughts about what others are doing; for example, Instead of "I feel like you're irresponsible," which includes an interpretation of another's behavior, say "I feel worried.".

Step 3—Needs: Feelings are caused by needs, which are universal and ongoing and not dependent on the actions of particular individuals. State your need rather than the other person's actions as the cause; for example, "I feel annoyed because I need support" rather than "I feel annoyed because you didn't do the dishes."

Step 4—Requests: Doable, immediate, and stated in positive action language (what you want instead of what you don't want); for example, "Would you be willing to come back tonight at the time we've agreed?" rather than "Would you make sure not to be late again?" By definition, when we make requests we are open to hearing a "no," taking it as an opportunity for further dialogue. Let us consider the following examples of AVM statement and understand the use of Observation (O), Feelings (F), Needs (N) and Request (R) while talking, and understand process of guessing FNR while listening :

Original statement: "You're irresponsible! You made me so worried when you didn't get home on time! If you come home late again, you'll be ......"

AVM statement: "When you came home at midnight after agreeing to come home at 10 p.m., I felt so worried because I need peace of mind about your safety. Would you be willing to spend time right now coming up with a plan that will give you the FREEDOM you want and also help me feel more peaceful?"

Thus while talking you have to include OFNR in your statement. While listening, you have to guess feelings, needs and requests of the speaker. For this you have to use empathic listening.

In AVM (NVC invented by Marshall Rosenberg), empathy is stated in the form of a question because we are guessing what may be going on in another person. Instead of trying to "get it right," we aim to understand.

In the example above, the teen's response may be, "No!" The parent can then switch from expression to listening with empathy:

"Are you feeling annoyed because you need your ability to choose how to spend your time to be trusted?"

From here, the dialogue can continue with empathy and expression until both people's needs for connection and understanding are met.

The process of non-violent communication can be summarized as follows:

SPEAKING:

1. Simply state what you OBSERVE without evaluation
2. Identify your FEELINGS and express
3. Find the NEED behind that feeling and express
4. Make the REQUEST that is not a demand and preferably useful for both the listener and speaker

LISTENING {Receiving an expression with sensitivity and **empathy** (guessing feelings & needs, and clarifying a request).

1. **OBSERVE** : State what you observe while listening **:** "When you see, listen or think...... (just the perceivable facts).
2. **Guess** the other person's **FEELING** (emotions): "Do you feel......?"
3. **Guess** HIS/HER **NEED** (fundamental and universal need, value, principle or intention): " Because you need......?"
4. **Guess** the **REQUEST** (something **HE/SHE might want you to do or say, right now): "** So you would like me to......?"

Some classical examples of Non-violent Communication:

A. Mother is upset because her son's toys are strewn about the living room:

1. SHE OBSERVES : Toys strewn
2. SHE IDENTIFIES HER FEELING: Anger.
3. FINDS underlying NEED that is causing this feeling: Desire for a neat and orderly living room.
4. She REQUESTS for the action.

The NVC statement: "I see toys strewn in living room. I feel angry because I want the living room to be clean. I'd feel so much better if you'd just put these toys away."

B. A boy having a dominating father, who is now asking him to go for a hair cut

1. Boy Observes: Demand from father to go to barber's shop today at 4:00 PM
2. He identifies his Feeling: Anger.
3. Finds underlying need that is causing this feeling: Respect.
4. He requests : Proper behaviour.

NVC Statement:

"You want me to go for hair cut. I feel like a servant because I need respect. Please ask me if I want a haircut before making a barbershop appointment for me."

C. You have come home from a busy day and your partner seems preoccupied with the newspaper.

1. You Observe : Spouse preoccupied with newspaper
2. You Identify your Feeling : Hurt.
3. You find underlying need that is causing this feeling: Desire for feeling close right now (insecurity, disconnected)
4. You request: Closeness right away.

NVC Statement:

"When I walked in the door after an especially trying day, you seemed busy reading. I feel hurt because I would like to feel close to you right now and instead I'm feeling disconnected from you. Are you willing to take time out for a hug and a few moments of sharing?"

D. Your teenager has been talking on the phone for one hour and you are expecting a call.

1. You Observe : Teenager has been talking on the phone for one hour and you are expecting a call.
2. You identify your feeling: Frustrated
3. You find underlying need that is causing this feeling: Desire for hearing somebody right now (insecurity, fear)
4. You request: Phone be released.

NVC Statement:

I see you tied up to phone for one hour. "When you've got the phone tied up for so long, other calls can't come through." "I'm feeling frustrated because I've been expecting to hear from someone." "I'd like you to bring your conversation to a close if that's all right."

In order to gain mastery over use of OFNR while talking and empathic listening, do the AVM Exercises in different settings. To improve your communication in AVM, increase your vocabulary about feelings and needs.

Remember to speak ***slowly*** and in a ***quiet*** tone of voice during communication with children.

"Slow and low"
should be your motto.

6
Husband -Wife Relationship

> The greatest thing you can do for your children is love your spouse
> Stephen Covey

Human beings are sensitive to influences caused by behaviour of others, but are relatively less sensitive/insensitive to influences caused by their own behaviour on others. The situation becomes more complex in relationship between opposite sexes. Human male and female differ genetically from each other in many respects. These differences are so stable that they cannot be resolved. A major cause of conflict between husband and wife is not respecting these differences, instead trying to change each other. A women's self esteem rises and falls in a cycle between 21 and 35 days A man also pulls back like a rubber band about the same time. It does not affect her effectiveness at job but it does affect her communication with those she loves and needs.

When negative feelings are suppressed, positive feelings become suppressed as well. Avoiding arguments and fighting are bad but not by suppressing feelings. Couples who never fight or argue suddenly divorce. When a woman's wave crashes, it is the time for emotional cleansing. Without this emotional cleansing she would lose her ability to love and grow. Some women who avoid dealing with their negative emotions and resist natural wave motion of their feelings suffer from premenstrual syndrome (PMS). PMS is strongly correlated with inability to cope negative emotions in a positive way.

Studies have shown that major factors which create conflict in husband-wife relationship are:

1. Lack of commitment
2. Trying to change the partner

3. Jealousy
4. Self pity
5. Negative expectations
6. Incompatibility
7. Communication problems

Both husband and wife should increase their awareness about marriage. Now take some time out to do the following:

1. Describe your marriage in one word
2. How do you show that you love your spouse?
3. Give 3 reasons why you believe in marriage
4. Name something you enjoy doing with your family.
5. What family holiday experience has left pleasant memories?
6. What is something you really need from your family?

1. Lack of commitment

Why do people not make commitments? They ask dis -empowering questions. Such questions enhance "Fear." What if there is somebody better out there? What if I commit myself now and miss out? These questions fuel the fear that others are better than me. They prevent you from enjoying what you have. How come you always do this to me? Why don't you appreciate me? What if I were to leave right now- how would that make you feel? What if I commit but the other person does not?

Marriage is not a business where you decide, "If you do this much then I will do this much". Commitment means you give 100 per cent no matter what. People think that commitment is difficult because it is a kind of slavery, why should they alone give, it is not valuable to give, and they are not capable to give. These assumptions are totally wrong. Commitment is not slavery because it is done willingly and not by force.

You should be first to give because you get what you give. If one partner gives then the other partner also picks up courage to give. Commitment is the foundation of family happiness. Commitment is usually done with some expectations. Both husband and wife expect. While a non-working wife may expect only 10 minutes of sharing time with understanding, a working wife may expect sharing time plus sharing of home chores. A working wife is usually more stressed because she is getting neither. In India, most of the wives go for commitment but unfortunately this is taken for granted. When a husband shows respect for his relatives but neglects his wife, then the wife intensely feels the insecurity which at times is so severe that she develops phobia, panic attacks or even depression. It is a pity that in India and a few other countries parents do trading while marrying their son or daughter. In such situations, wife loses respect for the inlaws and husband right from the beginning of relationship. Human females suffer from terrible amount of insecurity which is built-in since birth. When a husband sides with his mother/father and neglects his wife to prove how obedient a son he is, the wife suffers from deep emotional shock.

In the West, where in the name of women liberation, a wife enjoys more liberty, there is enormous decline in commitment due to insecurity. This has shaken the foundation of family happiness: single parenting depriving the child of love of both parents and the parents too suffering from myriads of psychological problems.

Make and carry out commitments. For this be clear on your values, and what do you want from your life? When inevitable happens ask, "What is good about this?" "What can I learn from this?" Failure is unbelievable gift if you use it to make better decisions in future. Don't focus on short term setback, choose to learn lessons that will give you ability to succeed in future. Stay committed to your decision but stay flexible in your approach. Enjoy making decisions and have an attitude of expectation. Make one easy and one a bit difficult decision. Show yourself what you can do.

Better ask:

1. What are my qualities that can enable me to keep my commitments?
2. How could I make my husband/wife/children love, like and respect me?
3. How did I get so lucky to have you in my life?
4. What do I love the most about my wife/husband/children?
5. How much richer our life be as a result of our relationship?

People don't ask better questions because of their "state". Questions can change the "state". Ask: "How can I change my state so that I am feeling happy and am being more loveable?" Even if the initial response is nil, go on asking the question with a sense of certainty and expectations, then eventually, you will get the answer you need and deserve.

2. Trying to change the partner

Husband or wife try to change thoughts, feelings and actions of each other. It is impossible to change a person. The only person you can change in this world is you. You have to change yourself so that your changed attitudes create a change in the environment which may encourage the other person to enhance his/her awareness of his/her attitudes and prompt him/her to bring change in his/her attitudes. Husband and wife forget that they have come from entirely different psychological environment and therefore their attitudes to a situation need not be the same. In stead of adopting an attitude of acceptance for each other (accepting husband as he is or accepting wife as she is), they take the different behaviour of the partner as his/her fault or weakness. Since attitude of misunderstanding comes to human beings automatically, husband/wife start judging each other much before realizing what they are doing. Judging quickly leads to blaming and blaming blooms into powerful negative emotions of various kinds. It is mostly the male who tries to change the female by force and promptly. The wife does not change because she feels that she is not good enough and that is why she has to change and she starts experiencing a fear for the change due to fear of failure. Further, the ways adopted by husband to change the wife hurt the wife immensely.

When feeling tempted to change his/her partner, the wife/husband should realize that it is not the behaviour of his/her partner that is hurting but it is one's own attitude which is creating bad feelings. Clearly, one has to work on one self rather than working on the other person. Working on circle of concern does not pay. One should work on circle of influence. Husband/wife should first change his/her attitude. Each partner should first change his/her Attitude of Misunderstanding (attitude of judging, blaming and non-acceptance) to Attitude of Understanding (attitude of acceptance, attitude of humanity, attitude of individuality). Husband/wife should give attention, respect and time to each other. Husbands sometimes commit blunders unknowingly. At a party if a husband keeps looking or staring at a smart lady, it immensely hurts an innocent wife. When the husband comments, " Look how smart she is. You should dress like her" It deeply hurts the wife because she does not like to be compared. A clever husband should praise and show acceptance for his wife and then ask, " who you think was the most smartly dressed person in the party?"

Husband and wife relationship is the relationship between two equals. None should try to become a controlling partner. Suppose the husband is non-vegetarian and wife is vegetarian. In this situation husband should never force his wife to eat or cook non-veg food. Husbands suffering from in-born inferiority usually try to become a controlling partner particularly in matter of sex. Many husbands accuse their wives for frigidity without knowing that they themselves are the cause of such frigidity. Women are more realistic about sex. They realize the consequences and importance of sex more fully than men. The so called scientific information about sex recommending sex whenever desired or having unnatural sex is incomplete and indeed unscientific. Such dangerous information mostly backed by money power has not only diminished physical powers but also the strength of character of both the partners. When a wife discovers that her husband cannot restrain sex, and falls easy prey to sex, she loses confidence in him and sinks deeper into her inborn feelings of insecurity. She always equates character with sex. It's a pity that most wives are regularly raped by their husbands. Should a rape victim be expected to love the rapist? Husbands should become more sensible in matter of sex. For a wife sex mostly is a serious matter. She gives sex to get love. For a husband sex is a matter of ultimate enjoyment. He loves to get sex. Since sex is the finest form of valuable meant for procreation, men should stop using this energy like a sleeping pill.

Both husband and wife should have willingness to develop positive attitudes. They must accept the other person, put himself/herself in the other person's circumstances and gather all the facts. Husband/wife should :

1. Develop patience.
2. See all the good points in the other person.
3. Not expect 100 per cent perfection in the other person
4. Stop judging each other.
5. Use mental programming techniques like affirmations, mental imagery etc.

3. Jealousy

Jealousy is feeling low of oneself. It is primarily caused by lack of love in childhood. While feeling jealous, the person suffers from low self esteem and feel that they are not important so nobody likes them. A husband may feel jealous of his wife if she is more attractive, educated or at a higher job position.

4. Self pity

Self pity is feeling sorry for himself/herself for what others did/ did not do for oneself. It occurs due to low self esteem and it is a learned response from the parents. The person under spell of self pity blames others for no valid reason. A self pity affected person suffers from psychosomatic disorders and makes the life of his/her partner a hell. Both jealousy and self pity can be controlled by:

1. Accepting oneself as a valuable person.
2. Setting goals and working on action plan to achieve those goals.
3. Making his/her partner feel important.

5. Negative expectations

Nearly 99 per cent marriages fail because of low expections from the marriage. Positive expectations can be achieved by:

1. Expecting high from the partner.
2. Never accusing the partner.
3. Encouraging the partner to believe in himself/herself. By repeatedly telling him/her, "I believe in you".

Most wives suffering from feeling of insecurity doubt their husbands. This weakens the moral strength of the husband who may take a path to self destruction especially when he happens to come from a loveless family.

6. Incompatibility

Both husband and wife come from a different family background. Further they are different from each other psychologically. The difference is so great that you may consider them psychologically different species. Such differences must be appreciated properly and sorted out delicately otherwise these differences can finally wreck a marriage. When a marriage fails it does not mean that the partners have failed. It means only that they are incompatible for a particular paring. To improve, both husband and wife should increase their self awareness. They must find out the purpose of their marriage and work out ways to achieve that purpose despite their differences.

7. Communication problems.

This has been detailed in earlier chapters. To enhance positive communication between family members a family mission statement should be jointly structured and the system to operate home parliament with weekly meetings should be followed. To improve child-parent relationship, one-to-one bonding between a parent and a child should be made.

The consistent conclusions of studies in the area of husband-wife relationship can be summarized and transformed into following universal laws:

1. Law of Male Stretch

A wife wants her husband to remain attached to her all the time. A wife should understand that her husband cannot sustain his focus on her without pulling away and focus on himself. When husband starts to pull away, it triggers wife's waves to crash. Her unresolved feelings surface up.

2. Law of Male Goal-Orientation

Husband and wife differ with regard to goal-orientation. A wife is not goal-oriented because of insecurity. A husband is goal-oriented (interested in achievements, personal accomplishments, technology etc.) because of inferiority.

3. Law of Male Ego Satisfaction

Husband and wife differ in respect of ego satisfaction. Ego satisfaction in wife depend upon being in loving relationship while ego satisfaction in husband depends upon looking competent. A husband forgets that others can have problems too because of his instinct: first take care of yourself before you can take care of any body else.

4. Law of Female Worry

Worrying for husband/others is one way wife expresses her love and caring. It is a way of showing love. Ironically, not worrying for wife/ others is one way husband expresses his love. A husband questions, "How can you worry about someone whom you admire and trust?" Men support one another by not worrying or minimizing their troubles. But, wife actually wants her husband to worry for her when she is upset. Without this awareness of different needs, husband minimizes the importance of her concerns which makes wife more upset. The wife should help herself to feel good so that she is helpful to her husband. Examples: read a book, listen to music, work in the garden, exercise, get a massage, listen to self improvement tapes, attend/organize workshops, seminars; treat yourself to something delicious, call a girlfriend for a good chat, write in a journal, go shopping, pray/meditate, go for a walk, see a therapist, watch TV/Video.

How should they behave when in problem? A husband must: 1. Validate her feelings. 2. Not make her feel ignored and unsupported. A wife must: 1. Not take his coping mechanism personally. 2. Express feelings properly. 3. Go for fun, shopping, encourage him.

5. Law of Needs and Neediness

The difference between need and neediness should be carefully understood by the wife.

Valid requirements are needs. Wife's helplessness and mistrust transform her valid needs into desperate expressions of neediness which communicate the message to him that she doesn't trust him to support her. A wife does not understand difference between need and neediness because she does not recognize that husband needs to be trusted.

Needing = openly asking for support in a trusting manner (assuming that he will do his best). It motivates male to give. Neediness = Desperately needing support because she doesn't trust that she will get support (she is feeling rejected and unappreciated). It pushes away male.

6. Law of Sharing of Feelings

It is to be remembered that when upset, a wife does not want immediate solution. Her first priority is to get relief. She gets relief by: 1. By expressing herself 2. By being understood. 3. By talking randomly about her problems.

A wife does not get relief/feel better by focusing on a problem. She feels better by talking about all possible problems without focusing on problem-solving. It is through this process that she can explore her feelings and gain greater awareness of what is really bothering her.

Sharing of her feelings is the only way a wife can find solution provided listener accepts her feelings and gives empathy. Expression of feelings require:

1. Generalization
2. Metaphor
3. Superlatives

That is why wife uses these three tools to express her feelings. Since for a husband, facts are more important than feelings, he does not require (like) these tools for expression of facts.

A husband dislikes tools used by wife to express her feelings because men mistakenly take these expressions literally. They misunderstand the intended meaning and therefore react in an unsupportive manner. Men are used to use using speech as a means of conveying only facts and information. They use brief, correct and direct words.

When upset what does a wife need most? She needs to feel that she is not alone. She needs to feel loved and cherished. Companionship is most important for her. She needs closeness, intimacy and sharing. Sharing help a wife because :

1. She begins to remember that she is worthy of love.
2. She feels that her needs will be fulfilled
3. Doubts and mistrust in her melt away.
4. She feels that she can relax, give less and receive more. She deserves as a female

Sharing a problem is a sign of love for wife. But sharing a problem is a sign of weakness for a husband. When a problem comes, a husband stops talking but he does watch TV, read news, go for games. Why? Because he alone focuses so much that he forgets everything and cannot give attention and share /accept feelings wife needs and deserves. Having still not solved his problem, he goes for the release from stress and tension by watching TV, news and games. When the husband doesn't talk about his problem, a wife wrongly thinks that he is ignoring her. She feels hurt when he watches TV, goes for news and games because she incorrectly interpret his stress coping mechanisms as an expression of how he feels about her. She does not cooperate with him to get what she wants/needs.

A husband resists when wife talks about problems because: 1. He feels he is being held responsible for her problems. 2. He doesn't know why she needs to talk her problems. 3. He has to struggle to find relevance of problems so he becomes impatient. She randomly changes from problem to problem while he is used to a orderly fashion of thoughts, so he becomes confused and frustrated.. 4, She talks too much details to feel good which prevents him from looking at the bottom line needed for solution. 5. Females commonly enjoy letting the suspense build because it brings more feelings. This frustrates males.

7. Law of Different Languages

Misunderstanding arises because husband and wife speak different languages. Take time to translate what your partner really means or wants to say. Men and women seldom speak the same language even when they use the same words. Expression of feelings is a difficult task for human mind, therefore, women use superlatives, metaphors and generalizations. Men mistakenly take these expressions literally. They misunderstand the intended meaning and therefore react in an unsupportive manner. Men are used to use using speech as a means of conveying only facts and information.

Wife: We never go out

Husband: That's not true. We went out last week.

Wife: Everyone ignores me

Husband: I am sure some people notice you

Wife: I am so tired. I can't do anything.
Husband: That's ridiculous. You are not helpless.

Wife: No one listens to me anymore
Husband: But I am listening to you right now.

Wife: I want more romance
Husband: Are you saying I am not romantic?

Men and women argue when they misunderstand each other. Men misunderstand because they don't understand that women express feelings differently. That is why they misjudge and invalidate women's feelings which leads to arguments.

Since men are not as vulnerable to uncaring comments and tones, he does not even realize how much he is hurting his partner and provoking her resistance. Similarly women do not realize how hurtful they become to a man. When challenged, her tone automatically becomes more mistrusting and rejecting. This rejection is most hurtful when man is emotionally involved.

A husband thinks that offering solution would help his wife. But wife does not need advise. She needs three things while talking: 1. No solutions from others. 2. Listening by husband with patience and empathy (this means an honour to her). 3. Husband's truly seeking to understand her problems.

The following can help a husband to learn listening to females?

1. He must understand why females talk more in random fashion
2. Listening with full support provides her emotional support
3. She just wants to talk about her problems and doesn't want husband to solve any of her problems.
4. Take a deep breath, relax and just listen.
5. Listening is healing for a female as watching TV, news, sports are healing for males.
6. Listening becomes easy when the husband reminds himself that he should listen without feeling blamed or responsible.
7. Listening will help him forget problems of the day, and bring a lot of fulfillment to his wife

8. Law of Different Primary Love Needs

The primary love needs of wife and husband are different. These needs must be first satisfied to receive and give other love needs. Conflicts arise and persist in absence of a clear understanding of these primary needs.

The Primary Love Needs

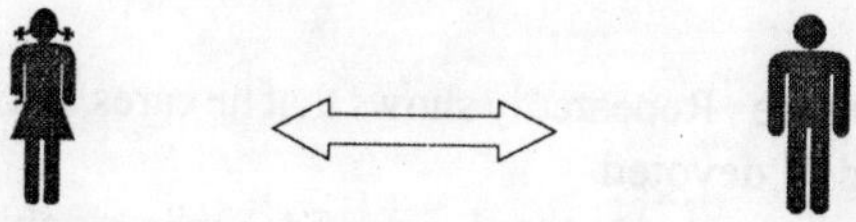

1. Caring 1. Trust

Caring: Show interest in her feelings and heartfelt concern for her well being

Trust : Positive belief in his abilities and intentions Unless she feels cared, she will not trust and vice versa. This holds good for all 11 other types of love.

2. Understanding ⟺ 2. Acceptance

Understanding : Listening without judgment but with empathy
Acceptance : Lovingly receiving him, without trying to change him

3. Respect ⟺ 3. Appreciation

Respect : Acknowledging and prioritizing her rights, wishes and needs

Appreciation : When she acknowledges receiving personal benefits and value from a man's efforts and behaviour

4. Devotion ⟺ 4. Admiration

Devotion : Giving priority to her needs and proudly committing himself to supporting and fulfilling her needs

Admiration : She is happily amazed by his unique characteristics and talents

5 Validation ⟺ 5. Approval

Validation : Accepts and confirms validity of her feelings
Approval: Acknowledging goodness in him andexpressing overall satisfaction with him

6. Reassurance ⟺ 6. Encouragement

Reassurance : Repeatedly shows that he cares, understands, validates, respects and is devoted

Encouragement: Expressing confidence in his abilities and character. Her attitude expressing trust, acceptance, appreciation, admiration and approval

When a wife does not know what her husband's primary needs are, and gives a caring love rather than trusting love, she is unknowingly destroying the relationship. Trust is most important and foremost need of the husband because he needs to prove himself that he is capable of accomplishing things without the help of others.

A wife gives advice because she feels herself responsible for growth and nurturing her husband. The unsolicited advice makes the husband feel very touchy, mistrusted, unloved, insulting, incompetent and weak. He stops caring and listening to his wife because he feels mistrusted and unappreciated. A husband needs acceptance to learn from his mistake. Advice makes him feel unloved and controlled.

9. Law of Male and Female Love Inadequacy

A wife should never criticize or offer advice unless he asks. She should give him loving acceptance. This is what he needs not the lectures. As husband begins to feel her acceptance, he will begin to ask what she thinks, but if he detects that she demands change in him, he will not ask for advice or suggestions. A husband needs to feel very secure before he can open up and ask for support.

Instead of blaming, a wife should: 1.Encourage husband by appreciating him for what he does give. 2. Continue asking for his support. 3. Trust him that he wants to give more. 4. Accept him

The husband is afraid of giving love because he suffers from feelings of inferiority. He has deepest fear that he is not good enough and incompetent. This wrong belief is formed in the childhood when he is expected to do better. Male is more vulnerable to this wrong belief which gives him fear of failure. He wants to give but is afraid that he will fail so he doesn't try.

When a wife talks about problems only, the husband feels that he has failed. When wife is unhappy over anything, he fees like a failure. Her unhappiness confirms that he is just not good enough. He wants to be her hero but he is just zero. A husband then does not listen to his wife.

10. Law of Sexual Restrain :

A husband who has no sexual restrain stands poor chances of receiving love from his wife. Sex means different things for male and female. While most women don't like porno and abnormal sex, most men may not agree with them. Too little research in human sexuality has encouraged manipulation of whatever little known in favour of commercial sex on internet and elsewhere. Look at anal sex, the way it is advertised and what the scientific truth is. The vagina has a thick multilayered cell lining that while not easily absorbing the semen from inside, is designed to withstand friction and sheering force. Further, there is a mechanism for secretion of lubricating mucus to withstand these forces. Furthermore, semen has clinical properties that will increase thickness and resistance of the lining membrane in vagina. On the other hand, rectum is lined with very thin and delicate cells. In the rectum the semen is retained and its extremely potent physiological properties are allowed freedom of action. Within the constituents of semen, there are substances that can overtake immune system of the host and force them to shut down.

Free and easily available sexual triggers have spoiled many male lives. "Enjoy sex whenever and wherever you wish, but wear a condom" Instead of telling the hard truth, we are substituting it with moral ambiguity. Are we not playing with universal principles? We must be bold enough to tell the society that we should not have sex whenever we wish and whomsoever we wish because it is wrong as it is against the universal principles. Sex-morality-character-commitment bond should be given highest importance to ensure happy husband – wife relationship. Because we have spent many thousand years as a race of rational human beings in discovering a truth that is compatible with universal principle of evolution, and this truth alone can evolve us from animality to divinity. The paradigm that marriage is for safe sex needs to be changed. What is a paradigm? A paradigm is the most basic understanding on which new knowledge is generated. For example the old paradigm that earth is flat was wrong. The new paradigm that earth is round has enabled us to design all maps, globes, recognize various stars and calculate distances more accurately for space travel. A new paradigm with regard to sex in married life is desperately needed. Today, too many wives are raped by their husbands.

Does a rapist deserve respect?

Six Fatal Mistakes a Wife Makes

1. Trying to improve his behaviour or help him by offering unsolicited advice.
2. Change/correct his behaviour by sharing her negative feelings(share feelings but not when attempted to manipulate or punish).
3. Not acknowledging what he does for her but complaining what he has not done.
4. Telling him what to do.
5. Expressing upset feelings indirectly with questions like "How could you do that?"
6. Correcting/criticizing him when he is making a decision or taking initiatives.

The result is that the husband feels unloved. Why? Look at the following tables.

Mistake by wife	*Why husband feels unloved*?
Trying to improve his behaviour or help him by offering unsolicited advice.	He feels that wife does not trust him anymore

Mistake by wife	*Why husband feels unloved*?
Change/correct his behaviour by sharing her upset or negative feelings(its OK to share feelings but not when attempted to manipulate or punish).	He feels that wife does not accept him as he is.

Mistake by wife	*Why husband feels unloved*?
Not acknowledging what he does for her but complaining what he has not done.	He feels that wife takes him for granted and does not appreciate what he does.

Mistake by wife	*Why husband feels unloved*?
Telling him what to do	He feels that wife does not admire him

Mistake by wife	*Why husband feels unloved*?
Expressing upset feelings indirectly with questions like" How could you do that?"	He feels that wife has taken away her approval of her. He no longer feels like a good person.

Mistake by wife	*Why husband feels unloved*?
Correcting/criticizing him when he is making a decision or taking initiatives.	He feels that wife does not encourage him to do things on his own

Husbands do not recognize the ways they communicate that are disrespectful and unsupportive to wife. A husband should become more sensitive to and respectful of her needs.

Six Fatal Mistakes Husbands Make

1. Not listening, getting easily distracted, not asking interesting/concerned questions.
2. Taking feelings literally and correcting her. Thinking that she is asking for solutions.
3. Listening but getting angry and blaming her for upsetting him or bringing him down.
4. Reducing importance of her feelings and needs. Thinking that his work is more important.
5. When wife is upset, explaining why he is right and why wife should not be upset.
6. Saying nothing or walking away after listening.

The result is that the wife feels unloved. Why? Look at the following tables.

Mistake by husband	*Why wife feels unloved?*
Not listening, getting easily distracted, not asking interesting/concerned questions.	Because she feels that husband is not attentive or showing that he *cares*.

Mistake by husband	*Why wife feels unloved?*
Taking feelings literally and correcting her. Thinking that she is asking for solutions.	Because she feels that husband does not understand her.

Mistake by husband	*Why wife feels unloved?*
Listening but getting angry and blaming her for upsetting him or bringing him down	Because she feels that husband does not respect her feelings.

Mistake by husband	*Why wife feels unloved?*
Reducing importance of her feelings and needs. Thinking that he makes children and work more important.	Because she feels that husband is not devoted to her and does not honour her as special.

Mistake by husband	*Why wife feels unloved?*
When wife is upset, explaining why he is right and why wife should not be upset.	Because she feels that husband does not validate her feelings but instead makes her feel wrong and unsupported.

Mistake by husband	*Why wife feels unloved?*
Saying nothing or walking away after listening.	Because she feels insecure as she doesn't get the reassurance she needs.

Techniques for improving relationship

Compliment. Everyone loves a good compliment. The best moment is when there are a lot of people around. Say it promptly, say it aloud. "You're looking good!" "Nice hair!" "Black suits you well!" "Your nails are gorgeous!" "Did you lose weight".

Reinforce. It sounds like a compliment, but it's more of a reinforcement or affirmation of something someone did well. "That was a nice thing to say." "Your performance was flawless!" "You were incredible out there!" "Hey, I couldn't have done it better!"

Empathize. Share feelings. If you were in his shoes, what words would you like to hear? "You must be very proud of your kids!" "I'm so happy for you." "This is so exciting!" "I'm enjoying this. Let's do this more often."

Sympathize. Show compassion. Be there and comfort. Condole. "I understand how you feel." "It's all right." "You'll be fine." "Things will work out. Don't worry."

Apologize. This takes not only timing, but also sincerity. An apology is one of the most powerful words that should never be left unsaid. It heals wounds, mends broken hearts, and brings back what otherwise would have been needlessly lost forever. Be sorry. Be honest. And say it. "I'm sorry." "Please forgive me." "It's my fault. It will never happen again."

Express. Translate expressions of love and happiness to words. The right moment presents itself all the time. Grab it before it goes away. Say how much you care. Express how happy you are. Share the feeling. Put it in words. "I really enjoy shopping with you." "It's so nice to see you again." "I'm so glad I work here." "I'm very proud of you, my son." "I love you very much."

Appreciate. Say the words that express appreciation, goodwill, and caring like. Thank you

Ways to Support a Husband Thinking about Something/Worrying

1. *Don't*
   (a) Disapprove of his need to for withdrawing
   (b) Try to help him solve his problem by offering solution
   (c) Try to nurture him by asking questions about his feelings
   (d) Sit close to him and wait for him to become normal
   (e) Worry about him or feel sorry for him

2. *Do*

Trust him that he can handle his problems otherwise his honour, pride and self esteem suffer badly. A husband wants his wife to be happy so that he has one less problem to worry about, and it helps him to feel loved by her.

When husband is upset, wife should not talk to him. When he begins showing signs of interest in her, it is the right time to talk to him. The wife may casually say, "When you feel like talking, I would like to spend some time together. Would you let me know when?" A husband feels supported when wife communicates in a way that says, "I trust you to handle things unless you directly ask for help".

Set boundaries

In the relationship, a wife should decide how much and what she can give without resenting her partner. To heal a relationship, following steps be taken:

1.Motivation: A wife should share and a husband should patiently understand her feelings. After she feels understood (heard and her feelings validated), both can proceed to the next step: after hearing her pain and unfulfilled needs, husband will feel motivated.

2.Responsibility: A husband should take responsibility for not supporting her wife. A wife should take responsibility for not setting limits/boundaries. A husband should apologize for the ways he had hurt her. A wife should realize that as he crossed her boundaries by treating her in disrespectful ways (yelling, grumbling, resisting her requests and invalidating her feelings) she had not set her limits. Once she accepts her inability to set her limits and her tendency to give more, she can become more forgiving and her resentment will be released.

3. Practice: (A) Both to learn to express honest feelings in a respectful way. Wife to set limits and husband to learn to respect her boundaries.

(B) Both to practice setting and respecting limits

(C) Both to know that at times they would make mistakes.

Example1: "Wife to practice saying:" I don't like the way you are talking. Please stop yelling or I will leave the room. After leaving room a few times, she will not need to do it anymore.

Example 2: When a husband makes a request that she later resents doing, a wife should practice saying "No! I need to relax or No, I am too busy today"

Example 3. When a wife says she wants to go on vacation, and husband says he was too busy, wife should practice saying, I would go alone (husband will suddenly shift his schedule and would want to go).

Example 4: When both talk and male interrupts, female has to practice saying, "I am not finished, please hear me out"

Example 5: Wife to practice asking or what she wants(most of females think why should they ask after all they give everything). She should make him responsible for knowing her wants. She should become responsible for getting her needs fulfilled.

Example 6: A husband should become respectful of her changes and not expect her to be the same accommodating partner he originally married.

They will become graceful as they practice. As a male experiences limits, he is motivated to give more. Through respecting limits, he is motivated to question effectiveness of his behaviour patterns.

When to Talk with a Husband?

Don't talk or get closer when he is pulling away. Let him pull away. After some time he will return. He will appear loving and supportive and will act as though nothing has happened. This is the time to talk. He wants intimacy and is actually available to talk.

A wife should be the first to begin the sharing even if her partner has little to say. A husband needs a reason to talk. He never talks for the sake of sharing. Further, in the beginning a husband has very little to talk though he is open for having a conversation, but when wife talks for a while, he will start to open up and share how he relates to what she has shared.

What Should a Wife do to Improve the Relationship?

1. Understand that husband's withdrawl doesn't mean that he doesn't love her
2. Be more accepting at those times when he is experiencing more stress.
3. Understand that for a male it is very hard to give his full attention sometimes.
4. Not take his preoccupation personally.
5. When he is bothered by a problem, it is not the right time for intimate talks but for fun, shopping and talking about friends.
6. Make him feel accepted and loved.

7. Make him feel needed(make him feel trusted to do his best to fulfill her) and appreciate his efforts.

How to stop trying to change husband?

1. Ignore that he is upset unless he wants to talk to you about it. Show some initial concern but not too much.
2. Trust him to grow on his own. Honest share feelings but without the demand that he changes.
3. Practice patience. Wait until he asks for your advice.
4. Show him that he doesn't have to be perfect to deserve your love. Practice forgiveness.
5. Do not depend on him to make you happy.
6. When sharing feelings, let him know that you are not trying to tell him what to do but that you want him to take your feelings into consideration.
7. Practice accepting imperfections. Make his feelings more important than perfection and don't lecture or correct him.

7

Child - Parent Relationship

Family Environment and Development of Child, Teenager and Adolescent

Divorce and child

Divorce has a disastrous effect on children. One out of every two marriages today ends in divorce and many divorcing families include children. Parents who are getting a divorce are frequently worried about the effect the divorce will have on their children.

While parents may be devastated or relieved by the divorce, children are frightened and confused by the threat to their security. Some parents feel so hurt or overwhelmed by the divorce that they may turn to the child for comfort or direction. Divorce can be misinterpreted by children unless parents tell them what is happening, how they are involved and not involved and what will happen to them. Children often believe they have caused the conflict between their mother and father. Many children assume the responsibility for bringing their parents back together, sometimes by sacrificing themselves. Vulnerability to both physical and mental illnesses can originate in the traumatic loss of one or both parents through divorce.

Young children may react to divorce by becoming more aggressive and uncooperative or withdrawing. Older children may feel deep sadness and loss. Their schoolwork suffers and behavior problems are common. As teenagers and adults, children of divorce often have trouble with their own relationships and experience problems with self-esteem.

Children will do well if they know that their mother and father will still be their parents and remain involved with them even though the marriage is ending and the parents won't live together. Parents' ongoing commitment to the child's well-being is vital.

Family Movement and Child

Moving to a new community can be a major stress-producing

experience Frequent moves or even a single move can be hard on children and adolescents. Children who move frequently are more likely to have problems at school. Moves are even more difficult if accompanied by a death, divorce, loss of family income, or a need to change schools.

Moves interrupt friendships. To a new child at school, it may at first seem that everyone else has a best friend or is securely involved with a group of peers. The child must get used to a different schedule and curriculum, and may be ahead in certain subjects and behind in others. This situation may make the child stressed, anxious or bored.

Children in kindergarten or first grade may be particularly vulnerable to a family move because developmentally they are just in the process of separating from their parents and adjusting to new authority figures and social relationships. The relocation can interfere with that normal process of separation by causing them to return to a more dependent relationship with their parents.

In general, the older the child, the more difficulty he or she will have with the move because of the increasing importance of the peer group. Pre-teens and teenagers may repeatedly protest the move. Some youngsters may not talk about their distress, so parents should be aware of the warning signs of depression, including changes in appetite, social withdrawal, a drop in grades, irritability, sleep disturbances or other dramatic changes in behavior or mood. Children who seem depressed by a move may be reacting more to the stress they are experiencing than to the relocation.

The more frequently a family moves, the more important is the need for internal stability. With the proper attention from parents, and professional help if necessary, moving can be a positive growth experience for children, leading to increased self-confidence and interpersonal skills. To make the move easier on children, take the following steps:

- Explain clearly why the move is necessary.
- Familiarize the children as much as possible with the new area with maps, photographs or the daily newspaper.
- Describe advantages of the new location (such as a lake, mountain or an amusement park).
- After the move, get involved with the children in social activities.
- If a child is a senior in high school, consider the possibility of letting him or her stay with a trusted family until the school year is over.
- Let children participate in designing or furnishing their room.

- Help children keep in touch with friends from the previous neighborhood through telephone, letters, e-mail, and personal visits.

Lying

Young children (ages 4-5) often make up stories and tell tall tales. This is normal activity because they enjoy hearing stories and making up stories for fun. These young children may blur the distinction between reality and fantasy.

An older child or adolescent may tell a lie to be self-serving (e.g. avoid doing something or deny responsibility for their actions). Parents should respond to isolated instances of lying by talking with the youngster about the importance of truthfulness, honesty and trust.

Some adolescents discover that lying may be considered acceptable in certain situations such as not telling a boyfriend or girlfriend the real reasons for breaking up because they don't want to hurt their feelings. Other adolescents may lie to protect their privacy or to help them feel psychologically separate and independent from their parents (e.g. denying they sneaked out late at night with friends). Lying that may indicate emotional problems:

Some children, who know the difference between truthfulness and lying, tell elaborate stories which appear believable. Children or adolescents usually relate these stories with enthusiasm because they receive a lot of attention as they tell the lie. Other children or adolescents, who otherwise seem responsible, fall into a pattern of repetitive lying. They often feel that lying is the easiest way to deal with the demands of parents, teachers and friends. These children are usually not trying to be bad or malicious but the repetitive pattern of lying becomes a bad habit.

There are also some children and adolescents who are not bothered by lying or taking advantage of others. Other adolescents may frequently use lying to cover up another serious problem. For example, an adolescent with a serious drug or alcohol problem will lie repeatedly to hide the truth about where they have been, who they were with, what they were doing, and where the money went.

Honesty and dishonesty are learned in the home. Parents are often concerned when their child or adolescent lies. Parents are the most important role models for their children. When a child or adolescent lies, parents should take some time to have a serious talk and discuss:

- the difference between make believe and reality, lying and telling the truth,

- the importance of honesty at home and in the community, and
- alternatives to lying.

Sports and Child

Sports help children develop physical skills, get exercise, make friends, have fun, learn to play as a member of a team, learn to play fair, and improve self-esteem. It is important to remember that the attitudes and behavior taught to children in sports carry over to adult life. Parents should take an active role in helping their child develop good sportsmanship. To help your child get the most out of sports, you need to be :

- providing emotional support and positive feedback,
- attending some games and talking about them afterward,
- having realistic expectations for your child,
- learning about the sport and supporting your child's involvement,
- helping your child talk with you about their experiences with the coach and other team members,
- helping your child handle disappointments and losing, and
- modeling respectful spectator behavior.

It is also important to talk about what your child observes in sports events. When bad sportsmanship occurs, discuss other ways the situation could be handled. While you might acknowledge that in the heat of competition it may be difficult to maintain control and respect for others, it is important to stress that disrespectful behavior is not acceptable. Remember, success is not the same thing as winning and failure is not the same thing as losing.

While you may not change a particular attitude or behavior of a coach, you can make it clear how you would like your child to be approached. Being actively involved and talking with your children about their life is very important. Being proud of accomplishments, sharing in wins and defeats, and talking to them about what has happened helps them develop skills and capacities for success in life. The lessons learned during children's sports will shape values and behaviors for adult life.

Television and Child

Television viewing has a tremendous influence on children and adolescents. While television can entertain, inform, and keep our children company, it may also influence them in undesirable ways. Television can be a powerful influence in developing value systems and shaping behavior. Unfortunately, much of today's television programming is violent. Hundreds of studies of the effects of TV violence on children and teenagers have found that children may:

- become "immune" to the horror of violence
- gradually accept violence as a way to solve problems
- imitate the violence they observe on television; and
- identify with certain characters, victims and/or victimizers

Extensive viewing of television violence by children causes greater aggressiveness. Sometimes, watching a single violent program can increase aggressiveness. Children who view shows in which violence is very realistic, frequently repeated or unpunished, are more likely to imitate what they see. Children with emotional, behavioral, learning or impulse control problems may be more easily influenced by TV violence. The impact of TV violence may be immediately evident in the child's behavior or may surface years later, and young people can even be affected when the family atmosphere shows no tendency toward violence.

While TV violence is not the only cause of aggressive or violent behavior, it is clearly a significant factor. Parents can protect children from excessive TV violence in the following ways:

- pay attention to the programs their children are watching and watch some with them
- set limits on the amount of time they spend with the television; consider removing the TV set from the child's bedroom
- point out that although the actor has not actually been hurt or killed, such violence in real life results in pain or death
- refuse to let the children see shows known to be violent, and change the channel or turn off the TV set when offensive material comes on, with an explanation of what is wrong with the program
- disapprove of the violent episodes in front of the children, stressing the belief that such behavior is not the best way to resolve a problem
- to offset peer pressure among friends and classmates, contact other parents and agree to enforce similar rules about the length of time and type of program the children may watch

Parents can also use these measures to prevent harmful effects from television in other areas such as racial or sexual stereotyping. Television viewing takes away time from important activities such as reading, school work, playing, exercise, family interaction, and social development. Children also learn information from television that may be inappropriate or incorrect. They often can not tell the difference between the fantasy presented on television versus reality. They are influenced by the thousands of commercials for alcohol, junk food, fast foods, and toys. Children who watch a lot of television are likely to:

- Have lower grades in school
- Read fewer books
- Exercise less
- Be overweight

Violence, sexuality, race and gender stereotypes, drug and alcohol abuse are common themes of television programs. Young children are impressionable and may assume that what they see on television is typical, safe, and acceptable. As a result, television also exposes children to behaviors and attitudes that may be overwhelming and difficult to understand. Parents can help by:

- Viewing programs with your children
- Selecting developmentally appropriate shows
- Placing limits on the amount of television viewing (per day and per week)
- Turning off the TV during family meals and study time
- Turning off shows you don't feel are appropriate for your child

In addition, parents can help by doing the following: don't allow children to watch long blocks of TV, but help them select individual programs. Choose shows that meet the developmental needs of your child. Children's shows on public TV are appropriate, but soap operas, adult sitcoms, and adult talk shows are not. Set certain periods when the television will be off. Study times are for learning, not for sitting in front of the TV doing homework. Meal times are a good time for family members to talk with each other, not for watching television.

Encourage discussions with your children about what they are seeing as you watch shows with them. Point out positive behavior, such as cooperation, friendship, and concern for others. While watching, make connections to history, books, places of interest, and personal events. Talk about your personal and family values as they relate to the show. Ask children to compare what they are watching with real events. Talk about the realistic consequences of violence. Discuss the role of advertising and its influence on buying. Encourage your child to be involved in hobbies, sports, and peers. With proper guidance, your child can learn to use television in a healthy and positive way.

Alcoholic Person in the Family and Child

Children living with alcoholic parents (elders) are at greater risk for having emotional problems than children whose parents are not alcoholics.

Alcoholism runs in families, and children of alcoholics are four times more likely than other children to become alcoholics. Most children of alcoholics have experienced some form of neglect or abuse.

A child in such a family may have a variety of problems:

1. Guilt: The child may see himself or herself as the main cause of the mother's or father's drinking.

2. Anxiety: The child may worry constantly about the situation at home. He or she may fear the alcoholic parent will become sick or injured, and may also fear fights and violence between the parents.

3. Embarrassment: Parents may give the child the message that there is a terrible secret at home. The ashamed child does not invite friends home and is afraid to ask anyone for help.

4. Inability to have close relationships : Because the child has been disappointed by the drinking parent many times, he or she often does not trust others.

5. Confusion : The alcoholic parent will change suddenly from being loving to angry, regardless of the child's behavior. A regular daily schedule, which is very important for a child, does not exist because bedtimes and mealtimes are constantly changing.

6. Anger : The child feels anger at the alcoholic parent for drinking, and may be angry at the non-alcoholic parent for lack of support and protection.

7. Depression : The child feels lonely and helpless to change the situation.

Although the child tries to keep the alcoholism a secret, teachers, relatives, other adults, or friends may sense that something is wrong. The following behaviours may signal a drinking or other problem at home:

- Failure in school
- Lack of friends
- Delinquent behavior, such as stealing or violence
- Frequent physical complaints, such as headaches or stomachaches
- Abuse of drugs,alcohol etc.
- Aggression towards other children
- Risk taking behaviors
- Depression or suicidal thoughts or behavior

Some children of alcoholics may cope with the alcoholism by becoming controlled, successful "overachievers" throughout school, and at the same time be emotionally isolated from other children and teachers. Their emotional problems may show only when they become adults.

These children and adolescents can benefit from educational programs and mutual-help groups such as programs for children of alcoholics. Early professional help is also important in preventing more serious problems for the child, including alcoholism. Child and adolescent psychiatrists can help these children with the child's own problems, and also help the child understand that they are not responsible for the drinking problems of their parents.

Discipline and Child

Children do not always do what parents want. Parents should begin by talking to each other about how they want to handle discipline and establish the rules. It is important to view discipline as teaching not punishment. Learning to follow rules keeps a child safe and helps him or her learn the difference between right and wrong.

Once rules have been established, parents should explain to the child that broken rules carry consequences. For example, *Here are the rules. When you follow the rules, this will happen and if you break a rule, this is what will happen.* Parents and the child should decide together what the rewards and consequences will be. Parents should always acknowledge and offer positive reinforcement and support when their child follows the rules. Parents must also follow through with an appropriate consequence when the child breaks a rule. Consistency and predictability are the cornerstones of discipline and praise is the most powerful reinforcer of learning.

Children learn from experience. Having logical consequences for misbehavior helps them learn that they are accountable for their actions, without damaging their self-esteem. If children are fighting over the television, computer or a video game, turn it off. If a child spills milk at the dinner table while fooling around, have the child clean it up. A teenager who stays up too late may suffer the natural consequences of being tired the next day. Another type of consequence that can be effective is the suspension or delay of a privilege. If a child breaks the rule about where they can go on their bike, take away the bike for a few days. When a child does not do chores, he or she cannot do something special like spend the night with a friend or rent a videotape.

There are different styles and approaches to parenting. Research shows that *effective* parents raise well-adjusted children who are more self-reliant, self-controlled, and positively curious than children raised by parents who are punitive, overly strict (authoritarian), or permissive. Effective parents operate on the belief that both the child and the parent have certain rights and that the needs of both are important.

Effective parents don't need to use physical force to discipline the child, but are more likely to set clear rules and explain why these rules are important. Effective parents reason with their children and consider the youngsters' points of views even though they may not agree with them.

Tips for effective discipline:

- Consider the limits of your child's age and stage of development.
- Make sure what you ask for is reasonable.
- Speak to your child as you would want to be spoken to if someone were reprimanding you. Don't resort to name-calling, yelling, or disrespect.
- Be clear about what you mean. Be firm and specific.
- Model positive behavior. "Do as I say, not as I do" seldom works.
- Allow for negotiation and flexibility, wherever appropriate.This can help build your child's social skills.
- Let your child experience the consequences of his behavior.
- Whenever possible, consequences should be delivered immediately, should relate to the rule broken, and be short enough in duration that you can move on again to emphasize the positives.
- Consequences should be fair and appropriate to the situation and the child's age.

More information on discipline is given elsewhere in this chapter.

Stepfamily Problems

New stepfamilies face many challenges. As with any achievement, developing good stepfamily relationships requires a lot of effort. Stepfamily members have each experienced losses and face complicated adjustments to the new family situation.

When a stepfamily is formed, the members have no shared family histories or shared ways of doing things, and they may have very different beliefs. In addition, a child may feel torn between the parent they live with most (more) of the time and their other parent who they visit (e.g. lives somewhere else). Also, newly married couples may not have had much time together to adjust to their new relationship.The members of the new blended family need to build strong bonds among themselves through:

- acknowledging and mourning their losses
- developing new skills in making decisions as a family
- fostering and strengthening new relationships between: parents, stepparent and stepchild, and stepsiblings
- supporting one another; and

- maintaining and nurturing original parent-child relationships

While facing these issues may be difficult, most stepfamilies do work out their problems. Stepfamilies can use grandparents (or other family), support groups, and other community-based programs to help with the adjustments. Parents should consider a psychiatric evaluation for their child when they exhibit strong feelings of being:

- alone dealing with the losses
- torn between two parents or two households
- excluded
- isolated by feelings of guilt and anger
- unsure about what is right
- very uncomfortable with any member of the original family or stepfamily

In addition, if parents observe that the following signs are lasting or persistent, then they should consider a psychiatric evaluation for the child/family:

- child vents/directs anger upon a particular family member or openly resents a stepparent or parent
- one of the parents suffers from great stress and is unable to help with the child's increased need
- a stepparent or parent openly favors one of the children
- discipline of a child is only left to the parent rather than involving both the stepparent and parent; or
- members of the family derive no enjoyment from usual pleasurable activities (i.e. learning, going to school, working, playing or being with friends and family)

Most stepfamilies, when given the necessary time to work on developing their own traditions and to form new relationships, can provide emotionally rich and lasting relationships for the adults, and help the children develop the self-esteem and strength to enjoy the challenges of life.

Children Alone at Home

There are many issues and potential risks and dangers that parent(s) should consider before a child is placed in this situation. Parent(s) should consider the following:

- Age readiness
- Parental "rules and expectations"
- How to access parent(s) or other adults (e.g. phone numbers)
- Potentially unsafe situations (e.g. medical emergencies, fire,

alcohol, drugs, strangers, guns, etc.)

- When and how to answer the phone or doorbell
- Use of phone, 911 for emergencies
- Use of computer (internet)
- Friends and visitors coming to the house
- Responsibilities for siblings
- Use of unstructured time (e.g. watch TV, videos, etc.); and
- Access to "adult" cable TV; internet chat rooms and adult web sites

Parent(s) must consider the child's level of maturity and past evidence of responsible behavior and good judgment. When a child is ready to be left alone, a graduated approach should be used starting with a very short period of time (i.e.1 hour). Being home alone can be a frightening and potentially dangerous situation for many children and adolescents. Parents should strive to limit the times when children are home alone. Parents should prepare their children in advance for how to deal with situations that may arise.

Parent(s) should talk with their youngsters to prepare them for each of the issues or potential problems listed above. In addition, parent(s) should strive to make their home as safe as possible from obvious dangers and hazards and rehearse the developed "emergency plan" with their children. Parents should also teach their child important safety precautions (i.e. locking the door, dealing with strangers or visitors who come to the house, use of the stove, etc.)

The Adopted Child

Parents with an adopted child wonder whether, when, and how to tell their child that he or she is adopted. They also want to know if adopted children face special problems or challenges.

Children should be told about their adoption in a way that they can understand. Telling a child too early may confuse the young child who can't really understand the information. Children should learn of their adoption from the adoptive parents. This helps give the message that adoption is good and that the child can trust the parents. If the child first learns about the adoption intentionally or accidentally from someone other than parents, the child may feel anger and mistrust towards the parents, and may view the adoption as bad or shameful because it was kept a secret.

Adopted children will want to talk about their adoption and parents should encourage this process. Several excellent children's story books are available which can help parents tell the child about being adopted. Children have a variety of responses to the knowledge that they are adopted. Their feelings and responses depend on their age and level of maturity. The child may deny the adoption or create fantasies about it. Frequently, adopted children hold onto beliefs that they were given away for being bad or may believe that they were kidnapped. If the parents talk openly about the adoption and present it in a positive manner, these worries are less likely to develop.

All adolescents go through a stage of struggling with their identity, wondering how they fit in with their family, their peers, and the rest of the world. This struggle may be even more intense for children adopted from other countries or cultures. In adolescence, the adopted child is likely to have an increased interest in his or her birth parents. This open curiosity is not unusual and does not mean that he or she is rejecting the adoptive parents. Some adolescents may wish to learn the identity of their birth parents. Adoptive parents can respond by letting the adolescent know it is okay to have such interest and questions, and when asked should give what information they have about the birth family with sensitivity and support.

Some adopted children may develop emotional or behavioral problems. The problems may or may not result from insecurities or issues related to being adopted. If parents are concerned, they should seek professional assistance. Children who are preoccupied with their adoption should also be evaluated.

The Anxious Child

All children experience anxiety. Anxiety in children is expected and normal at specific times in development. For example, from approximately age 8 months through the preschool years, healthy youngsters may show intense distress (anxiety) at times of separation from their parents or other persons with whom they are close. Young children may have short-lived fears, (such as fear of the dark, storms, animals, or strangers). If anxieties become severe and begin to interfere with the daily activities of childhood, such as separating from parents, attending school and making friends, parents should consider seeking professional help. One type of anxiety that may need treatment is called separation anxiety. This includes:

- constant thoughts and fears about safety of self and parents
- refusing to go to school
- frequent stomachaches and other physical complaints
- extreme worries about sleeping away from home

- overly clingy
- panic or tantrums at times of separation from parents
- trouble sleeping or nightmares

Another type of anxiety (phobia) is when a child is afraid of specific things such as dogs, insects, or needles and these fears cause significant distress.

Some anxious children are afraid to meet or talk to new people. Children with this difficulty may have few friends outside the family.

Other children with severe anxiety may have:

- many worries about things before they happen
- constant worries or concern about school performance, friends, or sports
- repetitive thoughts or actions (obsessions)
- fears of embarrassment or making mistakes
- low self esteem

Anxious children are often overly tense or uptight. Some may seek a lot of reassurance, and their worries may interfere with activities. Because anxious children may also be quiet, compliant and eager to please, their difficulties may be missed. Parents should be alert to the signs of severe anxiety so they can intervene early to prevent complications. It is important not to discount a child's fears.

Severe anxiety problems in children can be treated. Early treatment can prevent future difficulties, such as, loss of friendships, failure to reach social and academic potential, and feelings of low self-esteem. Treatments may include a combination of the following: individual psychotherapy, family therapy, medications, behavioral treatments, and consultation to the school.

The Depressed Child

Children and teenagers may have depression, which is a treatable illness. Depression is defined as an illness when the feelings of depression persist and interfere with a child or adolescent's ability to function.

Children under stress, who experience loss, or who have attention, learning, conduct or anxiety disorders are at a higher risk for depression. Depression also tends to run in families.

The behaviour of depressed children and teenagers may differ from the behavior of depressed adults. If one or more of these signs of depression persist, parents should seek help:

- Frequent sadness, tearfulness, crying
- Hopelessness

- Decreased interest in activities
- Inability to enjoy previously favorite activities
- Persistent boredom
- Low energy
- Social isolation
- Poor communication
- Low self esteem
- Guilt
- Extreme sensitivity to rejection or failure
- Increased irritability, anger or hostility
- Difficulty with relationships
- Frequent complaints of physical illnesses such as headaches and stomachaches
- Frequent absences from school
- Poor performance in school
- Poor concentration
- A major change in eating and/or sleeping patterns
- Talk of or efforts to run away from home
- Thoughts or expressions of suicide or self destructive behavior

A child who used to play often with friends may now spend most of the time alone and without interests. Things that were once fun now bring little joy to the depressed child. Children and adolescents who are depressed may say they want to be dead or may talk about suicide. Depressed children and adolescents are at increased risk for committing suicide. Depressed adolescents may abuse alcohol or other drugs as a way to feel better.

Children and adolescents who cause trouble at home or at school may actually be depressed but not know it. Because the youngster may not always seem sad, parents and teachers may not realize that troublesome behaviour is a sign of depression. When asked directly, these children can sometimes state they are unhappy or sad.

Depression is a real illness that requires professional help. Early diagnosis and medical treatment are essential. Comprehensive treatment often includes both individual and family therapy. It may also include the use of antidepressant medication.

Stress and Teenagers

Teenagers, like adults, may experience stress everyday and can benefit from learning stress management skills. Most teens experience more stress when they perceive a situation as dangerous, difficult, or painful and they do not have the resources to cope. Some sources of stress for teens include:

- school demands and frustrations
- negative thoughts and feelings about themselves
- changes in their bodies
- problems with friends and/or peers at school
- unsafe living environment/neighborhood
- separation or divorce of parents
- chronic illness or severe problems in the family
- death of a loved one
- moving or changing schools
- taking on too many activities or having too high expectations
- family financial problems

Inadequately managed stress can lead to anxiety, withdrawal, aggression, physical illness, or poor coping skills such as drug and/or alcohol use.

Teens that develop a "relaxation response" and other stress management skills feel less helpless and have more choices when responding to stress.

Parents should: (i) Monitor if stress is affecting their teen's health, behavior, thoughts, or feelings (ii) Listen carefully to teens and watch for overloading. (iii) Learn and model stress management skills (iv) Support involvement in sports and other pro-social activities

Teens can decrease stress with the following behaviors and techniques:

- Exercise and eat regularly
- Avoid excess caffeine intake which can increase feelings of anxiety and agitation
- Avoid illegal drugs, alcohol and tobacco
- Learn relaxation exercises (abdominal breathing and muscle relaxation techniques)
- Use neurolinguistic programming technique
- Develop assertiveness training skills. For example, state feelings in polite firm and not overly aggressive or pàssive ways: ("I feel angry when you yell at me" "Please stop yelling.")
- Rehearse and practice situations which cause stress. One example is taking a speech class if talking in front of a class makes you anxious.
- Learn practical coping skills. For example, break a large task into smaller, more attainable tasks.

- Decrease negative self talk: challenge negative thoughts about yourself with alternative neutral or positive thoughts. "My life will never get better" can be transformed into "I may feel hopeless now, but my life will probably get better if I work at it and get some help".
- Learn to feel good about doing a competent or "good enough" job rather than demanding perfection from yourself and others.
- Take a break from stressful situations. Activities like listening to music, talking to a friend, drawing, writing, or spending time with a pet can reduce stress.

Build a network of friends who help you cope in a positive way.

Music and Child

Singing and music have always played an important role in learning and the communication of culture. Most parents are concerned about what their young children see and hear, but as children grow older, parents pay less attention to the music and videos that hold their children's interest.

The sharing of musical tastes between generations in a family can be a pleasurable experience. Music also is often a major part of a teenager's separate world. It is quite common for teenagers to get pleasure from keeping adults out and causing adults some distress.

A concern to many interested in the development and growth of teenagers is the negative and destructive themes of some rock and other kinds of music, including best-selling albums promoted by major recording companies. The following troublesome themes are prominent:

- Advocating and glamorizing abuse of drugs and alcohol
- Pictures and explicit lyrics presenting suicide as an "alternative" or "solution"
- Graphic violence
- Rituals in concerts
- Sex which focuses on control, sadism, masochism, incest, children devaluing women, and violence toward women.

Parents can help their teenagers by paying attention to their teenager's purchasing, downloading, listening and viewing patterns, and by helping them identify music that may be destructive. An open discussion without criticism may be helpful.

Music is not usually a danger for a teenager whose life is happy and healthy. But if a teenager is persistently preoccupied with music that has seriously destructive themes, and there are changes in behavior such as isolation, depression, alcohol or other drug abuse, professional help should be considered.

Normal Adolescent Development

1. Movement Towards Independence

- Increased independent functioning
- Firmer and more cohesive sense of identity
- Examination of inner experiences
- Ability to think ideas through
- Conflict with parents begins to decrease
- Increased ability for delayed gratification and compromise
- Increased emotional stability
- Increased concern for others
- Increased self-reliance
- Peer relationships remain important and take an appropriate place among other interests

2. Future Interests and Cognitive Changes

- Work habits become more defined
- Increased concern for the future
- More importance is placed on one's role in life

3. Sexuality

- Feelings of love and passion
- Development of more serious relationships
- Firmer sense of sexual identity
- Increased capacity for tender and sensual love

4. Morals, Values, and Self-Direction

- Greater capacity for setting goals
- Interest in moral reasoning
- Capacity to use insight
- Increased emphasis on personal dignity and self-esteem
- Social and cultural traditions regain some of their previous importance

Teenagers do vary slightly from the above descriptions, but the feelings and behaviors are, in general, considered normal for each stage of adolescence.

Parenting can be the most rewarding work of adult life. Each age and stage of a child's development has specific goals and tasks. For infants, it is to eat, sleep, and explore their world. For adolescents, it is to become their own person with their own group of friends. Adolescents need many skills in order to successfully achieve their goal of increased independence. Some adolescents do not make this transition smoothly. Their movement toward independence can cause stress and grief for parents. Some aspects of this rough transition are normal and, while stressful, should not alarm parents.

Starting early is the best way for parents to prepare for their child's adolescence. The following are ways that parents can prepare themselves and their child for a smoother transition and greater success in achieving the tasks of adolescent development:

- Providing safe and loving home environment
- Creating an atmosphere of honesty, mutual trust, and respect
- Allowing age appropriate independence and assertiveness
- Developing a relationship that encourages your child to talk to you when upset
- Teaching responsibility for their belongings and yours
- Teaching basic responsibility for household chores
- Teaching the importance of accepting limits

A teenager's adolescent years will be less stressful when parents and child have worked together on these tasks throughout the child's earlier development.

The ability to talk openly about problems is one of the most important aspects of the parent and child relationship. Developing this relationship and open communication takes time, persistence, and understanding. The relationship develops gradually by spending time with the child. Meal times, story telling, reading, playing games, outings, vacations, and celebrations are important opportunities for parents to spend time with their child.

Parents should also go for bonding which means try to spend some individual time with each child, particularly when talking about difficult or upsetting things. This relationship creates the foundation for talking with the child when struggles and conflicts emerge during adolescence.

Parents investment of time and energy in the child's early years can prevent small problems of childhood from becoming larger problems of adolescence.

Alcohol, Drugs and Teens

Experimentation with alcohol and drugs during adolescence is common. Unfortunately, teenagers often don't see the link between their actions today and the consequences tomorrow. They also have a tendency to feel indestructible and immune to the problems that others experience. Using alcohol and tobacco at a young age increases the risk of using other drugs later. Some teens will experiment and stop, or continue to use occasionally, without significant problems. Others will develop a dependency, moving on to more dangerous drugs and causing significant harm to themselves and possibly others.

Adolescence is a time for trying new things. Teens use alcohol and other drugs for many reasons, including curiosity, because it feels good, to reduce stress, to feel grown up or to fit in. It is difficult to know which teens will experiment and stop and which will develop serious problems. Teenagers at risk for developing serious alcohol and drug problems include those:

- with a family history of substance abuse
- who are depressed
- who have low self-esteem, and
- who feel like they don't fit in or are out of the mainstream

Teenagers abuse a variety of drugs, both legal and illegal. Legally available drugs include alcohol, prescribed medications, inhalants (fumes from glues, aerosols, and solvents) and over-the-counter cough, cold, sleep, and diet medications. The most commonly used illegal drugs are marijuana (pot), stimulants (cocaine, crack, and speed), LSD, opiates, heroin, etc. The average age of first marijuana use is 14, and alcohol use can start before age 12.

Drug use is associated with a variety of negative consequences, including increased risk of serious drug use later in life, school failure, and poor judgment which may put teens at risk for accidents, violence, unplanned and unsafe sex, and suicide.

Warning signs of teenage alcohol and drug abuse may include:

1. Physical : Fatigue, repeated health complaints, red and glazed eyes, and a lasting cough.

2. Emotional: personality change, sudden mood changes, irritability, irresponsible behaviour, low self-esteem, poor judgment, depression, and a general lack of interest.

3. Family: starting arguments, breaking rules, or withdrawing from the family.

4. School: decreased interest, negative attitude, drop in grades, many absences, truancy, and discipline problems.

5. Social problems: new friends who are less interested in standard home and school activities, problems with the law, and changes to less conventional styles in dress and music.

Some of the warning signs listed above can also be signs of other problems. Parents may recognize signs of trouble. An effective way for parents to show care and concern is to openly discuss the use and possible abuse of alcohol and other drugs with their teenager. Parents can help through early education about drugs, open communication, good role modeling, and early recognition if problems are developing.

Consulting a physician to rule out physical causes of the warning signs is a good first step.

Parent-Child Relationship

Parent-child relationship is the most important phase in our life. We are marked for the entire life by the quality of interactions that take place between us and our parents in the formative years. Degree of success of parenting is the degree to which parents nurture self esteem of the children. Children need a continuous flow of high quality love from parents. Children die of infant grief death syndrome if they are not touched and talked to. Children's need for love is very critical. All psychosis, neurosis, schizophrenia can be traced to the first year of life. Children who do not receive high quality love in 3-5 years of age develop deficiency needs like vitamin deficiency. The psychological deficiencies developed in the childhood create lots of emotional problems in later life.

Things do not change, we change.

-Henry David Thoraue

Negative Habit Patterns

In 2-3 years of childhood, destructive criticism of the child leads to Negative Habit Patterns (NHP) that are carried to adult life. NHP develop due to fear. Three types of NHP are:

1. Inhibited NHP (I cannot, I cannot, I cannot)
2. Compulsive NHP (I have to, I have to, I have to ; fear of rejection, to gain approval of superior, as adult we do things to compensate for lack of approval from parents in childhood)
3. Double NHP (I cannot but I have to. The person is driven to perform but is afraid to try)

These three NHPs cause more damage than all the fears in the world. What causes NHP? Destructive criticism from superiors. Destructive criticism decreases self esteem, ability to perform well, and leads to hypersensitivity so the adult is not able to take any more criticism in life. From where do negative emotions come from? The answer is destructive criticism and lack of love in the childhood. When a child is born, he/she has no self concept, no fear, jealousy, anger, guilt, etc. As the child grows, the negative emotions come to the child from destructive criticism and lack of love. The child up to 5 years cannot differentiate between valid and invalid criticism, and therefore accepts the criticism as a fact. Once the child's conscious mind accepts the destructive criticism as a fact, it goes to the subconscious mind which also accepts and stores it in form of recording. The subconscious mind then makes all the words and actions of the child in subsequent years on a " negative pattern" consistent with the negative impression.

Most of us have been programmed negatively as a child, and we go on to act in a manner consistent with the programme. As life goes on, we go on accumulating negative emotions and putting brakes to our life. It is impossible to realize the full potential of human life without leaving negative emotions. It is like driving a car with emergency brakes on. There is so much stress and strain on engine, transmission, gear and differential that you might break some parts of the machine when you drive the car with emergency brakes on. We must discard negative emotions.

Relationship between youngers and elders in the family affect child development. In most cases, mistakes are committed by both elders and youngers.

Mistakes by elders :1. Do not trust the young ones. 2. Want young to live the way they lived. 3. Take modern living as disrespect. 4. Expect too much time, attention and respect from young. 5. Dislike freedom of young. 6. Blaming. 7. Not forgiving. .

8. Even little inconvenience done inadvertently is misunderstood. Interfere in life of husband-wife-children. Disrespect and criticism of parents of daughter-in-law

9. Unwanted directions, instructions, guidance..Requiring young to behave the way they behaved in their times. Forcing their likes and dislikes in food, dressing, social circle. 10. Making non-issue an issue. 11. Criticizing own family members to outsiders and relatives. 12. Poor listening skills. 13. Belittling young. 14. Avoiding joint problem-solving. 15. Not sharing joy of young, no gifts, praise, touch. 16. Verbal violence. 17. Comparing own children with others. 18. Worrying only for their own comfort. 19. Financial living according to their desires. 20. Insulting children before grand children and outsiders. 21. Giving more importance

to their own daughter/son in front of daughter-in-law/son-in-law. 22. Not realizing their mistakes but blaming young for that. 23. Pampering grand children 24. Not compromising

Mistakes by young: 1. Ignore elders in decision-making. 2. Insulting spouse in front of elders 3. Telling lies to hide mistake. 4. Not caring emotionally. 5. Not giving surprising gifts, praise. 6. Criticizing everything that is old. 7. Poor listening skills 8. Verbal violence. 9. Not providing food, etc according to needs of elders. 10. Provoking spouse against parents. 11. Not compromising. 12. Daughter treats in-laws as in-laws not as father/mother. 13. Suspecting elders. 14. Expecting work-sharing/finance too much. 15. Not involving parents in social circle/friends

16. Not seeking advice in relationship/other problems. 17. Lead personal life wrongly with no interference from elders. 18. Disrespect of relatives and friends of elders.

19. Keeping home command ignoring elders. 20. Not providing financial support

21. Not caring for peace and comfort of elders. 22. Enjoy their life at the cost of comfort of elders. 23. Not giving time to elders.

The Golden Time to Build Relationship

We remain unresponsive when others are behaving well or not misbehaving. We react immediately the moment other person behaves wrongly as if we were waiting for it. We give attention (mostly negative) to others when they are on the wrong track. We mostly interact negatively with others. In other words, we encourage others to misbehave so that they get attention. The other person may be a child/father/mother/boss/ subordinate/ anybody. Hold a 2 year old baby in your arms. The baby will calmly look at different things around but in less than every 2 minutes, he will look into your eyes to ensure that he is acceptable to you. Brain of a child needs stimulus/strokes/attention for its development on a continuous basis. Without these stimuli, the child will feel terrible pain. The hunger for such stimuli (praise, touch, attention, etc) persists even in the adult life.

The practical utility of this information is that by giving attention/ acceptance to a person while he is behaving properly/not behaving improperly, we can encourage him to maintain/increase his desirable behaviour. By doing this, we can also prevent him from getting into undesirable behaviours. Relationship can be easily build in peace not in war. Instead of ignoring or remaining quite while other person is behaving normally, we must immediately provide positive strokes (social reinforcement) to help him become a better human being. Alas, human beings could realize importance of conditional and unconditional social reinforcement in building superior human relationships. Why don't we do this? The reason lies in our childhood. We give what we get.

Self esteem in children

The way we interact with children on a daily basis influences the positive picture that they construct of themselves. Let them know through our language and our behaviour that they are capable and worthwhile and they will began to believe it. The messages we send to children influences the way they see themselves as well as our relationship with them. Heaping children with undeserved praise not based on accomplishment will not build real self esteem.

For parents the essential question is : What type of self image are you helping your children to construct ?While children have countless experiences in settings outside their home and receive messages from many sources including their peers, parents have a huge influence in the way children see them. In fact, when children are very young their sense of self is linked to their parents so a parents self-esteem is obviously important determinant in a child's self- esteem.

Children with a healthy level of self- esteem generally :

- Feel worthwhile (and lovable)
- Believe that they are capable
- Extend themselves as learners

Raising self esteem in children

Following steps can promote self- esteem in children –

1. Build on children's strengths. Point out to children their areas of expertise. This often is difficult with young children but as they progress through primary school they have more options for success available.
2. Give kids realistic responsibility. Develop self- help skills from an early age.
3. Develop the courage to be imperfect. Let them know that mistakes are part of learning.
4. Encourage sensible risk-taking. Help them to develop the attitude that anything is possible.
5. Establish an achievement board or corner in your house or room.
6. Develop a strong language of encouragement that focuses on

effort, improvement, and their contribution and displays your confidence in their ability to succeed.

7. Stick positive affirmations around the house. Use them yourself.
8. Tell children how you handled difficult situations in your life. This is extremely reaffirming for children.
9. Ask children's opinion on important family matters. It shows you value their input.
10. Mirror back a positive self – image or picture.
11. Self esteem comes from achieving success in high-risk areas so help them achieve in an area such as public speaking or drama.
12. Look for small victories or achievements and celebrate them.
13. Provide them with opportunities to take risks and make mistakes.
14. Remind kids that we only grow and improve when we take risks.
15. Help children set goals and stick to them.
16. Write letters or notes of appreciation. Leave notes under the pillow, in lunch boxes or on the computer in e-mail.
17. Help kids accept responsibility for their own actions ans their own fate.
18. Give objective feedback but begin with a strength or positive.
19. Compare them only to themselves.
20. Teach them how to reframe problems or see a situation from a positive point of view.

Praise and Self Esteem

Does praising appropriate behavior nurture self-esteem? Praise-should be reality-based, calibrated to the significance of the child's actions (in other words, not extravagant or grandiose), and directed at the child's behavior rather than his or her character. Sweeping statements such as "You're a perfect angel," or "You're always such a good girl," or "You're always so kind and loving," are not helpful; rather than nurture self-esteem, they tend to evoke anxiety, since the child knows there are times when they are not true.

Avoid turning a child into an approval-addict. We want a child to experience the intrinsic pleasure that flows from appropriate behavior. We want the child to become the source of his or her own approval, not always waiting eagerly for ours. So we must avoid bombarding a child with our "evaluations."

Doesn't a teacher's preoccupation with nurturing a student's self-esteem get in the way of academic achievement? That depends on the teacher's understanding of self-esteem and what is required to nurture it.

If a teacher treats students with respect, avoids ridicule and other belittling remarks, deals with everyone fairly and justly, and projects a strong, benevolent conviction about every student's potential, then that teacher is supporting both self-esteem and the process of learning and mastering the challenges. For such a teacher, self-esteem is tied to reality, not to faking reality.

Our two principal fears are: fear of failure and fear of rejection. They result from low self esteem which is brought on by negative experiences of childhood.

In contrast, however, if a teacher tries to nurture self-esteem by empty praise that bears no relationship to the students' actual accomplishments, then self-esteem is undermined and so is academic achievement. There is a significant relationship between self-esteem and academic achievement

Praise has transformed several lives. The story of Edna Buchanan is well known. This poor, awkward girl, who wore used clothes and other children always laughed at her became the famous journalist because her teacher praised her one home assignment.

Is it possible to have too much self-esteem? Having high self-esteem is equivalent to having good health. High self-esteem is well grounded in reality and balanced between an equal sense of worth and competence. Self-esteem is a particular way of experiencing the self. It is confidence in our ability to learn, to make appropriate choices and decisions, and respond effectively to change. It is also the experience that success, achievement, fulfillment-happiness are right and natural for us.

How much you like yourself is totally dependent on who you think you are

---

Obviously parents, teachers, and other adults can do a great deal to make the road to self-esteem easier or harder. Sometimes, where there are deep psychic wounds and traumas left unresolved since childhood, a decent level of self-esteem can be very difficult to achieve. In such cases, psychotherapy may be necessary.

Many factors influence our self-esteem. Certainly parental upbringing is important; parents can make the road to self-esteem easier or harder- but they cannot determine the ultimate level of their child's self-esteem. Neither can teachers or other adults. Neither can biology—nor birth experiences. Yet all these factors can play a role. And among these factors, none is likely to be as important as the influence of parents, primarily through the values they instill, which can lead a child toward or away from growing self-esteem.

Isn't self-esteem the consequence of approval from "significant others?" The answer is "No". When people betray their mind and judgment ("sell their souls") to win the approval of their "significant others," they may win that approval, but their self-esteem suffers. What shall it profit us to win the approval of the whole world and lose our own?

Doesn't the possession of good looks, popularity, and wealth almost guarantee self-esteem? No, these things guarantee nothing—if one does not have the self-esteem to support them.

Isn't it true that if you have high self-esteem, nothing bothers you? The answer is that. self-esteem can make one less susceptible to anxiety and pain, it cannot make one impervious. To offer a simple example: If someone you love dies, does having good self-esteem mean the loss won't bother you? Clearly not. Self-esteem is the immune system of consciousness. If you have a healthy immune system, you might become ill, but you are less likely to; if you do become ill, you will likely recover faster—your resilience is greater.

Once you've attained self-esteem, is it automatically maintained forever? No, every value pertaining to life requires action to maintain it. If we do not continue to breathe, the breathing we did yesterday will not keep us alive today.

Building self esteem

To increase self esteem, answer the following:

1. An important thing to know about me is ________.
2. I felt proud when I ________.
3. Other people like me because I am ________.
4. The thing I do best is ________.
5. I look ________.
6. If a new friend came to visit, the first thing I would show him/her is my ________.
7. I like myself because ________.
8. I do not feel important when ________.

Behaviours that Build Self Esteem

SMILES

HUGS

EYE CONTACT

TOUCHING
PRAISE
CCEPTANCE
WARMTH
LISTENING
QUALITY TIME
ENCOURAGING
BEING SUPPORTIVE
COMMUNICATING
NO PUT-DOWNS
COOPERATING
NON-JUDGMENTAL ATTITUDES
GIVING RESPONSIBILITY
RESPECTING OTHERS

The fastest way to build self esteem is: make the person feel that he/she is responsible for his/her life. We are 100 per cent responsible for our life after our childhood, no matter what kind of childhood we had.

People see in you what you see in yourself.

Ten simple ways to boost your self-esteem

1. De-bug your system

(A) Use the right programming language when you talk to yourself.

(B) Congratulate yourself when things go right – even little things like getting to work on time or remembering to call a friend on their birthday.

(C) If something is bothering you, whether it's a person, an incident, or something you did or didn't do, acknowledge it, learn from it and then delete it.

(D) Before you go to sleep, think of six things that made you happy during the day. It could be a smile, a piece of music, sunshine on your back or a cuddle.

(D) Use your sleeping time positively. If something's bothering you, ask yourself some questions about it before you go to sleep. Make sure you phrase those questions positively – don't ask yourself, 'why am I such a failure?' before you close your eyes. Ask, 'how can I be more successful/confident/happy?'

About 80 per cent fears are imaginary. They are product of your mind as they do not exist in reality

2. Start the Day Right

Put yourself in a positive frame of mind before you even get out of bed by asking yourself these questions:

- If I went to sleep last night with a question in mind, am I any closer to an answer now? (If you don't have that answer yet, don't chase it. Wait until it comes.)
- What am I happy about in my life? (It doesn't have to be large or wonderful. Small happiness counts.)
- What am I excited about?
- What am I proud of?
- What am I grateful for?
- What am I committed to?
- Who do I love?
- Who loves me?

3. Cultivate Your Social Life

Less you interact with other people, the more negative you'll feel about yourself and the less likely you'll be to put yourself in social situations. Break the negative circle by starting to include other people in your life. Join a voluntary organization or club and offer to help. This generates feelings of self worth.

4. Get Exercise

Working out outdoors, is a great way to generate your own 'feel-good' chemicals and will give you body confidence as well as energise you. Exercise regularly. If you have physical poise and strength, it's much easier to feel confident inside as well.

5. Relax

Learn to breathe like a relaxed and confident person, and it's the simplest habit you could ever learn. Take up meditation or yoga and become a master of poise and positive energy.

6. Make Your Own Choices

Take time out to assess a) your career and b) your relationships.

Ask yourself:

- Is this job/person giving me positive feedback?
- Do I enjoy this job/person?
- Does this job/person acknowledge and reflect my creativity and my strengths?
- Am I sticking with this job/person simply out of habit?
- Could I do better?

7. Review Your Situation

Include time for reflection in your daily schedule – praying if you're religions, meditating or writing a diary of your thoughts and feelings. *We often don't give ourselves enough time to process all the things that are going on in our lives.*

If you decide on a diary, instead of writing a list of what went wrong today, write down these headings first, and fill them in.

- Goals: set yourself a daily outcome and build up to larger goals.
- Achievements: what did you achieve today?
- Gifts: what happened, out of the blue, to cheer you?
- Insights: you may not get one every day – but when you suddenly spot a key to some piece of your behaviour, write it down.

8. Change Your Environment

Chances are, your environment reflects the way you feel, but, whether it's dull, cluttered or messy, you can change it. Any positive changes you make are going to have a positive effect on your mood too. Look at your desk, your home or even your wardrobe and see what you can do to make it more inspiring.

(a) Clear up the clutter (a good Feng Shui practice that will make you feel more energetic) and throw out stuff you don't use
(b) Give yourself a sound track – add some inspiring music
(c) Introduce new bold colours that you love

Excuses are useless as they only reveal your lack of faith in your ability to succeed

---

9. Give Yourself the VIP Treatment

Start treating yourself the way you'd treat your best friend. It comes as a shock to most people *how nasty and neglectful we can be to ourselves.* Give yourself encouragement and support. Take yourself out for a hairdo, a massage, even a clothes-shopping trip.

10. Find a Role Model

Pretend to be someone else? Think of someone you admire – it could be someone you know, or someone famous – and live your day as they would. How would they react to others? Would they be assertive? Relaxed? Confident? Fun and energetic?

Think back to when you were a child, you'll be able to come up with a time when you were happy with yourself and in control of your situation. In fact, if you can remember that time very well, why not be your own role model?

Art of Parenting

Is parenting a duty or burden for you? Let me give you the example of one of the best parents I met, Srivastavas. Dr. B. P. Srivastava, a world famous entomologist, my teacher and later my next door neighbour was blessed with a female child. Madhulika who unfortunately got slipped from the hands of doctors soon after birth and got severe spine injuries making her a handicap for the whole life. Madhulika developed a big hump at jer back, could never straighten her body and did not reach more than around 4 feet. She had a difficult time in school with children teasing her and lots of other problems.

Dr. Srivastava never worried about his daughter. He never criticized her, judged her or controlled her. Parenting was a joy for him.

Madhulika's self esteem always remained high. Getting enough time, attention, unconditional love and support from the parents enabled her to top in her biotechnology classes in JNU, Delhi, and earn a prestigious fellowship from USA. We uselessly force our desires on our children. Instead of becoming their partner we try to become their controller. We cannot take a single breath for our child, cannot think a single thought for our child, cannot feel a single feeling for the child, cannot dream a single dream for our child, cannot cry a single tear for our child, yet we foolishly try to control our child's life. We forget that the child lives for himself and that is his responsibility. Personal responsibility is the essence of self.

What happens we decide for the life of our child? The child stops taking responsibility for his thoughts and leaves his mind open for the whims of others. If a child senses he is a disappointment to those who should love him unconditionally, in desperation, he might seek approval elsewhere, often with negative and destructive peer groups.

We must show acceptance to our child by not judging, moralizing or guilt-tripping the child. If you judge your child then he will 1. do something you do not want him to do.

2. He will have no trust in you, and 3. His relationship with you will be weakened. We must respect individuality of the child. His feelings, needs and requests must be considered properly.

> Children are given to us on loan for a very short period of time.
> They come to us like packets of seeds with no guarantees.
> We do not know what they will look like, act like or have the potential to become.
> Our job, like the gardener's is to meet their needs as best as we can. To give proper nourishment, love, attention, caring, and to hope for the best

What to do when your son grows into a rebellious teen ? Take following steps:

1. Assume that you know nothing about your son. Start with a clean slate. Work on yourself. Take out all frustration, anger and judgment on a paper by writing.
2. Develop a sincere desire to understand your son. Don't try to shape him up or give advice to him.
3. Learn to love him unconditionally just the way he is rather than withholding your love until he shapes up.
4. Learn to listen within his frame of reference.
5. Apologize for your judgments and past mistakes. Be patient.
6. Repeat 4 and 5 until your son opens up and you recover your son.

Child-parent relationship is so crucial that it affects all other kinds of relationships in our life. Unfortunately, many of us rely almost exclusively on punishment when dealing with our children.

We must know what behavious are undesirable. A target behavior is habitual, frequently occurring, inappropriate, and distinctly observable. We can see or hear it. A checklist for target behaviours and their treatments are described below.

Target Behaviours

1. Not Doing as Told - Disobedience

When your child is told to do something, he may fail to respond or may choose to ignore your request because he may not have learned to pay attention when being addressed, or may be an expert at tuning out.

Treatment : Get the child to respond immediately following your calm and firm request. Be strict but not punitive. Use time out.

2. *Defying Commands - Defiance*

If a child replies, "No, I won't" or may do the opposite of what you asked Treatment: Defiance needs to be dealt with immediately. Use time out.

3. *Temper Tantrums*

If tantrums occur more than 4-5 times a year, then the behavior should be targeted. Treatment: Teach children to express their feelings assertively, such as "Mother, I'm angry at you because you aren't listening!" Use time out before undesirable behavour becomes a temper tentrum.

4. *Poor-Me Statements*

Examples are: No one loves me, you love my sister more than me, I'm stupid, I can't do anything right, Everyone has a better life than I do, You love the dog more than me, I want to die, I'm going to kill myself. Also included are pouting (hanging-lip syndrome), whining (puppy-dog syndrome) and crying (manipulatively, to get attention or to get his or her way). Treatment : If a child makes poor-me statements only rarely, you can comfort or console the child appropriately. But if poor-me's are frequent, nurturing will reinforce them and increase their frequency. If a child who has not previously expressed poor-me statements suddenly begins to show this behavior, attempt to learn if something specific may be troubling the child-perhaps a problem at school-and then try to remove it. Enhance self esteem of the child, touch the child and discuss his feelings.

5. *Negative Statements*

Examples are: Jeevan is a creep, I hate doing this, Why do we always have to do this? Do we have to go there? He's stupid, I hate you! I hope you go bankrupt. Treatment : Identify and correct these statements in early childhood.Enhance self esteem of the child.

6. Nagging

A child's nagging or repeatedly asking for something after he or she has been told no. Treatment : When you tell your child no, explain why you are saying no. If your reasonable answer is still no and the child continues to nag, time out should be used. Be patient.

7. *Interrupting*

The child who constantly interrupts when you are talking to others. Treatment : Allow interruptions to report only a dangerous situation.

8. *Physical Complaints*

When a child frequently complains of vague pains or of generally not feeling well but you have no indication of an actual medical disorder. Treatment: Physical complaints most often occur when a child wishes to avoid a normal but stressful situation, such as a test at school, an overly critical teacher, or a bully. In such cases if you can eliminate the problems, the complaints will disappear.

9. *Not Paying Attention - Inattentive*

Children with attention problems are experts at tuning out. Treatment: Attention has three parts: looking, listening, and remembering. The child's eyes should focus directly on a task or directly on the adult speaking and eyes should divert only very briefly. To check whether the child is listening, ask, "What did I just say?" If the child consistently cannot answer correctly, then listening should be treated as a target behavior. Most children with attention problems have been trained not to remember what they are told to do because parents repeat commands, nag, prompt, coach, or issue warnings. The child has little incentive to use his own mind. If your child constantly tells you, "I forgot," when you ask, "Why haven't you done this?" or "What are you supposed to be doing?" and his response is a completely bewildered look - then treat forgetting as a target behavior. The child can learn to remember. It is a learned skill. Stop repeating commands, nagging, prompting, coaching, or issuing warnings. Use time out.

10. *Helplessness and Dependency*

A. Task dependency: a child needing excessive support and prompting in order to begin or complete a task. B. Cognitive dependency : not thinking throughout the day. The child does not pay attention to how to behave correctly in different environments (restaurant, market or the classroom). He doesn't monitor his own behavior throughout the day. C. Emotional dependency is an irrational belief that one cannot be alone. The emotionally dependent individual experiences strong feelings of anxiety (fear) when alone. Treatment: Sitting with the child during homework and constantly prompting and guiding her work reinforces the child's task dependency. You can show them one or two times how to organize but do not continue to prompt and coach thereafter. Let the consequences do the work. They'll then learn quickly. When the coaching is eliminated and instead consequences are enforced, these children dramatically change in less than two weeks. The parents should not do everything for such a child but instead should teach him skill building: teach and require him to perform self-help skills, including making his own bed, cooking, doing laundry, etc. Use social reinforcement abundantly.

11. Dawdling

The child who begins tasks slowly and takes more time than necessary to complete them is a deliberate dawdler, for example, the dawdler isn't ready on time for the school bus. Parents then wind up rewarding the child by driving her to school. Dawdling when doing homework is very common. Treatment Cut one hour of play after school if child was driven to school by car (reinforcement removal). Use social reinforcement abundantly.

12. Poor Reading Skills

The reasons underlying reading problems are enormous and complex. Treatment : Relearning the fundamental reading skills taught earlier in school and approaching them slowly. Use social reinforcement abundantly.

13. Poor School Performance

Not paying attention has a lot to do with the poor academic performance. If school performance does not improve, teachers should deal with the following target behaviors: (a) Not staying on task (or not paying attention) : (i) not looking at the work or the teacher, (ii) not listening to instructions, (iii) not remembering what to do (b) Not finishing work on time (c) Not doing work neatly (d) Not doing work correctly and accurately and thus consistently getting lower grades. (e) In some cases, failing to be quiet – noisy (f) In some cases, not staying in seat - fidgeting and running around (g) Blurting out questions without politely raising a hand (h) Pushing in line rather than waiting and walking in line Treatment : Analyze and treat the problems at home. In school, use reinforcement as shaping. Use natural reinforcers.

14. Tattling

All children tattle occasionally. When tattling occurs frequently, treat it as a target behavior. Treatment: Tell the tattler to work things out with the other child. Working things out means being assertive and using good communication skills. Don't try to teach the skills at the moment a target behavior occurs, because that inadvertently reinforces or conditions the behavior It is best to try not to interfere, whether the problem involves playmates or siblings. Children develop social skills by trial and error. Tattling be allowed, if the child being tattled on is doing something dangerous or has become physically aggressive then use reinforcement removal. Use social reinforcement abundantly.

15. Fighting with Siblings

Discipline both parties immediately without asking questions. If you have observed directly who initiated the conflict, you may discipline that child only. Beware of a child who looks like an angel who may be guilty of secret taunting and teasing. Use time out for one party only if you have seen only that party initiating and indulging in the fight. Use reinforcement removal Allow children to work out their differences themselves. Use social reinforcement abundantly.

16. Aggression

violent contact with others, whether directly or using objects. Treatment: Aggressive children come from aggressive families. Treatment of adults is required. For children, use a strong method of discipline like reinforcement removal.

17. Lying

Decrease imaginary play considerably as the child approaches the age of ten. Use a strong method of discipline like reinforcement removal.

NO PUNISHMNT

Punishment is the application of an aversive (painful) stimulus, such as yelling and hitting, to decrease a behavior. Many of us rely more on punishment than reinforcement. Often we are not aware that we do this. Children receiving punishment, when discover their power as adolescents, rebel, and want to be away from you. Punishment damages relationships and does little to make your child warm and loving. Frequent punishment leads to severe alienation between parent and child. Reinforcing our child's good behavior works more slowly but the change is permanent. The major side effects of severe punishment include anxiety and nervousness (the nervous child does not learn well; tension interferes with new learning;

they have trouble sitting still and paying attention. So we call them hyperactive or highly misbehaving), emotional problems (vandalism, drug addiction, suicide), filled with anger and hostility, adaptation to pain, reinforcement of undesired behaviours, bad emotional health of punisher, and bad relationship between punisher and child.

Most of the time we express our anger in a setting we perceive as safe - usually at home. We do this, falsely believing we can get away with it when targeting our children or our spouse. But it does not work. A healthier alternative is to express feelings assertively.

Teach assertiveness to your child to say, "Mummy (Daddy), I'm mad at you because you're not listening to me!" instead of having temper tantrums Focus on every behavioral and motivational problem, including aggression that may occur both in the home and at school. Use a form of discipline that is neither punitive nor reinforcing to undesirable behaviors. The first step in behaviour change programme is correct identification of target behaviours. The second step is to select a correct method of treatment. It is better to use first the mild methods and then move on to strong methods if required except for aggression and lying.

Important methods of treatment are as follows:

I. Reinforcement : 1. Social Reinforcement 2. Material Reinforcement
II. Disciplining : 3. Ignoring 4. Time Out 5. Reinforcement Removal

1. Reinforcement

The true secret to success lies in the positive interactions between parent and child. Reinforcement is the key ingredient for working successfully with a child. Once a child's behavior improves, discipline becomes less necessary. Once youngsters' behavior patterns become positive, they are treated positively, which helps them feel better about themselves.

Reinforcement involves procedures that either maintain or increase desirable behaviors. Reinforcers can be divided into two broad categories - Social and Material. Material reinforcement may be divided into two categories - activities and objects.

Social reinforcers include personal interactions between you and your child likepaying attention, spending time with the child, looking at the child, talking to the child, praising, touching, listening,just plain showing a response.

Material reinforcers include various objects and activities like: watching television, having free play, going outside, riding a bike, playing games, enjoying special privileges, attending a special event, and having prized objects such as toys, favorite foods, money.

Social Reinforcement

It is better to use social reinforcement over material reinforcement because:

(A) Social reinforcement during early childhood develops a close relationship between parent and child. (B) Material reinforcers generally produce the quickest improvements in behavior, but they often fade rapidly. (B) Material reinforcers promote a payment expectancy. Ability to work willingly, lovingly, and voluntarily at home to fulfill our responsibilities to our family does not grow. (D) Social reinforcement helps children develop a more positive self-image - more self-esteem. Youngsters develop their primary attitudes about themselves from how their parents treat them and what their parents say to them.

Some basic principles that underlie changing our children's behaviors through reinforcement are:

1. Immediate social and material reinforcement is more effective in changing behaviors than delayed reinforcement. 2. If reinforcement is to be effective, the parent must reinforce correct responses consistently. Here are a few examples:

You say, "Please pick up your toys and get ready for dinner." If the child immediately begins to put his toys away. Reinforce by saying, "I'm really proud of you for listening to me and doing as you are told so quickly. I'm very proud of you."

Suppose you say "no" for something and the child says "OK" and quietly walks away and he has a history of temper tantrums. Use this moment and say, "Son, wait a minute. I want to give you a hug and a kiss. When Dad said no you didn't blow up and you accepted what I said in such a nice way. I love you, son."

Or if you hear Jeevan and his sister Maya settle a dispute without fighting, go in the room and say, "Jeevan, Maya, I was listening to you two settle your difference in a nice way. Jeevan, you asked Maya to play with her keyboard and when she said no you gently told her you'll be careful with it. I'm so proud of you for asking so nicely and without threatening your sister. And Maya, you said no at first, but you listened to what your brother had to say and even changed your mind so he could practice on your keyboard. You didn't whine or cry but instead you handled it like a big girl. I'm so proud of you. I'm so proud of the both of you. I love you."

Training new behavioral patterns requires a lot of work at first, but it is easer and faster later.

Every elder must reinforce consistently when an appropriate behavior is being learned. Consistency requires that you reinforce behaviors when the child is in different situations - restaurants, temple, market etc. You can praise a child anywhere and at any time.

3. Contingency means that consequences exist for target behaviors. Reinforcement is given as a consequence of the child's responding correctly; discipline is provided as a consequence of the child's not responding correctly. Both conditional reinforcement (praise for performance) and unconditional reinforcement (telling the child "I love you") should be practiced abundantly. Children who are abundantly reinforced will be more comfortable and secure about themselves and thus will be less likely to spend their lives searching for approval. Unfortunately, much of this interaction is negative. At home and at school, when children are quiet and being well behaved, we ignore them. When they do or say something inappropriate, we immediately give them our attention - the negative kind. If you wish to make unconditional reinforcing statements to your child, make them while your child is behaving well. and say, "I love you.". When socially reinforcing a behavior, use descriptive statements such as these:

"I like the way you're sitting at the dinner table. You're being quiet and asking for things in a nice way."

When your son brings you his homework after completion say,

"You did a beautiful job on your homework. Your writing is nice and neat, just the way Mummy showed you."

"Jeevan, I'm glad that you picked up your toys when Mummy asked you, without making a fuss. I'm very proud of you."

We wait for children to misbehave and then we interact with them negatively by yelling and describing what they did wrong. Negative statements are the predominant way parents and teachers treat children. Parents use descriptive statements all the time, but usually in a negative way, such as:

"Why didn't you pick up your toys like I asked you? " "Why don't you ever listen to Mummy ?" "Stop making those sounds at the dinner table. I want you to sit quietly and keep your mouth shut."

Have you noted that misbehavior often gets gradually worse until we explode? For example, Jeevan may kick the table leg and we try to ignore him. Then he hits his sister - then we explode. To prevent escalation of misbehaviors, learn vigilance. Use positive description statements before the child does anything wrong. An example is, "Jeevan, you're sitting so quietly tonight at the table. I'm proud of you." Do this before he starts banging on the table. Reinforce the child as early in the sequence as possible.

Children are not motivated to perform well in school. They hate school. A positive teacher using shaping techniques is crucial in getting these children to like school, that is, to motivate them to want to do well. If a child becomes positively motivated to perform well in school, the problematic patterns will disappear.

A teacher should walk around the classroom while the children are on task and touch their shoulder, praise them, and smile at them for their efforts and for their skill improvements. *Praising the child for effort is an important motivating tool.* When stopping to help students, the teacher can also prompt them on the next step while praising them for having improved a skill by one or more steps. This requires only a few seconds with each child.

Material Reinforcement

The principles of immediacy, consistency, and contingency that apply to social reinforcement apply to material programs as well. Here are additional principles reserved specifically for objects and activities:

1. Identify what your child finds reinforcing. All children have a wide variety of reinforcing objects and activities. With the list from your observations you can begin the program and be successful.

2. To avoid lapses due to satiation, update and monitor on a continuous and ongoing basis. Removing a particular reinforcer for a while can increase its effectiveness. As you probably already know, when you deprive a child of an object or activity, the youngster finds it desirable. For example, if you do not allow your child to use her bicycle, it probably won't bother her for a few days. Eventually she will most likely begin requesting it more and more. At that point, having use of her bicycle will be useful for controlling a behavior because it will have regained importance to your child.

Primary Reinforcers like food, water, shelter, or clothing may not be withheld. All other reinforcers - a bicycle, a football, a favorite doll - are called secondary reinforcers and can be useful in controlling undesirable behaviors.

3. If a child fails to get one reinforcer, he is not allowed to substitute something else in its place. For example,

Becausse seven-year-old Mohan dawdled every morning, he missed the bus and his mother had to drive him to school. This made his mother late for work. Waking him up earlier did not remedy the situation. Yelling, pleading, and threatening did not help either.

Mohan loved to ride his bicycle, so we gave him the contingency that if he was ready for school on time, exactly at 6:45 A.M., he could ride his bike after school from 3:30 to 5:00. If he failed to be on time in the morning, he would not be allowed to ride his bike or do anything else-no substitutions-on that day during those ninety minutes. This meant that from 3:30 to 5:00 Mohan was deprived of contact with friends, phone calls, and most especially, homework, which meant he had to do it all later in the evening and miss his favorite TV show. This means that we want to change inappropriate behaviors to appropriate behaviors in the briefest possible time.

Each day is a fresh start. This means that Mohan can make choices: be ready and on time the next day and be allowed to ride his bike, be late again and not ride his bike, or get his homework done early.

If Mohan can't ride his bike but can play with his video games, the consequences to him are meaningless. The removal of homework is also important because if he completes his homework in this time period, he's free later to pursue fun activities. Allowing children to do their homework when an activity has been lost indeed neutralizes the effectiveness of the treatment.

4. Do not offer to buy the child something special if he improves a behavior. Getting a new bicycle for good grades means bribery and extortion. Instead, make the child earn the reinforcers that are already part of their environment or part of their daily routine. Examples of natural reinforcers are: watching one hour of television at night, talking to friends on the telephone, playing football with friends, going outside for free play after school for an hour or two, and eating a favorite dessert after dinner.

Each of these can be useful when we have to deal with some very important behaviors. In fact, these reinforcers should be used to improve school performance.

4. Social reinforcement must also be given abundantly whenever the child's performance is correct. Even when using material reinforcers, we must still reinforce socially. Material programs will fail quickly unless correct behavior is also rewarded with praise, a hug, a kiss, and touch.

The real success is in the social reinforcement. Consistent social reinforcement is the key to success. Without it, no form of discipline will work. When actively reinforcing behaviors you'll begin to see incorrect target behaviors subside and new appropriate behaviors begin to emerge.

DISCIPLINE

Children dislike and avoid zero stimulation - the absence of reinforcement or punishment. The discipline techniques based on zero stimulation are not only highly effective but lack the detrimental effects of traditional forms of punishment.

First, actively reinforce all forms of positive behavior. No matter what method of discipline is employed, no long-lasting gains will occur unless parents reinforce the child for good behaviors. This includes deliberate praise for specific improvement and unconditional expressions of love and caring when the child is behaving well. Even parents working full-time must make the time for talking to and for having fun with their children. All children must have individual attention. Without abundant reinforcement no success will be achieved.

For any method of discipline to succeed, the following be ensured.

(i) Discipline should be applied immediately following misbehavior. (ii) Correct misbehavior that occurs outside the home. (iii) Consistency : it cannot be sporadic or haphazard. (iv) No Nervousness, no Humiliation

Discipline should not produce tension or anxiety within the child. If you yell often, watch out when your child becomes an adolescent. He has learned from you how to yell, and your teenager will yell back. Frequent yelling also teaches a child to tune out.

(v) No unintended reinforcement. The best methods of discipline require as little person-to-person interaction as possible. An additional interaction inadvertently reinforces the behavior you're working on.

The three methods of discipline based on zero stimulation are:

I. Ignoring - the mildest form of discipline - is only useful for the mildest forms of misbehaviors.

II. Time Out is the most frequently used and successful method and is used if reasoning fails or if the behaviors are too strong for ignoring.

III. Reinforcement Removal is used for behaviors that are highly resistant to treatment, for example, lying and more severe misbehaviors such as aggression.

2. Ignoring

Ignoring, which means removing social reinforcement, is useful only for very mild target behaviors (those you can tolerate without losing control).Target behavior can worsen immediately following the beginning of ignoring. Ignoring is very inefficient and slow. It requires in finite patience and works only

3. Time Out

It means removing the misbehaving child from all material and social reinforcement and from all negative attention. When in time out, the child gets little or zero stimulation. In other words, it is completely boring. Time out can begin at age three, although it has been used with even younger children. The following rules be followed:

- Use Time Out for Even a Hint of Misbehavior
- Choose a Suitable Environment
- Avoid Reinforcers near the Time Out Chair
- Use Time Out Everywhere
- Choose the Right Amount of Time
- Do Not Talk to Your Child While in Time Out
- Never Physically Put a Child in Time Out
- Deal with "I Need to Go to the Bathroom"
- Insist that the Child Remember the Misbehavior
- Respond to Misbehaving on the Way to Time Out
- Reinforce Correct Behavior
- Be Tough Consistently - Allow No Testing
- Don't Bargain
- Be Consistent with the Other Parent
- Respond Early and Quickly
- Offer No Warnings
- Treat Siblings Equally
- Explain Time Out to Your Child

Designate a large, comfortable, overstuffed chair for time out and move it away from windows. The ideal place for a time out chair is in a forma' living room. Your goal is to make the area around the chair as boring as possible. A competing reinforcer may be a television the child can watch from a distance. Simply moving the chair a couple of feet will be desirable or turn off TV.

To use time out away from home, simply designate a convenient place such as a bench, an empty table at a restaurant or a corner of a grocery store; then ask your child to come to you. Firmly whisper in his ear to go to time out. Try to do this away from observers. If you embarrass your child, you may control the misbehavior but risk psychological and emotional scarring. Choose the right amount of time. Consult the following table.

Age	Minimum Time
3 to 4	3 minutes
4 to 5	5 minutes
5 to 11	10 minutes

If children misbehave in time out, do not let them out while acting up, even if the time limit has been reached. That reinforces the misbehavior. Instead, when they finally sit up and behave, time one extra minute of quiet and then let them out. For children ages five to eleven, the average time for the first day is about nineteen to twenty minutes. Within three days, almost every child behaves within the minimum time.

Avoid physically putting children into time out or physically taking them out If your child refuses to go to time out, do the following: Remove all reinforcing objects from his room. Put a lock on the outside of his door. Install a one-way peephole to allow you to check on his safety. He then has a choice - either go to the time out chair or go to the room. If he refuses to go to the chair, physically put him in his room, lock the door, and follow all the same procedures as you would when using the chair. Insist that the child remember the misbehavior. When children come out of time out, they are required to tell you what they did wrong. Ask them, "Why did you go to time out?" After they tell you, then command them to do what they were supposed to do. Unless they comply immediately, they go back to time out and the time starts from zero.

They also return to time out if they can't remember what they did wrong. Begin the timing from zero. When the youngsters emerge, ask again, "Why did you go to time out?" For three- and four-year-olds, you can be less strict. If they cannot respond, it's all right for you to tell them. But after age four, they must assume the responsibility for remembering what they did to be sent to the time out chair.

What should you do if your child misbehaves on the way to time out by stomping a foot on the floor, kicking a chair, or cursing under her breath? When time is up, ask why she went in the first place. If the answer is correct, ask a second question: "What did you do on the way to time out?" Tell your child to go back to time out for the full time. Then ask, "Why did you have to go to time out a second time?" Once again she must tell you what she did wrong and then perform the behavior she was supposed to have done in the first place.

No form of discipline will work if the parent does not reinforce correct behavior. Time out will reduce inappropriate behavior, but it will not teach the child new correct behaviors. Reinforcement - especially social reinforcement - will teach the child correct and appropriate behaviors.

As a result, when they come out of time out and tell you what they did wrong, you say, "Now give Daddy a kiss, and do what you're supposed to do." In this way they learn that you judge their behavior to be wrong but in no way have they lost your love.

The technique of counting "one, two, three" is a warning. This reminds the child to pay attention. When you warn or correct they will comply with the correct behavior, but five minutes later they will resume their "not thinking" pattern, which is exactly what we are combating. Getting them to think is crucial. Sending the child to time out immediately, with no warning and no counting, is probably the most important rule to follow in the correct use of time out. Do it at all times.

Explain time out only on two occasions: the night before you start and the night after you start. Never explain it again; experience will teach it well enough. You want your child to remember the rules. When you finish explaining, ask your child to explain it back to you. Clear up any misconceptions.

Keep the explanation simple. Don't review each target behavior. Otherwise, if you forget one or two you may hear: "But you didn't say that." Simply tell your child that he will go to time out for any and all misbehavior and will stay in for exactly ten minutes (or the minimum time mentioned earlier) if behavior is perfect while in the chair. Explain that if he misbehaves while in time out, he will stay in until his behavior is proper and quiet.

Tell your children that they must think about what they did wrong whenever they go to time out and that they must tell you what it was when they come out. Say, "If you can't remember what you did wrong, then you will have to go back until you do remember." Do this only when explaining time out. Do not repeat this for each incident. Important information:

1. Your child may start to resume old habits. If so, you are probably being lax by not reinforcing enough or letting testing behaviors slip past you. Stay alert for warning signs that your child is starting to test you. Expect testing.

2. Spontaneous reappearance of target behaviors is likely. Don't become dismayed. Simply enforce the time out rules, and the testing will disappear quickly.

3. Matters will get worse before they get better. Because time out removes both social and material reinforcers, target behaviors will get worse and new misbehaviors, or new testing behaviors, will emerge. This generally gets rough for three or four days. If you hang on, you will see dramatic improvement by the fourth or fifth day.

5. Most important of all, the key to success is love-social reinforcement for behaving correctly.

4. Reinforcement Removal

Reinforcement Removal is the technique of taking away material reinforcers for a long period of time. For younger children the loss may be a week; for older children the loss is for longer periods of time - a month or even a year. Time periods that work best for reinforcement removal depend on age: a week for three- and four-year-olds, a month for five- to seven-year-olds, and a year above the age of eight. It must be used precisely.

Process of Reinforcement Removal

Step 1. Make a list of at least seven objects and activities that are most important to your son or daughter. Examples are using the telephone to talk to friends, riding a bicycle, playing video games, listening to favorite CD's, watching a favorite TV show, going to the movies, or going camping. Do not choose things that are impractical to take away, such as reading.

Step 2. Prioritize the list, with number (1) being the most important to the child and number (7) also being very important but the least important on the list.

Step 3. Explain to the child that if he engages in a serious act such as aggression, he will lose an item for a long period of time. For example, "Rishi, if you hit your sister, or anyone, you'll lose your bicycle for a month. If you do it again remember the other items on our list." This method has been successfully used with aggressive teenagers - some referred because their aggression had reached very dangerous levels.

Step 4. Begin with the loss of item (7) and for each act move up the list. Each aggressive act serves as an increasingly uncomfortable loss. Keep a record for yourself of the starting date as a reminder.

Step 5. It's also important to have a backup if your child uses an item while it is confiscated. The back-up must be particularly strong and thus very meaningful. Two methods that work well are (1) to be permitted no contact with friends for a week and (2) to give away or sell the item. Use this only after the first method has failed twice and warn your child ahead of time that this will be the consequence. Example

Gopal was an eleven-year-old whose mother was feeling extremely guilty and desperate. She loved her child, but at the same time she "hated" him. Gopal's mother was struggling financially, working extremely hard as a nurse, raising two younger children The stress was taking its toll on her.

Different methods of behaviour control brought all target behaviors under check except aggression. On a daily basis Gopal's behaviors at home improved. He readily did as he was told, his poor-me's and whining stopped, he no longer nagged, and he stopped interrupting his mother's conversations. His schoolwork improved. He paid attention in class, completed all his work, stopped acting like the class clown, and was polite to his teacher. However, he continued to lose his temper on rare occasions. In addition, loss of temper and violent rage are such powerful emotions that they are more difficult for a child to contain. Aggression is actually very resistant to almost all forms of traditional treatment. Here, the use of reinforcement removal is very effective.

Gopal's aggression occurred only about twice a month. He would use his fist to hit other children or even his mother, sometimes with an object in his hand. Reasoning with Gopal about his aggressiveness failed. He promised repeatedly to do better but did not. Therefore reinforcement removal was applied. Each aggressive act meant the loss of an item for one year; dates were recorded in a notebook. His mother listed the following seven items:

1. Police Station computer game. 2. Guitar playing. 3. Watching television. 4. Riding his bicycle. 5. Calling his friends. 6. Going to the movies. 7. Eating candy

If he was found using an item when it had been taken away, he would then not be permitted contact with his friends for one week. This is a strong backup technique.

The aggression persisted through the first six items. His mother managed to carry out the contingencies to the letter. Finally at item (1), the aggression halted. Now, most children stop the aggression after the loss of three items.

Several weeks later in a follow-up session, Gopal was very happy. His uncle had bought him an expensive pen as a gift, and they had started going swimming together. Gopal had never been treated this way.

Generally, for children below the age, of five, the combination and judicious use of time out and social reinforcement - control aggression extremely well. From the age of five through age twelve, reinforcement removal has to be added.

Whether the method of discipline is ignoring, time out or reinforcement removal, do not forget to actively reinforce your child when he is behaving well. Discipline suppresses the target behaviors, but learning new and more appropriate behaviors requires very active social reinforcement.

Handling an Attention Disordered Child

1. Frequent yelling at your child or other family members trains children to tune out. A loud home trains children to not pay attention to anything.

Treatment: Talk in a normal tone at all times. When telling your child to do something, speak in a calm, normal, firm tone.

2. Frequently hitting or spanking children teaches them to tune out the discomforts of their surroundings. It also makes them nervous and agitated, which interferes with learning and increases problem behaviors.

Treatment: Use time out, also reinforcement removal when the target behavior is severe (aggression).

3. Being inconsistent confuses children trying to learn right from wrong. They don't understand when they are behaving as they should or shouldn't.

Treatment: Be consistent with praise for doing things correctly and with using time out for doing things incorrectly.

4. Doing everything for your children trains them not to think, not to problem solve, and not to be independent.

Treatment: Consequences should require children to think, to remember, and to be attentive. Teach them to do things for themselves and to help with family responsibilities. Then require them to not only do all of these things but to remember when these tasks are to be performed.

5. Serving as your children's reminder machine teaches them how not to think for themselves.

Treatment: Use praise for remembering and time out for not remembering.

6. Warning your children of the effect of their misbehavior is similar to reminding them and contributes to their not thinking.

Treatment: If they fail to do something, send them directly to time out.

7. Sitting with your children while they do their homework teaches them dependency.

Treatment: Set up strong consequences if the school reports that a child's homework was poorly done or incomplete. With strong enough consequences, such as loss of free play after school with no substitutions.

8. Failing to praise your children when they are behaving nicely reduces their motivation to behave correctly - motivation to do their schoolwork and their chores, to problem solve, and to take the initiative.

Treatment: Problem children are poorly motivated, and this can only be remedied with a high dosage of daily praise.

9.Unintentional neglect is a prime cause of problem kids. Because we fail to train children in appropriate behavior, we fail to tenderly nurture their values. Our stressful, busy lives steal from our children the quantity and quality of love and attention they need from us.

Treatment: Give not only quality time but sufficient time (quantity) each and every day. Children need our attention.

10. Failing to make education and reading important places your child at a lifelong disadvantage.

Treatment: 1. From preschool on, take a deep and sincere interest in your children's day at school. Sit and talk with them about their day and also share with them how yours went. A great time for this is dinnertime, with everyone gathered at the dining table instead of in front of the TV. Yes, a good education is an important ingredient to getting a good job, but education in and of itself is important. If you convey excitement about your own learning as well as theirs, you'll be transmitting an important message. Time, love, attention, and interest in school, learning, and education are crucial if you want your child to pay attention and behave well in school. This is how values are taught. 2. Offer lots of opportunities for educational enrichment. Take family visits to zoos, museums, plays, live-music concerts, historical sites, nature and science activities, and college campuses. In other words make learning new things fun, exciting, and an important family value. 3. Make reading a basic value in the family. Kids who love reading rarely display attention problems.

Education

Take your child on short educational trips. Visit museums, college campuses, and historical places. Make learning about nature important and fun. Take trips to scenic places. Go camping and teach your child camping skills. Go hiking. Get up early to watch the sun rise. Buy a telescope and scan the heavens. Instead of toys, buy microscopes, chemistry sets, or ant colonies and experiment with them with your child. Have your child help plant flowers and shrubs. Visit planetariums. Show an enthusiastic interest in your children's schoolwork. Talk with them every day about their day in school. Show your pleasure when they get a good grade.

Demonstrate your love for music. Take your child to plays. Go as a family and you'll have fun, too.

Reading

It is vitally important to help your child become a reader. Readers perform better than nonreaders in school and on national tests. Reading is so very important throughout life.

To get children to become readers it is important to help them learn to love reading. To do this we have to make reading a fun activity, so here are ten helpful hints to make that happen:

1. Read to your children and choose subjects of interest to them. When you read to them, select materials that are at or above their current reading level

When you read to them from more challenging books, you can expose them to more advanced vocabulary that will help with word-recognition skills and make it easier for them to decipher new words. Developmentally, children have excellent auditory learning skills that help with language learning..

2. When they read on their own, select material that is equal to or lower than their current reading level. Reading is much more fun when a child doesn't trip over every other word. Let them get into enjoying the content of the material. If they enjoy it, they'll do it. If they develop the reading habit, their reading skills will automatically improve.

3. Allow children to read in bed for thirty minutes at bedtime. If they ask to do anything else-draw or play with a toy, for example-your answer should be a flat no. Only reading is allowed. Reading before bed or for pleasure should be easy and fun, not the chore that reading can be at school.

4. Take trips to the library at least every other week. Let them choose books on subjects they like. Gently encourage them to explore new topics, but don't insist. Again, select reading material at relatively easy levels.

5. Subscribe to children's magazines and newsletters. Children are thrilled when the mail arrives bringing subscriptions in their name. Many magazines include fun exercises for children to do alone or with you.

6. Allow comic books - they are perfectly fine. Don't be persuaded by the myth that they hurt reading ability. If children enjoy them, comics can contribute to making reading a joy. Look for those that are fun to read and appropriate to the child's age.

7. During quiet periods with your children, ask them about their reading. But do not push such conversations or pressure your child. If he seems excited and talks about the reading material, then listen and share the excitement.

8. If you can afford to, buy books children can read and enjoy. Build a library for them. Teach them to treat books with tenderness and love. Teach them that books are sacred treasures.

9. Take time to read for your own enjoyment and set an example that will foster a love for the written word. Shut off the television in the evening and sit and read as a family.

10. Leave magazines around the house. Choose them wisely so they are suitable for children.

8
Tests and Techniques

A. Personality and character

1. The Egogram : Ego states of your personality

[CP = Critical Parent NP = Nurturing Parent A= Adult, NC= Natural Child LP = Little Professor AC = Adaptive Child]

Instructions:

(a) The test is to be performed quickly.

(B) The tentative limits of desirable ego states are as follows:

CP should be 0-5
NP more than 12
A around 18
NC around 15
LP around 12
AC should be 0-5

(c) Bold numbers are column numbers of Table-A, wherein the score is to be written

(d) Rating system: Almost never = 0, Rarely =1, Sometimes=2, Frequently =3, Very frequently = 4

(e) Please score each question on the first thought, no second thought required

QUESTIONS

1. I give reason when unable to complete a work. **3**
2. I feel bad about something that people say or do to me or something that I say or do to others. **6**
3. I expect people to do what I say **1**

4. I consciously make search to get needed information. **4**
5. I do what my superiors say to do even when it is difficult **6**
6. I feel guilty about some thing (not getting a job on time; coming late; working too hard)**6**
7. I assume without bothering to gather real data. **5**
8. I approach people with a pleasant smile. **4**
9. I suggest that a ill person see the doctor or take rest. **2**
10. I insist that things be done my way. **4**
11. I hear a voice in my head like," those people should.." **2**
12. Knowing that a job cannot be done when I want it, I repeatedly ask to complete that job ahead of schedule. **4**
13. I find ways to make a boring task interesting. **5**
14. I attend classes, workshops, lectures and do self-study to improve my job skill and knowledge. **3**
15. I get the feeling of something unusual that is about to happen before it happens. **5**
16. I plan ways to do things that might be considered harmful, illegal or unethical. **3**
17. I think or say: "What would you do without me". **2**
18. I feel happy when I enter a friend's office or work-area. **5**
19. I correct subordinates when they fail to perform up to standard. **1**
20. I cleverly find out how to get what I want at the cost of others. **5**
21. I keep calm in an emotionally charged atmosphere. **3**
22. I help others by doing something for them by going a little out of way. **2**
23. When I feel hurt, I go somewhere to be myself. **6**
24. I insult people without thinking. **1**
25. I frequently take some rest when doing a long work, and I enjoy the feeling that I am relaxing. **4**
26. I say 'Please' and "thank you" wherever required. **6**
27. I say or think: "I will do it for them, they cannot be expected to handle it" **2**
28. I talk about logic or facts when other person needs comfort. **3**
29. I take the last biscuit left in the plate. **4**
30. To make an accurate interpretation, I gather necessary information and then use my imagination. **5**
31. I help a co-worker in emergency. **2**
32. I insist that others should take care of themselves **2**
33. I always answer the phone in pleasant voice. **6**

34. I cunningly find out a way to avoid a job assigned to me. **5**
35. I set people straight when they are not doing their job properly. **1**
36. I set standards for proper performance of subordinates. **1**

Please enter your rating in te concerned column for each question.

Q. No.	1	2	3	4	5	6
1						
2						
3						
4						
5						
6						
7						
8						
9						
10						
11						
12						
13						
14						
15						
16						
17						
18						
19						
20						
21						
22						
23						
24						
25						
26						
27						
28						
29						
30						
31						
32						
33						
34						
35						
36						

CP (total of col. 1) = NP (total of col. 2) = A(total of col. 3) =
NC (total of col. 4) = LP(total of col. 5) = AC(total of col. 6) =

2. Assessment of Interpersonal Relationship – Johari Windows

Joe Luft and Harry Ingham developed a conceptual model to help us understand what might be going on in interpersonal relationships. The name of their model is the JoHari Window.

There are four aspects of personality ranging from known to unknown. The model has a square window with four panes. The two columns of panes are labeled "What I know about me" and "What I don't know about me" and the rows are labeled "What you know about me" and "What you don't know about me." The window looks something like this:

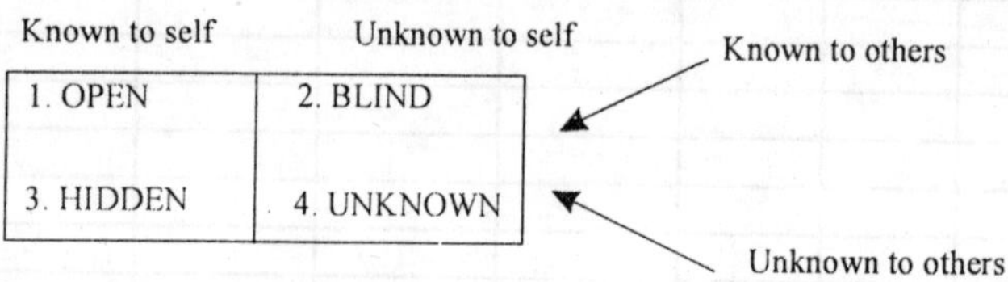

WINDOW 1 (Open window): Self is known to you and you share it with others. Person is open, spontaneous, confident about self image. It is accepted by self and others.

WINDOW 2 (Blind window): Self is with blind spots: Others see your actions, feelings and behaviour, but you are blind to them. Others can tell you what they see. You may not like what others tell you. But you can listen and respond if you decide.

WINDOW 3 (Hidden window) Self is known but part in shadow. Shadow part is subconscious. Here you dream out your potential, hopes and unfulfilled fantasies. You don't share these with others but you work out of this hidden aspect when appropriate or when you want to respond to any change in your life.

WINDOW 4(Unknown window): Unknown self : A mystery not known to self and others. You can learn new insights in this area if you enlarge 1, 2 and 3 by working at your self (exploration and personal growth).

This model can be used to find out self awareness in interpersonal relationship. To use the model, answer the following 20 questions according to the instructions given below.

Instructions

For each question there are two categories: A and B. Both categories are to be scored as follows:

1. Give A 5 points if A is completely characteristic of what you will do and give B 0 point if B is completely uncharacteristic
2. Give A 4 points if A is considerably characteristic of what you will do and give B 1 point if B is somewhat characteristic
3. Give A 3 points if A is slightly more characteristic of what you will do than B and Give B 2 points
4. Give A 0 point if A is completely uncharacteristic of what you will do and give B 5 points if B is completely characteristic
5. Give A 1 point if A is somewhat characteristic of what you will do and give B 4 points if B is considerably uncharacteristic
6. Give A 2 points and Give B 3 points if B is slightly more characteristic than A of what you will do

Question 1

A friend had conflict with a person known to him and me. It is important for my friend to get along with that person. I would:

(A) Tell my friend that he was partially responsible for the problems with that person and try to let my friend know how that person was being affected by my friend.

(B) Not get involved because I would not be able to get along with both of them once I entered in any way.

Question 2

If I had heated arguments with a friend and find that he is uncomfortable with me from that time on, I would:

(A) Avoid discussing his behaviour and just let the whole thing drop, so that things do not get worst.

(B) Talk about his behaviour and ask him how he felt, and how the argument affected our relationship.

Question 3

If a friend began to avoid me and acted in a withdrawing manner, I would:

(A) Tell him about his behaviour and suggest that he tells me what is in his mind

(B) Reduce my contacts and remain aloof since this seems to be what he wants

Question 4

If two of my friends and I were talking and one of the friends slipped and brought up a personal problem that involved the other friend, of which he was not aware, I would:

(A) Change the subject and signal my friend to do the same
(B) Fill my uninformed friend in on what the other friend was talking about and suggest that we go into that later.

Question 5

If a friend tells me that in his opinion I was doing things that made me less effective than I ought to be in social situations, I would:

(A) Ask him to describe what he observed and suggest changes I might make
(B) Resent his criticism and let him know why I behave the way I do

Question 6

If a friend of mine aspired for an office in our organization, for which I felt he was unqualified, and if he has been tentatively assigned to that position by the President of organization, I would:

(A) Not mention my feelings to my friend or President, and let them handle in their own way.
(B) Tell my friend and the President of my feelings and leave the final decision to them

Question 7

If I felt that one of my friends was being unfair to me and his other friends, but none of them had mentioned anything about it, I would:

(A) Ask several of these people how they perceived the situation, to see if they felt he was being unfair
(B) Not ask others about how they perceived our friend, but wait for them to bring it up with me

Question 8

If I were preoccupied with personal matters and a friend told me that I had become irritated with him and others and that I was jumping on him for unimportant things, I would:

(A) Tell him I was preoccupied and would probably be on edge for a while and would prefer not to be bothered
(B) Listen to his complaints but not try to explain my actions to him.

Question 9

If I heard some friends discussing an ugly rumour about a friend of mine which I knew could hurt him, and he asked me what I knew about it, if anything, I would:

(A) Say," I didn't know anything about it and tell him no one would believe a rumour like that anyway."

(B) Keep my opinions to myself rather than be seen as interfering in things that are none of my business.

Question 10

If a friend pointed out a fact that I had personality conflict with another friend with whom it was important for me to get along, I would:

(A) Consider his comments out of line and tell him I did not want to discuss the matter any further

(B) Talk about it openly with him to find out how my behaviour was being affected by this.

Question 11

If my relationship with a friend has been damaged by my repeated arguments on an issue of importance to us both, I would:

(A) Be cautious in any conversations with him so the issue would not come up again to ruin our relationship

(B) Point to the problems the controversy was causing in our relationship and suggest that we discuss it until we get it resolved.

Question 12

If in a personal discussion with a friend about his problems and behaviour, he suddenly suggested that we discuss my problems and behaviour as well as his own, I would:

(A) Try to keep the discussion away from me by suggesting that other closer friends often talked to me about such matters

(B) Welcome the opportunity to hear what he felt about me and encourage his comments

Question 13

If a friend of mine began to tell me about his hostile feelings about another friend whom he felt was being unkind to others (and I agreed wholeheartedly) I would:

(A) Listen and also express my own feelings to him so he would know where I stood

(B) Listen, but not express my own negative views and opinions because he might repeat what I said to him in confidence.

Question 14

If I thought an ugly rumour was being spread about me and suspected that one of my friends had quite likely heard it, I would:

(A) Avoid mentioning the issue and leave it to him to tell me about it if he wanted to

(B) Risk putting him on the spot by asking him directly what he knew about the whole thing

Question 15

If I had observed a friend in social situations and thought he was doing a number of things which hurt his relationships, I would:

(A) Risk being seen as a busybody and tell him what I had observed and my reactions to it.

(B) Keep my opinions to myself rather than be seen as interfering in things that are one of my business.

Question 16

If two friends and I were talking and one of them inadvertently mentioned a personal problem which involved me, but of which I knew nothing, I would:

(A) Press them for information about the problem and their opinions about it

(B) Leave it to my friends to tell me or not tell me, letting them change the subject if they wished.

Question 17

If a friend seemed to be pre-occupied and began to jump on me for seemingly unimportant things, and to become irritated with me and others without any real cause, I would:

(A) Treat him with kid gloves for a while on assumption that he was having some temporary personal problems which were none of my business

(B) Try to talk to him about it and point out to him how his behaviour was affecting people

Question 18

If I had begun to dislike certain habits of a friend to the point that it was interfering with my enjoying his company, I would:

(A) Say nothing to him directly, but let him know my feelings by ignoring him whenever his annoying habits were obvious

(B) Get my feelings out in the open and clear the air so that we could continue our friendship comfortably and enjoyably

Question 19

In discussing social behaviour with one of my more sensitive friends, I would:

(A) Avoid mentioning his flaws and weaknesses so as not to hurt his feelings

(B) Focus on his flaws and weaknesses so that he could improve his interpersonal skills

Question 20

If I knew I might be assigned to an important position in our group and my friends' attitude towards me had become rather negative, I would:

(A) Discuss my shortcomings with my friends so I could see where to improve

(B) Try to figure out my own shortcomings by myself so I could improve

Fill your ratings in the following

RECEPTIVITY TO FEEDBACK	WILLINGNESS TO SELF DISCLOSE
Q2 B	Q1. A
Q3 A	Q4 B
Q5 A	Q6 B
Q7 A	Q9 B
Q8 B	Q11 B
Q10 B	Q13 A
Q12 B	Q15 A
Q14 B	Q17 B
Q16 A	Q18 B
Q20 A	Q19 B
TOTAL	TOTAL

Inter-Personal Risk Taking = Receptivity to Feedback + Willingness to Self Disclose

Now plot the total for receptivity to feedback on axis of x, and total for willingness to self disclosure on axis of y. For example if total for receptivity to feedback is 30, and total for willingness to self disclosure is 25, then plotting will be as follows:

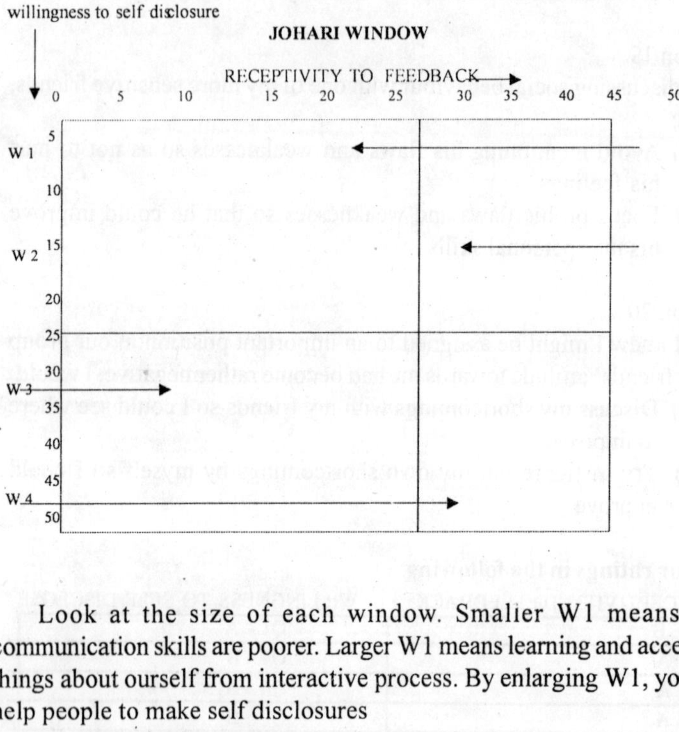

Look at the size of each window. Smalier W1 means that communication skills are poorer. Larger W1 means learning and accepting things about ourself from interactive process. By enlarging W1, you can help people to make self disclosures

To increase window 1:

1. Accept information from others (W2 reduced)
2. Give information to others (W3 reduced)
3. Reveal previously unknown or unconscious information to others (W4 reduced)

In an interactive process, considerable energy is required to block, hide or deny behaviours. When other person tells you his perception of something you do but you are not aware of doing it, the other person is coming from his W3 to reflect an aspect of a blind spot W2.

Opening up from a hidden area to blind spot produces swift learning- we learn who we are. When you feel that things are going wrong or you are being misunderstood, ask for help from other person to understand your effects on the context.

3. Assessment of components of "Freedom to choose"

3 A. Assessment of gross self awareness

Rate the following according to the scale:

0= Never, 1 = Between Never and Sometimes, 2 = Sometimes, 3= Between Sometimes and Always, 4 = Always

Statement	*Rating*
1. I can stand apart from my thoughts or feelings and examine and change them	
2. I am aware of the way I think about things and the impact it has on my attitudes and behaviours and the results I am getting in my life.	
3. I am aware of a difference between my biological, genealogical, psychological and sociological scripting- and my own deep inner thoughts.	
4. When the response to other people to me - or something I do-challenge the way I see myself, I am able to evaluate that feedback against deep personal self-knowledge and learn from it.	
TOTAL =	

3 B. Assessment of gross conscience

Rate the following according to the scale:

0= Never, 1 = Between Never and Sometimes, 2 = Sometimes, 3= Between Sometimes and Always, 4 = Always

Statement	*Rating*
1. I sometimes feel an inner prompting that I should do something or that I should not do something I am about to do.	
2. I do sense the difference between " social conscience"- what society has conditioned me to value- and my own inner directives.	
3. I do inwardly sense the reality of universal principles such as integrity and trustworthiness.	
4. I do see a pattern in human experience-bigger than the society in which I live- that validates the reality of principles.	
TOTAL =	

3 C. Assessment of gross imagination

Rate the following according to the scale:

0= Never, 1 = Between Never and Sometimes, 2 = Sometimes, 3= Between Sometimes and Always, 4 = Always

Statement	*Rating*
1. I do think ahead.	
2. I do visualize my life beyond its present reality.	
3. I use visualization to help reaffirm and realize my goals.	
4. I look for new, creative ways to solve problems in a variety of situations and value the different views of others.	
TOTAL =	

3 D. Assessment of Gross Independent Will

Rate the following according to the scale:

0= Never, 1 = Between Never and Sometimes, 2 = Sometimes, 3= Between Sometimes and Always, 4 = Always

Statement	*Rating*
1. I am able to make and keep promises to myself as well as to others.	
2. I have the capacity to act on my own inner imperatives even when it means swimming upstream.	
3. I have developed the ability to set and achieve meaningful goals in my life.	
4. I can subordinate my moods to my commitments.	
TOTAL =	

The total for each component of Freedom to Choose is to be assessed as follows:

(A) 0-7 = Poor
(B) 8-14 = Average
(C) More than 14 = Good

4. Self Esteem Index

Rate the statements as follows:

0=Not True, **1**= Somewhat True or True only part of the Time, **2**=Fairly Tru or True about half the time,

3=Mainly True or True most of the time, **4**=True all the time

1. I don' t feel anyone else is better than I am.
2. I am free of blame, shame and guilt.
3. I am a happy carefree person.

4. I have no need to prove I am as good as or better than others.
5. I do not have a strong need for people to pay attention to me or like what I do.
6. Losing does not upset me or make me feel "less than" others.
7. I feel warm and loving toward myself.
8. I do not feel others are better than I am because they can do things better, have more money or are more popular.
9. I am at ease with strangers and make friends easily.
10. I speak up for my own ideas, likes and dislikes.
11. I am not hurt by others' opinions or attitudes.
12. I do not need praise to feel good about myself.
13. I feel good about others' good luck and winning.
14. I do not find fault with my family, friends or others.
15. I do not feel I must always please others.
16. I am open and honest, and not afraid of letting people see my real self.
17. I am friendly, thoughtful and generous toward others.
18. I do not blame others for my problems and mistakes.
19. I enjoy being alone with myself.
20. I accepts compliments and gifts without feeling uncomfortable or needing to give something in return.
21. I admit my mistakes and defeats without feeling ashamed or "less than".
22. I feel no need to defend what I think, say or do.
23. I do not need others to agree with me or tell me I am right.
24. I do not brag about myself, what I have done, or what my family has or does.
25. I do not feel "put down" when criticized by my friends or others.

Total of
Ratings=

SELF ESTEEM INDEX		
95 or above	=	Sound Self Esteem
90 - 94	=	Good SE
under 90	=	Disadvantage
75 or less	=	Serious handicap
50 or less	=	Crippling lack of SE

5. Testing Self image of Your Child.

Does your child possess a good self image? How would your child answer the following questions:

- Are you good?
- Are you lovable?
- When you try something new, do you expect to succeed?
- Do you think you have a unique contribution to make to the world that no one else can make?
- Are you proud to be Indian?

Give 20 marks to each "yes" and work out percentage

6. Focus on Qualities for Boosting self Esteem

Make a list of your qualities. Take your time in preparing your list. The list should contain at least 15 important qualities that you possess. Keep this list handy with you so that you could read the list anytime anywhere. Make it a point to read the list in all different situations in a day.

7. Remind Card for Positive self Concept

Duplicate the following card. Keep it in your pocket and read it in the day as frequently as you can:

Your inner feelings about yourself are the hub from which your emotional reactions generate
Never sabotage your basic good feelings about yourself If you love yourself, you will find it easier to love others
Do not extend harshness to yourself
No one is perfect. Mistakes are a part of life and that's the way it is.
Be sympathetic to yourself and lenient towards your efforts
Talk to yourself in a sympathetic voice
Make it a habit to remember your best self, your best images of the you and your best inner speech
From your internal photograph emanates your personality constellation
Overhaul your self portrait

8. Choosing to be Positive

Most people like to be around those who have positive attitudes about themselves.

- Put "P" in front of the sentence that shows a **positive** attitude.

Put "N" in front of the sentence that shows a **negative** attitude.

I like myself.

I am generally bored with life.

I am an important member of my family.

I enjoy spending time with my friends.

I dislike my looks.

I really do not like myself.

I enjoy going to school.

I have nothing to contribute to a group.

- Write a positive statement that you often say about yourself.
- Write a negative statement that you often say about yourself.

- Try to think about yourself in positive rather than negative ways.
- Try to talk about yourself in positive rather than negative ways

9. Neurolinguistic Programming for Changing Self Image

1. Place both hands in front of your face at about 15 inches with palms facing you.
2. Imagine the "old you" in a typical scene in your mind.
3. Frame the undesirable picture and place it in palm of left hand.
4. Make sure the picture shows all scars and flaws both mental and physical.
5. Imagine "new you"
6. As step 3.
7. As step 4.
8. Focus on "old you" picture in black and white, as dull, not animated, fuzzy and undesirable and slowly shrinking.
9. Focus on "new you" picture in bright colours full of sound and animation. Find it delightful and desirable and beginning to expand in size.
10. Focus on left hand and quickly bring right hand in front of it right up to your face saying "swish" in a loud, firm, confident voice. Burst in old image with new image.
11. Repeat step10 each time saying "see this" (seeing at left hand) and "do this" (seeing at right hand), and "swish".
12. Continue until old picture quickly triggers new picture and the positive feelings associated with it
13. Perform the exercise 10 times in quick succession each day for a week.

10. Neurolinguistic Thought Stopper

1. Close eyes. Make a medium sized black and white picture of your behaviour you want to change.
2. Frame it and mentally place it out in front of you at 12 inches.
3. Make a small bright coloured picture of behaviour you want to develop.
4. Place the desirable picture in between posts of a large sling shot lodged in ground a few feet away.
5. In your mind see desirable scene being pulled farther and farther away from you with rubber sling being stretched further and further.
6. At absolute limit, let it go.
7. See new picture explode through old picture in front of you and penetrate your brain.
8. Repeat word "swishs" as it becomes part of your consciousness.

11. Mirror Technique for Reduction of Critical Parent

Soon after getting up in the morning, look into the mirror, look into your eyes and smile. Keep smiling and remembering past good happenings of your life. Finally, speak twenty times with faith : I LIKE MYSELF.

12. Wellness Chanting Technique for Reduction of Critical Parent and Adaptive Child

Chant any mantra on beads but keep your mind fixed on past good incidences (happy moments) of your life. Do at least one round daily in first two hours of the day.

13. Alpha Wellness Technique for Disease/Disorder Management

Sit straight in the bed in the morning when you feel awake. Focus eye balls at a point in front of you at least 45 degree up. Keep eyes open without blinking. Close eyes when thoroughly tired, but keep eye balls in upright position even after closing the eyes. Now go silently for reverse counting from 100 to 1, 20 to 1, and 5 to 1 @ one count per second. Keep your mind focused on the counts. During counting, if any distracting thought appears, simply watch it, and bring your attention back to the counts.

After finishing the counts, visualize a rectangular white screen 6'x 4' in front of you at a distance of approximately 6 feet. See on this screen as vividly as possible all good events of your life happening again. Make the scenes as lively as possible. Try to even hear and touch and smell.

(Do not worry, if you cannot see a screen or any thing happening on the screen).

Speak orally with full confidence, twenty times: I LIKE MYSELF. Now say mentally, "I am going to count from 1 to 5, and when I arrive at 5, I will open my eyes. After opening my eyes, I will like myself and I will feel very good". Start counting mentally from 1 to 5. Open eyes at 5, feel mentally five times that you like yourself and feel mentally five times that you are feeling very good. Leave the bed.

Pei form this technique once more anytime in the day and one more time before sleep.

14. Silent Self Talk for Mind Programming

Listen to your mental dialogues very carefully every minute of the day. Remember your subconscious mind talks to you every second without your awareness of this fact, and you keep replying very fast without even becoming aware that you are talking to your subconscious mind. This kind of talking which goes on every second involuntarily is independent of other conscious functions. The entire process is called "silent self talk. "Latest researches show that whatever you reply to your subconscious mind gets immediately recorded in our subconscious and influences our current thinking, feelings and actions.

Strangely 90 per cent of thoughts, feelings, hunches or flashes that our subconscious mind gives us while talking, is negative. And we also mostly reply in negative without being aware of our replies.

To make new positive recordings so that old powerful recordings do not push us to negativity, we have to immediately bring every negative dialogue of subconscious mind into our awareness. After.bringing into our awareness, we have to head-on attack the negative thought and speak positively to our subconscious mind.

15. Compliment Book Technique for Boosting Self Esteem

Write daily in a diary the date, name of the person who praised you and the exact words used in your praise. Read and write this diary daily preferably before sleep or in the morning. Remember that praise is your's and other's life line. Thank the person who praises you by saying, "Thank you, I am glad you liked my.............."

16. Listening to your Success Tape for Boosting Self Esteem

Tape all the successful events of your life on a audio cassette. Keep the cassette handy so that you could listen to it in your car or walkman.

17. Self Speak Technique for Mind Programming.

Talk to yourself on a specific issue. If the problem concerns relationship with other person then play the role of that person and continue conversation. Another good way is to look into the mirror, smile, greet yourself and talk about plans of the day. Talk to yourself in a positive manner. Still another way is to get a tape made for you using expertise of a counselor/psychotherapist/psychologist. Such tapes have your voice along with the fortifying messages of the therapist. The tape can be effectively used to reduce anxiety, fear, feelings of inferiority, insecurity, body weight, etc.

18. Five Power Technique for thought Control

Step 1 LISTENING IN : Listen to internal dialogue. Identify any negative dialogue and go to step 2.

Step 2: UNDERLINNING: Say to yourself that this negative thought has come from some incidents of my childhood to punish me but I am not going to be punished by it. Immediately go to step 3.

Step 3. STOPPING. Say immediately with full force, STOP, STOP, STOP. Go immediately to step 4.

Step 4: SWITCHING. Remember your switching sentence and go to step 5

Step 5. REORIENTING. Say mentally: this negative thought came to distract me from my goals but I am nearing my goals.

SWITCHING SENTENCE: A sentence constructed in advance and is used every time the technique is applied. It is a 2-3 lines statement based on your qualities.

19. Autogenic Conditioning (Technique Developed by Johannes H. Schultz)

Step 1: Find a quite place.

Step 2: Relax your mind and body.

Step 3 :Say repeatedly the behavioural change you want detailing the new belief

Step 4: See yourself exhibiting specific behaviour in full details.

Step 5: Accept the scene and the change as being part of your life..

Step 6: Feel the positive feelings this new achievement generates.

Step 7: Execute an anchor (e.g. a fist) and repeat "yes, I can" over and over in a firm and confident manner

For step2 follow these steps::

(a) Sit in a comfortable chair

(b) Close eyes gently

(c) Imagine you are in an elevator going down slowly through a series of levels to a place of total peace and tranquillity

(d) Count 1 and feel that your face including eyelids forehead, cheeks, jaws, ears are totally relaxed.

(e) Count 2 and feel more deep relaxation on face.

(f) Count 3 and feel neck, shoulders and back totally relaxed

(g) Count 4 and feel arms, hands and wrists totally relaxed. Also realize that your breathing has become slower, deeper and more easy.

(h) Count 5 and feel the elevator going further down, you are experiencing deep relaxation, you are calm, comfortable and at peace with the world.

(i) Count 6 and feel that your buttocks and thighs are totally relaxed, and the tension is evaporating from the whole body and extremities.

(j) Count 7 and feel that your legs feet and tips of toes are relaxed.

(k) Count 9 and feel that you are going deeper and deeper, and closer to your special place of peace. You feel calm all over your body.

(l) Count 9 and you are almost there.

(m) Count 10 and you have arrived. You are in your special place. Enjoy the feeling of peace and serenity.

For step 3 you have to use affirmations. In each instance actually see yourself acting in the prescribed fashion and getting the desired results. You can use any one affirmation for 7-21 days:

- Today, I have eliminated criticism and impatience from my life and replaced them with praise and tolerance.
- Today, I enjoy happy harmonious relationships with my spouse and children. We show love and respect for each other by our verbal exchanges and sympathetic behaviour.
- Today, I totally believe in myself. I believe I am capable and worthy of high achievement. 1.
- Today, I manage my time effectively. I know every time is precious and irreplaceable and must be used to the best advantage.
- Today, I have a service-minded approach towards my employment and fellow human beings. I always do more than what is expected of me, knowing I will receive more of what I want in return..

- Today, I am effective in all my interpersonal relationships. I believe people take priority over problems, and that they deserve my total respect and attention. For step 3 follow:
- Today, I am pursuing a personal development programme. I dedicate at least 1 hour everyday towards improving me.

Some useful affirmations for improving relationships with others are:

1. I love. Like and enjoy.......(name of the person)
2. I am flexible and tolerant in all my relationships with others.
3. I experience joy from my present friendships and pleasures in making new ones.
4. I give to others same love, respect and helpfulness that I desire for myself.
5. I am filled with love, understanding, friendship and forgiveness. I hold no resentment, hate, judgment or self pity.
6. I am in complete harmony with all and within, for I know I van forgive because I can ask forgiveness.
7. I find all people interesting.
8. Because I now accept myself positively and unconditionally, I know that others will accept me in the same manner.
9. I love, believe and trust and respect my children so whole heatedly that I vonvey this confidence in all my relationships with them.
10. I am patient, skilful and understanding in dealing with all members of my family.

Some affirmations for banishing negative attitudes are:

1. I let go of all limiting thoughts of anxiety and doubt.
2. I am free of all (use proper word like malice, hate, jealousy, grudges, confusion, frustration, tension, conflict, inferiority, etc). I replace it with—
____
3. I give up every harmful thought, false belief and negative emotion that has found its way into my body and mind.

While doing the technique, you have to become fully associated with the experience. Imagine being yourself looking out through your eyes, getting precise results you want. Feel positive emotions associated with the new belief throughout your body. Tingle with excitement. Realize you are more than what you ever thought you were, that you are what you believe and say you are.

20. Catharsis (Venting, Discharging, Expressing emotions).

Sharing our secrets often provides relief. Methods for uncovering, venting, and reducing emotions are needed because once you accumulate intense emotions, then you may need to discharge those strong feelings harmlessly.

You need to let go of your feelings, i.e. your heartfelt emotions must be expressed openly, not just described in well measured words. Also your disclosure must be received by accepting, not critical people. Sharing your feelings and problems by talking or writing is helpful and healthy. Likewise, keeping traumas a secret is unhealthy. A method that can be used when all alone is as follows:

STEP ONE: *Become more aware of your feelings.*

If you are inclined to avoid feelings, do the following exercises to sharpen your awareness of feelings:

Find a quiet, private place to talk to yourself about feelings. Talk out loud. When you notice a feeling, stay with it and let it grow to its full strength. Often we shut off feelings so they won't get stronger but now let them grow or even exaggerate them. If you feel a little anxious, say you are terrified and try to feel it. If you are irritated, say you are really mad, shout, and pretend to hit something. If you feel bored, feel depressed and look for things you hate to do. Practice tuning in on your feelings and expressing them.

All forms of art express feelings. Indeed, many of us are more emotionally responsive to stories in books, movies, TV, paintings or music than we are to real life events. We can be touched by an unlucky character in a song but remain untouched by a classmate or co-worker who has a misfortune. Make use of your emotional responses to stories, films, and music for a better understanding of your emotions.

Make a list of what situations you respond to emotionally—what TV stories? What songs? What parts of novels? What art? What situations or interactions seem to generate what feelings? What common themes lead to joy? to commitment? to sadness? to anger? to crying? to loneliness? to self-criticism? to self-satisfaction? All of this helps you focus on your strongest or favorite feelings and become more aware of them. It helps you understand your feelings, e.g. suppose you especially enjoy movies where teenagers defy and outwit police and other authorities. What does this say about your relationship with parents or teachers and about your emotions?

After observing the specific connections between human events in movies, stories, music, etc. and your emotions, try to figure out the factors in your past (and/or in your current situation) that contribute to these emotional responses. Does the divorce of your parents make you uncomfortable when a couple fight in a movie? Does a successful, beautiful older sister make you disinterested in or resentful of movie stars? Does a smart brother make you avoid hard classes? These are clear memories, what about less obvious connections?

Take an emotional reaction you have, say joy when someone is especially thoughtful of others, and go on a fantasy memory trip. Let your mind wander back to any associations this emotion takes you to. What kind of childhood events does this emotion remind you of? Talk out loud about these memories. Don't concern yourself with "Did this really happen?" or with "Don't be so critical." In fact, if no memories occur to you, make up what might have happened. This can remind you of real memories or bring out hidden wishes and fears and feelings about specific people.

You could ask your parents and older siblings where your emotional reactions, such as fears of authority or a quick temper, might have come from. The idea is to gain a greater interest in, awareness of, and understanding of your emotions. Keeping a diary and doing daily ratings that focus on feelings would be very helpful.

It is best to explore feelings with a friend. That person should choose you as a sounding board, because the two of you should reverse roles as needed. The person experiencing his/her feelings should say whatever comes to mind, but focus on feelings and express them strongly. The idea is: to feel more, you need to express more. If you feel like hitting something, hit a pillow. Lie on the floor and scream or cry or grunt if you feel like it. Or, just talk about your feelings.

The listener just listens. Being empathic is helpful. But the crucial thing is to listen with concern, understanding that the other person needs to express his/her feelings. Avoid giving reassurance prematurely; don't give advice; don't ask about the details of the situation (When did this happen?) or the causes (Why did he/she do that?). If you provide any focus at all, encourage him/her to express his/her feelings. Remember, the person probably wants to feel—to re-experience and vent—some emotion, even a very painful one. It feels good to share feelings. Give them plenty of time.

STEP TWO: *Learn how to overtly express overly inhibited or scary emotions*

Re-learn to cry. Crying is so important that techniques have been developed to re-learn how. Some people cry every day, not because they are suffering some great loss but because they feel better afterwards (more relaxed, fewer headaches, less eye strain).

A method to cry : Place one hand on your collarbone, right where your neck joins your chest. Breathe very shallowly, only as deeply as your hand. Breathe rapidly and make a whining or sobbing sound, like a baby crying. Try to get into feeling sad. Think of things that make you feel very distraught. If necessary imagine something very sad—leaving your family or friends or loss of a loved one. Let yourself sob until the need is met. The emotionally inhibited (constipated) person has been called "intellectually honest, but emotionally a liar."

When you can experience anger to social situations, the next step is to learn to get angry about everyday things in your life. Make a list of irritating situations. Describe some scenes in detail, like the war scene, and repeat them to yourself over and over and get mad. After you have learned to detect and internally experience your anger, then you can start learning to be assertive.

You may need a friend to give you "anger training" to express anger more thoroughly by getting your whole body into it. The friend might tell you to kick, growl, frown, and use whatever parts of your body that are not involved. Don't turn the exercise into a game. It is a hard, serious task. When you have practiced getting angry for a few times, you are ready for the next step.

STEP THREE: *Vent the unwanted emotion full force until it is drained*

Approach 1 : If angry, find a private place where you can make noise. Obtain an object you can hit: a punching bag, a large pillow, a bean bag chair, a bed, a sofa. Be sure you will not hurt yourself as you hit the object. Some people prefer to hit with an object rather than their fists, using a tennis racket to hit a bed works well.

Go into a rage. Shout, scream, cry, snarl, growl, shake your fists, kick, bite, and above all hit and hit and hit, until you are exhausted—completely drained of hate. Do it again and again, after you catch your breath, if necessary to feel the anger has been completely discharged. The idea is to drain out or use up the anger (or other emotion), so that in the end you are calm and more able to cope.

Approach 2 : Throw a temper tantrum. Lie on your back and kick the floor or the bed with your feet and hit the floor with your fists. Shake your head and yell, "No, no, no, hell no! I hate you. Don't stop until you are drained.

Approach 3: Do hard physical work or play a sport, like tennis, when you are angry. If it works, that's fine. Remember: this is never to encourage violence to another person, it is to drain us of anger and, thus, prevent violence.

Women may be less comfortable with physical aggression compared to verbal aggression. Verbally aggress more vigorously and longer than usual, so you are emptied and ready to handle the situation more rationally.

Approach 4 : If you are sad or disappointed, try crying it out. Find a quiet, private place. Start remembering everything that has gone wrong. Let yourself feel deeply disappointed and sad. Cry without holding back. Moan and breathe heavily; tell yourself how awful it is. Talk to yourself about how bad you feel, how crushed, how depressed, how gloomy. Cry until you are cried out. Completely out of control, hysterical expression of intense emotions should be avoided, unless you are supervised by a professional.

Approach 5: Release your anger in writing or in humor. Abraham Lincoln recommended writing down your negative feelings—then throwing the paper away and in the process reducing your anger. It is also helpful to write a poem or a note to someone when you are sad. If one is in the midst of a terrible personal trauma, like the breaking up of a relationship, it may be helpful to write out a detailed explanation of what happened—then file the "report" away and forget it.

Lincoln, Churchill and others also used their sense of humor to handle anger.

STEP FOUR: *Tell yourself the emotions have been reduced to manageable size and make plans to cope with the situation*

After thoroughly discharging your feelings, shift your attention to considering reasonable, constructive action you can take (including forgetting the whole thing). Make specific plans and carry them out (use "I" statements).

21. Flexibility Test

The life of a tree is sometimes dependent on whether or not it can bend with the wind in a storm. How about you? Do you bend with the wind in the day-to- day storms of life?

Please respond and then total your scores. Responses : 5 = Always
4 = Usually
3 = Often
2 = Some
times

1 = Rarely
0 = Never

1. It upsets me when someone tries to cut in front of me in traffic.
2. I don't like criticism.
3. I really hate losing.
4. I object to someone trying to sell me something.
5. I am very competitive.
6. I resist compromising differences if I know I am right.
7. I get frustrated when someone will not consider an idea I suggest.
8. It irritates me when someone tries to prove I am wrong.
9. When I find a product I like I avoid trying another brand.
10. I am persistent when I am supporting my viewpoint.
11. It bothers me when people do not respect my opinion.
12. I resist change when I do not agree with it.
13. I am stubborn.
14. If someone disagrees with me it is easier for me to justify my opinion than it is to understand the other person's opinion.

Add up the ratings. A score higher than 30 means that flexibility needs to be increased.

22. Emotional Intelligence Quotient Test

1. T F... I do not get angry when verbally attacked.

2. T F... I am comfortable with others' grief, even those in close relationship to me.

3. T F... I get angry or fearful when physically threatened.

4. T F... I am able to decide to love another and then do so.

5. T F... I am comfortable with others' anger and hate.

6. T F... I worry regularly in some circumstances.

7. T F... At times and in some circumstances I feel shame.

8. T F... My anger keeps coming back in certain situations or with specific people.

9. T F... For some things I have done in the past, I feel guilty.

10. T F... At times I feel degraded and humiliated.

11. T F... Regularly I get anxious about some situations.

12. T F... Sadness keeps recurring for me over specific issues.

13. T F... Jealousy is sometimes a part of my life.

14. T F... I get blue or depressed regularly.

15. T F... In my life there is stress that never ends.

16. T F... I am comfortable hugging other adults of either sex.

17. T F... I regularly allow my own wracking sobs and tears

18. T.F...With a particular partner I am able to express all of the following: emotional love, physical love, words of love and lusty sexual love.

19. T F... Once my sobs and tears have been released, I feel great.

20. T F... I am comfortable saying the words "I love you" to men, women and children in a feeling way.

Questions one through five are true, questions six through fifteen are false, and questions sixteen through twenty are true.. Give 5 marks for each correct answer and work out percentage.

23. The Anger Quotient Test

For each question, choose the answer that best fits your method of coping with anger.

1. **If I become Frustrated when Something I'm Attempting to fix does not Work, I**

a) Keep my cool.
(b) Verbally express displeasure.
(c) Hide my anger inside.
(d) Physically take it out on the thing I am trying to fix.
(e) Strike out at anyone or anything that happens to be close.

2. **When I am Verbally Criticized, I**

(a) Listen and try to understand their point of view.
(b) Walk away.
(c) Pout and sulk.
(d) Become argumentative and verbally attack.
(e) Physically strike out at the person.

3. **When unjustly accused of something, I:**

(a) Stand up for myself.
(b) Assume a passive position and stay silent.
(c) Complain to someone else.
(d) Become verbally aggressive.
(e) Become physically assaultive.

4. **When Peers Tease me, I**
   (a) Ignore them.
   (b) Tease back.
   (c) Leave the group and sulk.
   (d) Counterattack aggressively.
   (e) Physically attack my tormentor.

5. When I Fail at Something that I Thought I could Succeed at, I:
   (a) Accept it and try to learn from the experience.
   (b) Rationalize, and become defensive.
   (c) Brood about it.
   (d) Put the blame on someone else, where it belongs.
   e) Take my anger and disappointment out on myself or on someone else.

6. When I Feel that I Am being Pushed to Change, I:
   (a) Try to recognize that I may really need to change.
   (b) Ignore those trying to push me.
   (c) Take it personally.
   (d) Dig in my heels and resist all suggestions.
   (e) Become physically or verbally assaultive.

7. When I Feel that People are Setting Limits on me, I:
   (a) Try to understand what is being requested and why.
   (b) Passively accept the limits, and generally don't question the need.
   (c) Become defensive, resistant and argumentative.
   (d) Openly defy or ignore them.
   (e) Become physically assaultive, or figure out ways to get even.

8. If I am Rejected when I am Trying to Help, I:
   (a) Accept that others might not want my help.
   (b) Try harder to help.
   (c) Take it personally.
   (d) Tend to become verbally judgmental of them.
   (e) Take it as a personal putdown and often take out my anger on myself or someone else.

Scoring Key

For each question: If you answered with A add 5 points; B = 4 points; C = 3 points; D = 2 points; and E = 1 point.

Total your points.

32-40 points - Good for you...you seem to handle your anger well. **24-31 points** - Well...you do have some ability to handle your anger, but it looks like you may want to make some changes. **23 points or less** - You need to work on your anger

24. Rational Emotive Imagery Technique for Anger Control

Imagine a situation in which you get angry. Imagine that the condition is getting worse and you are becoming angrier. See your anger reaching extreme level. Feel for a few moments your maximum anger level and then turn with full might the anger into feelings of frustration and helplessness. To convert anger into feelings of frustration and helplessness, you will have to challenge the four irrational believes(this situation is awful, I cannot tolerate this situation, he/she should not have behaved in that manner, and the person has behaved badly hence must be punished). When you have succeeded in converting anger into feelings of frustration and helplessness through your concentrated efforts, then carefully note what mental activities you performed to achieve this change. Note carefully what precise changes you made in your thinking process to change your four irrational beliefs. Acquaint yourself fully with the new rational beliefs formed as a result of your efforts. Repeat the whole exercise- see yourself becoming angry, boost your anger, experience it and convert it into feelings of frustration and helplessness, and not what did you do to achieve this conversion of anger. Practice this daily in the morning for 10 minutes. Amazing results will come after a few weeks.

25. Desensitization Technique for Anger Control

Write down various situations in which you get angry. In some situations you get mild anger, in others you get anger more strongly, and in still other situations your anger is so high that it is almost a rage. Arrange them sequentially from low-anger producing to high anger-producing situations. First take mild anger-producing situation. Imagine yourself getting angry and the moment you start feeling angry, interrupt the feeling of anger by relaxation. For relaxation, inhale while counting from 1 to 10, hold breath counting 1 to 5, and exhale counting from 1 to 15. Use 8-10 cycles of breathing. Master the technique to control anger in low anger-producing situation. On acquiring ability to control anger in low anger-producing situation proceed to the next situation which produces anger more than the earlier one.

26. Emotional Training Technique for Anger Control

The moment you start feeling anger at a person, immediately start recollecting the enjoyable moments/good time spent with that person. Sharpen these good experiences in your imagination and on basis of this memory, start feeling sincerely good wishes/feelings/gratitude for that person. Repeat again and again in your imagination the good experiences you had with that person, and get good feelings for the person. Now allow the good feelings for the person to dominate on the anger at the person.

27. Paradoxical Intentional Technique for Anger Control

If a person is not listening to you / annoying you then exaggerate your feelings of anger at that person in imagination as follows:

"No doubt this person will have to agree to do what I say. I have 100 per cent control over his behaviour. If he will not do as I desire, I will chain him and whip. If I demand. He will arrange any how a sum of Rs. 10 crore, or rub his nose on ground daily in front of me. He has no other option but to do as I desire. He will have to do whatever I desire because he has no other option but to agree to me.. I can get anything done from him. If he will not agree with me then I will finish him with my powers"

You will realize that when you will exaggerate your controlling power to unbelievable and funny level, a change will occur in your feelings about the situation of that person, and you will feel that you cannot do whatever you wish against that person.

28. Referenting Technique for Anger Control

This technique is particularly suitable in a situation where you feel angry at a person by merely looking at him/her. Draw a table blank with three columns. In the left column list all bad behaviours of the person (he is useless, dishonest, lazy, horrible, work-shirker etc.). List in the central column the good qualities of the person (mostly honest, behaving according to his viewpoint, behaving to defend/benefit himself, as I also do, determined, sometimes behaving very nicely, behaves well with others, generally caring for others, remains informed for his benefit as I also do, etc.). In the left column, list the neutral behhaviours (he has hobbies like.., he is deeply interested in.., he is a very good …., etc.).

Now write a paragraph below the table that includes all aspects taken out from all the three columns like.

Mr./Ms./Mrs. .... is a person who is horrible and who behaves nicely. He/she is sometimes dishonest but mostly honest. He/

she has virtues as well as vices. Mr./ Ms/Mrs is 6 feet tall and she/he does so many things,. He is deeply interested in music and is a very good orator. He keeps a good company. He is suffering from diabetes. He has written many good books.

The truth is that people and their behaviours are two different things. The mistake that we commit is that we judge people by their behaviour. This wrong referenting creates biases and the process of anger begins. The above technique corrects our perception about others.

29. Confidence Building Through Neurolinguistic Programming

Step 1. Stand in a quite room, imagine yourself feeling supremely confident, totally at ease with yourself and your surroundings. For this, recall a past occasion when you felt most confident.

Step 2. Consider how you would stand, breathe and look in this hightened state of well-being.

Step 3. Become aware of your positive back straight, shoulders set, and head high.

Step 4. Make fist of one hand and smash it into palm of other several times with great force each time shouting out loud in most confident voice " Yes I can".

Step 5. Become aware of your breathing in this state of absolute confidence, feel your breath slow deep and from abdomen.

Step 6. Repeat step 3 and 4.

Step 7. Become aware of your facial expressions, eyes, jaws, teeth, all set in a confident and comfortable manner.

Step 8. Consider your physiology for a few seconds and experience this enhanced state of awareness.

Step 9. Perform this exercise 10 times in a day for one week. Later, recall this exercise whenever you want by simply forming a fist and repeating the affirmation even in a soft voice.

B. Phobia, Fear and Anxiety

30. Phobia Bursting through Neurolinguistic Programming

Step 1. Follow first eight steps of the earlier technique.

Step 2. Believe you can overcome any hardship/ordeal since you are wearing a suit of shinning armour which cannot be penetrated by outside forces. Anchor this feeling by forming a fist.

Step 3. Imagine sitting in the center of a cinema hall, rising out of body, floating in the air, and entering into the projection room. From here.

Looking down at yourself and then looking up at the screen.

Step 4. Your other self is seeing a large black and white still picture of yourself as you are just prior to your normal phobic response.

Step 5. See step 4 running into black and white movie at high speed from beginning to end of phobic experience. Hear music of your choice.

Step 6. See step 5 at fast reverse at a very high speed. Note how comical it all looks.

Step 7. Freeze the film at very beginning and form a fist.

Step 8. Float back down, enter into your body sitting in the seat.

Step 9. Stand with greater confidence, walk up to the screen and jump inside the picture.

Stepp 10. Look out of your own eyes, run the same film forward in your favourote colours at normal speed and go through the same experience, only this time see. Hear and feel every thing going perfectly well.

Step 11. Replay the film in imagination several times, each time experiencing only positive feelings

Step 12. Acknowledge that you are in perfect control. Form a fist.

Step 13. Wait for a moment and try to recall what it was you were phobic of ....

31. Dealing with Excessive Fears and Anxieties

Step One: *Arrange for support.* Have a supportive friend/ Psychologist to help you. Select a friend who can cheer you on and give advice like a coach.

Step Two: *Expose yourself to the scary situation*

Approach the scary situation. If you can go all the way at first, then do it and stay in the situation until the fear declines. If you can't stand to go all the way at first, get as close as you can stand, wait until the fear declines at that point, and then advance a little further as you can tolerate it. Example: if you are afraid of elevators, perhaps you can just get on and ride all day until the fear subsides. If you can't get on it and ride immediately, you can stand outside it, then stand on it without going up or down, then go only one floor, etc.

Step Three: *Experience the fear completely until it loses its strength*

If needed hold your friend's hand, but approach the frightening situation so that the fear is intense. Don't try to reduce the fear, rather try to experience the fear fully. Tell yourself you want to feel it, not run away. Focus on the fear, not on the situation and not on your urge to run. Concentrate on your physical reactions (shaking, sweating, rapid heart beat, etc.) and on your thoughts about all the awful things that might happen. Recognize how unrealistic the thoughts and fears are.

Try to arouse the fear to its full fury, study it (telling yourself you can stand more), and challenge it to become even more intense. Welcome it. Be determined to stay right there as long as it takes to overpower and shrink the fear response. The fear will decline after some time, maybe after a couple hours or maybe after 10 or 12 hours.

Some fears you can not create, so you may need to use your imagination. Examples: speaking to large crowds or flying or fires or death. Make the fantasies as scary as possible. You might want to include terrible consequences, like being rejected by friends and parents, loosing self-respect, being insulted and put-down, or dying. Continue until the anxiety reaches tolerable levels. Then, when appropriate, expose yourself to the real-but-not-dangerous situation.

Step Four: *Continue the exposure until the fear is conquered*

Don't give up. Don't be intimidated by the fear. Repeatedly have the experience if one exposure is not enough. Also, continue to have the experience occasionally, otherwise the fear may return.

Caution: Be prepared for qualified, technical assistance

C. Stress

32. Strategies for Stress Management

Stress occurs when the pressures upon us exceed our ability to cope with those pressures. The increasing pressure results in stress. While many people are resigned to living a stressful life, it doesn't have to be that way. Here are some steps you can take immediately to control stress by (1) reducing the pressures or (2) increasing our ability to cope with life's demands.

1. Exercise. Engage in some form of cardiovascular exercise at least three days per week, for a minimum of 20-30 minutes per day. Pick an activity that you enjoy doing, and have fun!
2. Enjoy a healthy diet. In addition to reducing stress, a healthy diet will also lower your risk of disease. Eat more living foods, such as vegetables and fruits. Reduce your consumption of animal products, caffeine and refined sugar.
3. Increase your awareness. Be more attentive to your body's reaction to the demands placed on it, and act accordingly. Notice the events or habits are causing increased stress, as well as activities that are effective in alleviating pressure.

4. Do something enjoyable. Make time for activities that you are truly passionate about. Be creative, and engage in a hobby or other interest!

5. Relax. Engage in "quiet time" on a regular basis—daily, if possible. This routine could take the form of yoga, meditation, a warm bath, deep breathing exercises, prayer, or just sitting quietly or listening to relaxing music.

6. Enhance your support structures. Improve the quality of the relationships with people whom you enjoy and who support you. Surround yourself with pictures, plants, or a favorite quote that helps to keep things in perspective.

7. Maintain a positive attitude. Thoughts have a powerful effect, either positive or negative. Make sure that your thoughts (and words) are serving you. For support in this area, read motivational or inspirational books, or listen to audio tapes.

8. Get enough sleep. Lack of sleep can adversely affect quality of work, and also lead to ill health. Be sure that you are adequately rested at the start of each day. Use hypnotic sleep tape in the night.

9. Learn to say "no." While this seems especially challenging today, saying "no" to excessive requests is essential. Choose your activities carefully, and filter out the rest.

10. Smile and laugh. Laughing is indeed a special kind of internal jogging. Doing so will not only reduce stress, but can have a positive affect on others, too.

33. Emotional Management Technique

1. Acquaint yourself with the 13 treatment points

0 = The Sore Spot - On your chest where you would pin a medal or a brooch. Gently push with your finger tips to find an area that feels tender, rather than sore.

1 = Start of The Eyebrow - Where the bone behind your eyebrow turns into the bridge of your nose.

2 = Corner of The Eye - On the bone in the corner of your eye.

3 = Under The Eye - On the bone just below your eye, in line with your pupil if you look straight ahead.

4 = Under The Nose - Between you nose and your upper lip

5 = Under The Mouth - In the indentation between your chin and your lower lip

6 = Collarbone - In the angle formed by your collarbone and the breastbone

7 = Under Arm - in line with a man's nipples on the side of the body

8 = Thumb - all finger points are on the side of finger,in line with the nail bed.

9 = Index Finger, 10 = Middle Finger, 11 = Little Finger

12 = Life Point - on the side of your hand, roughly in line with your life line.

13 = Gamut Point - just behind and between the knuckles of your ring and little finger.

2. Learn the "Tapping" : The 13 treatment points are stimulated by tapping on them. The strength of tapping should be comfortable, but you should be able to feel a resonance from the tapping spreading out across a reasonable part of that side of your face.

3. Contacting the Problem - To direct the releasing effects of the tapping to the required area, we focus the mind on the problem by using a statement of the problem: "I am afraid of heights." Preferably, this is spoken out loud to engage as much of the neurology as possible and to contact the problem as directly as possible.

4. Process:

Step 1: Take the SUD (Subjective Unit of Disturbance) Test..

Ask yourself: on a scale of 10 to 0, 10 being the highest imaginable pain/freak out/fear/sadness/dis-comfort, and 0 being completely calm, pain free, tranquil, relaxed and happy, how would you rate what you are experiencing at this moment?

This works for emotions as well as for physical sensations and even for beliefs which might be a problem:

On a scale of ten to zero:

- how depressed are you right now?
- how painful is your leg?
- how bad is your fear of heights?
- how distressing is this memory?
- how much do you hate this person?

Step 2: Preparatory: Sit straight. Take a deep breath, close eyes, touch upper pallet with the tip of tongue, keep mouth closed, insert index finger in each ear, slowly exhale, producing a humming sound from back of the throat. Feel the sound, touching top of your head. Perform this three times.

Step 3: The Set Up. Now that we've named the problem, we can start with the Set Up. Use the following routine:

Find the sore spot on either side of your chest; rub it round gently and say:

"Even though I (insert problem statement),
I deeply and profoundly accept myself."

For example, if you decided your problem was "My back is killing me", you would say as your Set Up Statement:

"Even though my back is killing me,
I deeply and profoundly accept myself."

Repeat this three times, rubbing the Sore Spot continuously as you do so, and please do endeavour to put some meaning and energy into the "I deeply and profoundly accept myself" part.

Step 4: The Round. Tap all the points, 7 times, starting from the top (eyebrow) and ending up with the Karate Chop Point on the hand. As you tap each point, repeat a shortened version of the Set Up Statement which is called the reminder phrase; so if your set up statement was,

"Even though I hate and despise my boss,
I deeply and profoundly accept myself",

you say the reminder (shortened version) phrase:

"I hate and despise my boss"
on each point at the same time as you tap.

Step 5: **This is the middle part of the process. You tap continuously on the Gamut point, and then do the following:**

1. Move your eyes from the floor to the ceiling without moving your head and back again.
2. Move your eyes from left to right and back again
3. Move your eyes in a big circle and back again
4. Hum - Happy Birthday To You (or another tune or just a scale) for about one bar;
5. Count - one two three four five
6. Hum again
7. Take a deep breath in and out.

Step 6: As you do these things, repeat the statement in between as best you can to keep yourself focused on the problem in hand.

The eye movements are linked to various brain functions and the reason for the humming-counting-humming is to switch between hemispheres quite quickly; both are designed to "wake up" your neurology so the tapping can go to work on the problem

Step 7: Then, repeat the Round one more time, tapping all the points from the eyebrow to the karate chop point again. Take a deep breath and allow yourself a moment to reflect on how you feel now.

Step 8: Take SUD test again.

It's a good way to be able to assess how well the treatment has worked and if you need to repeat the treatment. If you start with 8, 9 or 10 and after a round of tapping, the severity is reduced to a 4 or a 5, this means that the treatment is beginning to work but there's more to be done.

Step 9: Subsequent Treatment Rounds

If the original set up statement was something along the lines of, "Even though I have this problem" and you have tapped a first round on "this problem", and upon checking with yourself, this problem is not as severe anymore but still noticeable, change the start up affirmation to:

"Even though there is still some of this problem remaining",

or

"Even though I still have some of this problem".

Step 10: When you're down to a rating of "Oh its a tiny little bit now" which would be a 2, 1 or a half on the subjective rating scale, a third round can be done with the opening statement of,

"I want to completely overcome this problem
and I fully and completely accept myself".

Any tapping you do stimulates the meridians, relaxes you, calms you and makes you feel a little better. Even if you get totally the wrong opening affirmation and the original problem has not yet shifted, just try again with a different start up phrase, or think about what the truth about the problem might be.

SUMMARY OF EMOTIONAL MANAGEMENT TECHNIQUE

Step 1. Take a SUD test

Step 2. Preparatory.

Step 3 - Find the sore spot on either side of your chest; rub it round gently and say:

"Even though I (insert problem statement),
I deeply and profoundly accept myself."

For example, if you decided your problem was "My back is killing me", you would say as your Set Up Statement:

"Even though my back is killing me,
I deeply and profoundly accept myself."

Repeat this three times, rubbing the Sore Spot continuously as you do so, and please do endeavour to put some meaning and energy into the "I deeply and profoundly accept myself" part.

Step 4 - Now tap all the points, (7 times each point) starting from the top (eyebrow) and ending up with the Life Point on the hand. As you tap each point, repeat a shortened version of the Set Up Statement which is called the reminder phrase;

Example : "My back pain is killing me", on each point at the same time as you tap.

Step 5- Following tapping all the points about 7 times from the top of the eyebrow to the life point, you tap continuously on the Gamut point, and then do the following:

- move your eyes from the floor to the ceiling without moving your head and back again.
- move your eyes from left to right and back again
- move your eyes in a big circle and back again
- hum - Happy Birthday To You (or another tune or just a scale) for about one bar;
- count - one two three four five
- hum again

Step 6 - Take a deep breath in and out.

As you do these activities - repeat the statement in between as best you can to keep yourself focused on the problem in hand.

Step 7- Then, repeat the Round one more time, tapping all the points from the eyebrow to the life point. Take a deep breath and allow yourself a moment to reflect on how you feel now.

Step 8. Take SUD test again.

Ask yourself:

- On a scale of 10 to 0, 10 being the highest imaginable pain/freak out/fear/sadness/dis-comfort, and 0 being completely calm, pain free, tranquil, relaxed and happy, how would you rate what you are experiencing at this moment?

Step 9. Subsequent Treatment Rounds. Change the start up affirmation to:

"Even though there is still some of this problem remaining",

or

"Even though I still have some of this problem".

Step 10. When you're down to a rating of "Oh its a tiny little bit now" which would be a 2, 1 or a half on the subjective rating scale, a third round can be done with the opening statement of,

"I want to completely overcome this problem
and I fully and completely accept myself".

(D) Knowledge about your family

34. Family knowledge

The following questions test your knowledge about families, parenting and ways we still remain "hung up" on our childhoods. Answer all the questions..Check your answers.

1. About 97 per cent of us grew up in at least somewhat dysfunctional families:

True False.....

2. Authoritarian messages from a parent to a child are usually harmful in the long run:

True False.....

3. The most frequent childhood trauma is NOT the highly abusive kind of trauma:

True False.....

4. Compassion and humaneness are often blocked in the AVERAGE person when following directions given by someone in authority:

True False

5. Children receiving authoritarian messages are more likely to be violent later on:

True False.....

6. Most of us are at our most neurotic when visiting families of origin:

True False

7. Millions of mothers are often sexist too, believing that their spouses are inherently just not as capable at being parents:

True False.....

8. One root cause of many societal ills is the abdication by fathers of parental responsibility:

True False.....

9. Children who have lived through parental divorce have many more problems statistically than those children without such experience:

True False.....

10. Children of working mothers have more difficulties than those with stay-at-home mothers:

True False.....

11. Latchkey children (those without after-school adult supervision) have more problems than peers with such supervision:

True False.....

12. Most of us knowingly and unknowingly continue to search for parental approval decades after childhood is over agewise:

True False

13. One important role of the elderly is to become more self-centered and introspective:

True False.....

Answers: False: 2, 5, 10. All others are true.

35. Eight-week intimacy building program for the married couple

Week 1: Think Before you Act.

Marriages don't die overnight, they die a slow death based on each choice we make. Every word we speak affects the quality of our marriage. We can choose to think before we open our mouths or just say what comes to mind. The impact of this choice over time is cumulative. Before you speak or make any kind of response to your spouse, try pausing to ask yourself: "Will this bring us closer together or will it push us further apart?

Week 2: Give Two Compliments before Bed.

Every night before going to bed tell your spouse two things you appreciate about him or her. It sounds simple but requires a little effort, especially after all the obvious things have been said over the first two weeks.

You'll need to look a little more carefully at your spouse and pay more attention to all the wonderful things you may have been missing.

As you get into the habit of noticing and expressing the positive qualities and actions of your spouse, you will experience a heightened sense of closeness. You will also find it very difficult to go to bed mad.

Week 3: Find Out what Makes your Husband Respected and Your Wife Feel Loved.

A man's primary need is to be respected and supported by his wife. A woman's primary need is to feel loved. Each partner should compile a list of things that make him feel respected and her feel loved. For example, he appreciates her hanging up the phone and greeting him when he comes home from work; she likes when he surprises her with a special evening or short getaway that he has planned himself.

We can't read each other's minds, so it's good to spell out what you want from your spouse.

Week 4: Have a Personal Request Meeting.

We all have personal needs within the marriage relationship. It can be very difficult for people to ask their spouses for what they want. The two biggest obstacles that block us from expressing our needs are fear of rejection and shame.

A husband or wife who feels uncomfortable for any reason about expressing his or her needs runs the risk of feeling angry and resentful, two emotions which foster anything but intimacy. The goal is to be assertive and to have the courage to ask for what we want. For example, "I feel more secure when you drive slowly," or "I need more help with the children at bedtime," or "I want you to accept my weakness in this area and stop berating me."

In order to facilitate this process, it helps greatly to schedule regular times to discuss your needs. The scheduling of a meeting makes it okay to ask; it's a way of giving each other permission to discuss your needs, thereby minimizing the two main obstacles of fear and shame.

Week 5: Do Things that give your Spouse Pleasure.

Consciously choosing to give your spouse pleasure is one of the most powerful ways of increasing closeness. This exercise calls for acting on the information we have gotten from our spouses over the last two weeks.

Select at least three things that your spouse wants or needs and give it to him or her.

If you think that "planned giving" is not spontaneous and therefore detracts from the genuineness of the act, ask yourself, "Would I rather get what I want through planning or not get it at all?"

Week 6: Do Something Together that you both Enjoy.

This one requires a lot of effort because we are all so busy that we tend to put "having fun with my spouse" last on the list of things we need to do.

This week, make the decision and plan to do something really enjoyable. Don't discuss any stressful subjects or business concerns. Focus on making it relaxed and pleasurable and enjoy the gift of having a life partner.

Week 7: Get Into the Gratitude Attitude

As a rule, most of us do pretty poorly when it comes to having the proper degree of gratitude for all the good things our spouses constantly do for us.

This week, make a list of fifty things that your spouse does for you that you tend to take for granted, such as making dinner, washing the car, picking up the dry cleaning, driving the carpool, etc. Pick one thing each day and say thank you. If you strive to master the gratitude attitude, your intimacy quotient will increase exponentially.

Week 8: Have an Encouragement Meeting

We all need encouragement. One of the most loving and caring things couples can do for one another is to express support for one another as they go through life.

Life's battles are tough and we need to know our spouse is solidly behind us, rooting for us and taking our side. At your encouragement meeting, take two minutes to say all the supportive and kind things you can think of to your spouse, while your spouse remains quiet. For example, "I don't tell you enough how much I admire your getting up so early to learn every morning. I know how tough it must be when that alarm goes off." Then your spouse can make comments and say thank you for all the nice words before taking his or her turn doing the same.

It may be difficult at first if you are not used to encouraging one another, but the payoff in increased intimacy should fuel your effort to continue.

36. Ensuring that your relationship is staying vibrant

Answer the following 10 questions by filling in the answer most consistent with your point of view.

Possible Answers :

9-7 = definitely true

6-4 = moderately true

3-1 = not at all true

(I) I tell my partner all the reasons why I love him/her?.

9

8

7

6

5

4

3

2

1

definitely true / moderately true / not at all true

(II) I compliment my partner.

9

8

7

6

5

4

3

2

1

definitely true / moderately true / not at all true

(III) I appreciate and thank my partner for what he/she does for me.

9
8
7
6
5
4
3
2
1

(IV) definitely true / moderately true / not at all true

37. Instead of nagging, I make my requests with loving sensitivity.

9
8
7
6
5
4
3
2
1

definitely true / moderately true / not at all true

(V) I flirt with my partner in lots of creative ways..

9
8
7
6
5
4
3
2
1

definitely true / moderately true / not at all true

(VI) I do thoughtful, loving things for my partner..

9
8

7
6
5
4
3
2
1
definitely true / moderately true / not at all true

(VII) I am considerate of my partner's needs and desires.

9
8
7
6
5
4
3
2
1
definitely true / moderately true / not at all true

(VIII)I touch my partner in loving ways..

9
8
7
6
5
4
3
2
1
definitely true / moderately true / not at all true

(IX) I plan fun activities for my partner and I to do together.

9
8
7
6
5
4

3
2
1
definitely true / moderately true / not at all true

(X) I let others know how lucky I am to have found my partner..
9
8
7
6
5
4
3
2
1
definitely true / moderately true / not at all true

Add up your ratings. Major changes required if the total is less than 60.

38. Has your marriage dried up?

Directions : Answer the following 10 questions by filling in the answer most consistent with your point of view.

Possible Answers :
9-7 = definitely true
6-4 = moderately true
3-1 = not at all true

(I) I focus on my partner's best qualities..
9
8
7
6
5
4
3
2
1
definitely true / moderately true / not at all true

(II) I never nag or complain because I know it creates disharmony.

9
8
7
6
5
4
3
2
1

definitely true / moderately true / not at all true

(III) I look forward to going to bed with my partner at least cuddling.

9
8
7
6
5
4
3
2
1

definitely true / moderately true / not at all true

(IV) I enjoy doing fun things with my partner.

9
8
7
6
5
4
3
2
1

definitely true / moderately true / not at all true

(V) I love it when my partner touches me throughout the day..

9
8
7

6
5
4
3
2
1

definitely true / moderately true / not at all true

(VI) I do creative things to keep the romance alive..

9
8
7
6
5
4
3
2
1

definitely true / moderately true / not at all true

(VII)I only say flattering things about my partner to others.

9
8
7
6
5
4
3
2
1

definitely true / moderately true / not at all true

(VIII)I speak kindly toward my partner when we are out in public.

9
8
7
6
5
4
3

2
1
definitely true / moderately true / not at all true

(IX) I look for ways to help my partner around the house.
9
8
7
6
5
4
3
2
1
definitely true / moderately true / not at all true

(X) I love being married to my partner..
9
8
7
6
5
4
3
2
1
definitely true / moderately true / not at all true

Add up your ratings. Major changes required if the total is less than 60.

39. Technique to encourage closeness between parents and children

To encourage teenagers to talk more to their parents and keep channels of communication open – play the following game. Both parents and children should pick up one question turn by turn and answer the question. Both parents and children should pick up one question turn by turn and answer the question. To play the game, cut the questions one on each slip and put the slips in a basket. The players now pick one slip turn by turn and answer the question.

1. What do I think people admire most about me?
2. How do I feel about my appearance?

3. What things embarrass me?
4. What do I like the best and least about my personality?
5. If I could do or be anything, what would that be?
6. What's fun about being silly?
7. What have I been afraid to share with you?
8. How could we better resolve our difference?
9. What do I wish we could do more?
10. What's good about curfews, and what's bad?
11. When is it the most difficult to tell you the truth?
12. What was my best moment this week and what was my worst?
13. What do I do that I always regret later?
14. What do I like most about being with my friends?
15. What could we do to spend time together?
16. When do I feel the least understood?
17. What is a secret dream of mine?
18. What do I like about you?
19. How does it make me feel when you tell me you love me?
20. What are some of my greatest fears?
21. What makes me feel really dumb?
22. If I could change places with you, what would I do?
23. How do I feel when you're angry at me?
24. How do I feel about physical shows of affection?
25. What's it like me when we talk about money?
26. Why am I lucky to have you as my parents (or child)?
27. It embarrass me when you ________?
28. What do I not understand about you?
29. What's one of the craziest things I ever did?
30. What do I like best about our vacations?
31. What's something we've never done that I think we'd like?
32. What do I think people think of me?
33. What's one of the bravest things I ever did?
34. What does it feel like when you blame, judge or criticize me?
35. What have been our best times together?
36. What's the worst thing that ever happened to me?
37. What's the best thing about being me?
38. What new things would I like to learn?
39. What do I wish I was better at?
40. What am I most grateful for?

40. Questions to be asked for improving relationships

1. What are some of the most romantic times we've shared?
2. What's the best thing about being me?
3. How can I tell you I love you from across a crowded room?
4. What do you do that makes me smile?
5. When do I feel the most joyful?
6. What fun activities should we do more often?
7. What would I like to do for my work if money was not a consideration?
8. What's the best part about being in love?

41. Alpha Wellness Technique for Improving Relationship

Sit straight in the bed in the morning when you feel awake. Focus eye balls at a point in front of you at least 45 degree up. Keep eyes open without blinking. Close eyes when thoroughly tired, but keep eye balls in upright position even after closing the eyes. Now go silently for reverse counting from 100 to 1, 20 to 1, and 5 to 1 @ one count per second. Keep your mind focused on the counts. During counting, if any distracting thought appears, simply watch it, and bring your attention back to the counts.

After finishing the counts, visualize a rectangular white screen 6'x 4' in front of you at a distance of approximately 6 feet. visualize yourself adopting attitude of understanding for others specially the person you don't like. Make the scenes as lively as possible. Try to even hear and touch and smell. (Do not worry, if you cannot see a screen or any thing happening on the screen).

Speak orally with full confidence, twenty times: I always hold an attitude of understanding for others or for .....(name of the person).

Now say mentally, "I am going to count from 1 to 5, and when I arrive at 5, I will open my eyes. After opening my eyes, I will like myself and I will feel very good". Start counting mentally from 1 to 5. Open eyes at 5, feel mentally five times that you like yourself and feel mentally five times that you are feeling very good. Leave the bed.

Perform this technique once more anytime in the day and one more time before sleep.

43. Measure your Communication

Fill the following table.

	A	B	C
1. I hold meaningful discussions or meetings regularly with others.	weekly	twice a month	Occasionally
2. I manipulate others by planning things to say that will get them to act a certain way	almost never	sometimes	often
3. I comment nicely on individual accomplishments of others	almost always	sometimes	often
4. I criticize people in front of others	almost never	rarely	sometimes
5. I make fun of others in a joking way	almost never	when done to me	often
6. I sit down and discuss a person's progress, problems and activities with that person	regularly	sometimes	rarely
7. When talking with a person about the person's problems, I spend time	75 per cent	50-75 per cent	25-50 per cent
8. When talking with a person, I allow distractions	almost never	sometimes	frequently
9. I exaggerate or distort the facts a bit to make the desired impression	almost never	sometimes	often
10. I get feedback from people to find out what they want or expect me to do	often	occasionally	rarely
11. If I sense something is wrong with a person, I ask the person right away if something is wrong	almost always	sometimes	rarely
12. I encourage a person to express his/her view if it is one with which I do not agree	almost always	occasionally	rarely
13. I interrupt others when I have an important point to make	almost never	sometimes	often
14. I cut a person short if I am busy and the person wants to talk to me to kill time	almost never	sometimes	usually

15. I communicate negative thoughts as an outlet for my own hostilities, anger or prejudices	almost	usually never	often
16. I make sure that associates are the first to know of any contemplated change and that information comes from me	almost always	usually	often
17. When in private conversation with a person, I ask questions	almost	usually always	rarely
18. I take the initiative for getting in touch with a person	often	sometimes	rarely
19. When any important information comes up, I inform it in writing and then reinforce verbally	almost always	sometimes	rarely
20. I point out when others are wrong even though it serves no useful purpose	almost never	sometimes	almost always
21. I find out other's interests, hobbies, views, likes. dislikes, family etc. to guide my communication in that direction	almost always	sometimes	rarely
22. If policies and rules are an important part of relationship, I make sure that others are completely aware of them	almost always	sometimes	rarely
23. I communicate by telephone, personal letters, cards, or notes with others	almost always	periodically	rarely
24. I communicate even when I am fearful of the other person's reactions	almost	sometimes	rarely
25. I believe I am sensitive and responsive to other's emotions in my communications	almost always	sometimes	rarely
TOTAL	______	______	______
	x 3	x 2	x 1
=	______	______	______

GRAND TOTAL =

43. Test for Finding out Mistakes in Communication in Husband - Wife Relationship:

For the Wife

Tick the ones that you say:

1. How can you think of buying that. You already have one.
2. Those dishes are still wet. They will dry with spots.
3. Your hair is kind of getting long. Isn't it ?
4. There is a parking spot over there, turn around.
5. You want to spend time with your friends, what about me?
6. You shouldn't work so hard. Take a day off.
7. Don't put there. It will get lost.
8. You should call a plumber. He will know what to do?
9. Why are we waiting for a table? Didn't you make reservations?
10. You should spend more time with kids. They miss you.
11. Your office is still a mess. How can you think in here? When are you going to clean it up?
12. You forgot to bring it again. May be you could put it in a small place where you can remember it.
13. You are driving too fast. Slow down or you will get a ticket.
14. Next time we should read the movie reviews
15. I didn't know where you were?
16. Somebody drank from the juice bottle.
17. Don't eat with your fingers, you are setting a bad example.
18. Those potato chips are too greasy they're not good for your heart.
19. You are not leaving yourself enough time.
20. You should give me more advance notice. I can't just drop everything and go to lunch with you.
21. Your shirt doesn't match your pants.
22. Harish called you three times. When are you going to call him back?
23. Your toolbox is such a mess. I can't find anything You should organize it.

These questions are just examples of ways a wife unknowingly annoys her husband by offering advice or seemingly harmless criticism. *Deduct one mark for each tick and work out your Annoying Index by computing the percentage.*

Why a wife gives unsolicited advice or criticism instead of simply sharing her needs, providing information or making a request. Since she does not know how to directly ask the husband for support, or constructively share a difference of opinion, she feels powerless to get what she needs without giving unsolicited advice or criticism. Give acceptance not advice or criticism.

Understand that he is not rejecting your needs but the way you are approaching him. Take rejection less personally and explore more supportive ways of communicating you needs. Remember a husband wants to make improvements when he feels he is being approached as the solution to a problem rather than as the problem itself

For the Husband

Tick the ones that you say:

1. You shouldn't worry so much
2. But that is not what I said.
3. It's not such a big deal
4. O.K. I am sorry. Now can we just forget it?
5. Why don't you just do it?
6. But we talk.
7. You shouldn't feel hurt. That's not what I meant.
8. So what are you trying to say?
9. But you shouldn't feel that way.
10. How can you say that? Last week I spent the whole day with you. We had a great time.
11. OK then just forget it.
12. All right I will clean up the backyard. Does that make you happy?
13. I got it this is what you should do.
14. Look, there is nothing we can do about it.
15. If you are going to complain about doing it, then don't do it.
16. Why do you let people treat you that way? Forget them.
17. If you are not happy then we should just get a divorce.
18. All right, then you can do it from now on.
19. From now on, I will handle it.
20. Of course, I care about you. That's ridiculous.
21. Would you get to the point?
22. All we have to do is....
23. That's not at all what happened.

These questions are just examples of ways a husband unknowingly annoys his wife by invalidating or attempting to explain the upset feelings or offer solutions designed suddenly to change her negative feelings to positive feelings. Deduct one mark for each tick and work out your Annoying Index by computing the percentage.

44. Use "I" statements

Whenever you are tempted to judge, criticize or blame someone. Convert your "you" statements into "I" statements as shown below:

You statements	"I" statements
Blaming: "You make me so mad."	"I feel angry when you ____." Or, "I have chosen to let it bother me when you ____."
Judging or labeling: "You are an inconsiderate, hostile, arrogant creep."	"I feel betrayed when you criticize me in front of others."
Accusing: "You don't give a damn about me!"	"I feel neglected when you avoid me."
Ordering: "You shut up!"	"I feel annoyed when you call me names and make fun of me."
Questioning: "Are you always this flirtatious?" or "Why did you do that? I feel like slapping your face."	"I really feel insecure about our relationship when you flirt."
Arguing: "You don't know what you are talking about."	"I feel convinced it is this way."
Sarcasm: "Of course, you are an expert!"	"I would like you a lot more if you were a bit more humble."
Approving: "You are wonderful."	"You are attractive." "I really am impressed with your ____ and besides I like you. I am attracted to you."
Disapproval: "You are terrible."	"I feel crushed when you seem only interested in spending my money."
Threatening: "You had better..."	"I'd like it if you'd ..."
Moralizing: "You ought to ..."	"I think it would be fair for you to..."
Treating: "You need to rest and..."	"I'd like to be helpful to you."
Supporting: "It will get better."	"I'm sorry you feel ..."
Analyzing: "You can't stand to leave your mother!"	"I'm disappointed that you are so reluctant to leave..."

45. Steps to become a good empathizer

STEP ONE: *Be an active listener.*

You should really want to know the other person. Further, avoid all the 12 barriers (mentioned in chapter on communication) to good listening

STEP TWO: *Understand what is involved in empathy responding.*

A good listener will let the talker know that he/she was understood. This responding is empathy. A good empathizer focuses on the talker's feelings, not on his/her actions or circumstances. Example: when talking with someone who has just been left by a lover, the empathizer will not ask "What did he/she say?" or "When did you first suspect?" but instead attend to and reflect the feelings, "It really hurts" or "You feel abandoned and lost." This focus on feelings encourages the talker to explore the core of the problem—his/her emotions. It is necessary to work through and handle our feelings before one can concentrate on solving the problems. Good empathy responses include accurate reflection of what the talker just said and tentative comments that help the talker understand him/herself.

46. Identification of levels of empathy responding. Empathy responses have 5 levels. Identify your level of empathy response and improve it.

Level 1.0: Inaccurate reflection or distracting comments.

1. *Changing-the-topic response*—a friend is complaining about a school assignment and empathizer says, "There was a good movie on Doordarshan last night."

2. *"I know better than you" response*—these are god-like pronouncements, such as "There's nothing wrong with you. You'll feel better tomorrow" or "The real problem is that your mother spoiled you" or "You are so in love, you can't see what a jerk he is."

3. *Judgmental response*—a person tells you they had several beers last night and you say, "I hope you didn't drive afterwards—you could kill someone." This may be a responsible reaction but it isn't empathic.

4. *Advising response*—a 35-year-old tells you he is scared to go back to school and you immediately tell him what college to go to, what courses to take, what notebook paper to buy, etc.

5. *Discounting and premature reassurance* —a co-worker tells you that her husband didn't come home last night and you comment, "Oh, everybody has little spats, don't worry about it. He'll be home tonight." This is a little like saying, "Don't talk to me about it any more."

6. *Psychoanalysis*—a male friend describes his fear of getting married and you explain to him that he was too emotionally involved with his mother and that he is scared that a wife would dominate and smother him like his mother did. This may be true, but let him self-explore and discover it on his own.

7. *Questions* —a friend hints at some problem in his/her marriage and you start the inquisition, "Do you two talk?" "Do you go out?" "How is sex?" Questions control and guide the conversation. Let the talker tell his/her story in his/her own way. On the other hand, questions that seek to clarify what the talker has just described are not controlling and encourage the talker to talk more.

8. *Telling your own story* —your friend's problem reminds you of a similar experience which you share (that's not so bad, unless you forget to return to your friend's concern).

Many others of us divert attention away from any serious problem as soon as we detect it. This is really terrible thing to do to a friend.

Level 2.0: Correct understanding of the other person's feelings and circumstances, but other significant factors are misunderstood or overlooked.

Examples: At this level, the listener doesn't entirely understand the talker's feelings. This may discourage the speaker from expressing more feelings unless the listener clearly indicates an interest in clarifying exactly what the talker is experiencing. Suppose a colleague tells you how mad he is at the boss and you respond, "You feel like going in and telling her off" but he responds, "Oh, no, I'm mad but not stupid!" You failed to understand that the talker was also feeling helpless and afraid to disclose his true feelings to the boss

It is usually our emotional reactions to what has been said that causes our misunderstandings. Example: the talker says something that triggers our anger, insecurity, hurt, defensiveness, or other emotion (not necessarily related to the speaker), which distracts us.

Level 3.0: An accurate empathy response captures the essence of the talker's feelings.

You have put yourself "in talker's shoes." Your comments reflect exactly what the talker has told you. Be brief. Use simple words and your own words, called paraphrasing; otherwise, it may sound like you are thoughtlessly "parroting" him/her. In this way, the talker knows you are attending closely and that you care.

Empathy statements are really questions, therefore, be tentative.. For example, when you say, "You are feeling down" you are really asking "You are feeling sad, right?" When you are slightly off the mark, it isn't awful, it gives the talker a chance to immediately "set the record straight" and get you precisely in tune with him/her.

It is important to make frequent comments reflecting your understanding of what has just been said. If the talker gets no comment from you for two or three minutes, he/she doesn't know "where you are at" and may conclude that you have lost interest, disapprove of what he/she is saying, or don't understand.

Example: if a friend says what a terrible day she has had—the car wouldn't start, co-workers were talking about her, she heard a rumor that her company was going broke, and she found out she has herpes—and you respond, "You really feel overwhelmed, like everything is out of control and going against you." If she says, "That's exactly how I feel," your comment was a 3.0 empathy response. If she says, "Well, frankly, I was pissed off all day and I'm still steaming," you get a 2.0 or a 2.2 rating although you made a good guess.

Level 4.0: Adding to the talker's self-understanding.

It is possible for an empathizer to understand (guess) what the talker is feeling even before the talker has recognized and/or expressed his/her own emotion. As soon as the empathizer questions if the talker might be feeling a certain way, the talker may readily recognize the underlying emotion and accept the interpretation. This can add greatly to the talker's insight, awareness or understanding of his/her feelings and the situation.

If you give an interpretation too soon it may seen too personal or critical and turn the talker off. Interpretations are always guesses, so be tentative: "Could it be..." or "I'm wondering if...."

Example: when a friend says, "I thought marriage would solve all my problems. I was so happy for a while but now everything is going wrong," you might respond, "Right now your marriage is causing you a lot of pain but marriage is so important to you that I'm wondering if it isn't really scary to think it might end?" The friend might tearfully respond, "You're so right. I remember what a terrible time it was for me when my parents divorced." (So, you made a 3.5 or a 3.8 response.) But he/she might say, "Oh, what a terrible thought. I don't want to think about that, so don't say something like that again." (Well, I really was off the track there, maybe a 1.5 or a 2.0 response.)

Level 5.0: Fantastic insight.

After knowing a person well for a long time, one may be able to provide some brilliant insight occasionally. Great insight is a rare event, however. Example: if your roommate has had a series of love relationships which end about the time they are getting intimate and serious, you may have observed that all of the boyfriends have a striking similarity to her father who divorced her mother when she was 5. You might suggest that her association of her boyfriends with her father and rejection may make intimacy especially scary to her. If she agrees and decides to select a different kind of boyfriend or to recognize that this is an irrational association which she can deal with, you may have given a 5.0 empathy response. If she tells you to forget that "stupid psychology crap," you have a 1.5 response and some work to do to rebuild the relationship.

47. Giving Empathic Responses

Use role-playing with two friends. Take turns being (1) the listener giving empathic responses, (2) the talker pretending to have a variety of problems and (3) the rater giving feedback to the empathizer using the 5-point empathy scale. The rater must rate every response given by the empathizer. Stop the interaction after 4 or 5 empathic responses have been rated. All three can discuss the good responses and how certain comments could have been more effective.

With experience you will learn to develop better and better guesses about the talker's feelings. These hunches come from three major sources:

Listen to and watch the talker:

(a) Hear the talker's words and tone of voice, but, also, observe his/her facial expression and other non-verbal messages. Read "between the lines" for subtle suggestions of feelings

(b) Remember any hints about possible causes of the talker's feelings, e.g. a talker might comment that his father was reluctant to play father-son softball with him when he was 12 or 13 because he was such a poor player. This information may be helpful when discussing the talker's lack of confidence.

Listen to your own gut reactions:

(a) Place yourself mentally in the talker's situation; then imagine what you would do and notice how you are feeling. This is one of the most powerful techniques for generating "intuition" about the talker's emotions.

(b) If you have had experiences similar to the talker's, then you can recall and mentally re-create the feelings you had. It is reasonable to assume that the talker may be feeling the same way you did in the same situation.

Make use of your memory

(a) You have a general notion about how persons similar to the talker would respond in certain circumstances. This accumulated wisdom grows as you study psychology, especially case studies, and have more life experience, *if* you store the memories away.

(b) You may have known others who have had the same problem as the talker. If so, remember how they acted and felt. This may suggest what the talker is experiencing.

Practice giving empathy responses in real-life situations.

Don't forget to be empathic with people you dislike or with whom you are having a conflict. Empathy not only calms the other person but you will discover that every human being, even the very worst, is understandable when you see the world the way he/she does.

Guard against advising, questioning, analyzing, judging, interrupting, etc. Be accepting of all feelings; private feelings don't hurt anyone.

Remember empathy is a *brief* response aimed at the gut (or heart – feelings), like "it's really upsetting," "you can't figure out what to do," "it seems like there is no way to win," and "it really seems unfair."

Build your "feelings" vocabulary so you can use words different from those the talker has used, but which connote the same meaning.

When you think you understand the other person's emotions very well, then give an empathy response that aids the talker's self-understanding ("You feel ______ because ______). Practice continuously. Keep a diary of your experiences establishing deeper, helping relationships with others.

48. Testing non-violent communication

TALKING

Exercise 1: Observation or Evaluation?

Do you state what you observe or mix evaluation to your observation?. Answer whether following statements reflect observation or not.

- 1. "Jeevan was angry with me yesterday for no reason."
- 2."Yesterday evening Natasha bit her fingernails while watching television."
- 3."Sohan didn't ask for my opinion during the meeting."

- 4. "My father is a good man."
- 5. "Jatin works too much."
- 6. "Hena is aggressive."
- 7. "Pawan was first in line every day this week."
- 8. "My son often doesn't brush his teeth."
- 9. "Leela told me I didn't look good in yellow."
- 10. "My aunt complains when I talk with her."

Exercise 2: Expressing Feelings

Do you *verbally* express feelings? Answer whether following statements express feelings or not.

- 1. "I feel you don't love me."
- 2. "I'm sad that you're leaving."
- 3. "I feel scared when you say that."
- 4. "When you don't greet me, I feel neglected."
- 5. "I'm happy that you can come."
- 6. "You're disgusting."
- 7. "I feel like hitting you."
- 8. "I feel misunderstood."
- 9. "I feel good about what you did for me."
- 10. "I feel worthless."

Exercise 3: Acknowledging Needs

Do you *verbally* express your needs? Answer whether following statements express needs or not.

- 1. You irritate me when you leave company documents on the conference room floor.
- 2. "I feel angry when you say that, because I am wanting respect and I hear your words as an insult."
- 3. "I feel frustrated when you come late."
- 4. "I'm sad that you won't be coming for dinner because I was hoping we could spend the evening together."
- 5. "I feel disappointed because you said you would do it and you didn't."
- 6. "I'm discouraged because I would have liked to have progressed further in my work by now."
- 7. "Little things people say sometimes hurt me."
- 8. "I feel happy that you received that award."
- 9. "I feel scared when you raise your voice."
- 10. "I am grateful that you offered me a ride because I was

needing to get home before my children."

Exercise 4: Expressing Requests

Answer whether the following statements clearly express request or not.

- 1. "I want you to understand me."
- 2. "I'd like you to tell me one thing that I did that you appreciate."
- 3. "I'd like you to feel more confidence in yourself."
- 4. "I want you to stop drinking."
- 5. "I'd like you to let me be me."
- 6. "I'd like you to be honest with me about yesterday's meeting."
- 7. "I would like you to drive at or below the speed limit."
- 8. "I'd like to get to know you better."
- 9. "I would like you to show respect for my privacy."
- 10. "I'd like you to prepare supper more often."

Listening

Exercise 5: Differentiating receiving empathically from receiving non-empathically.

State whether empathy is expressed or not.

- **1. Person A:** "How could I do something so stupid?"
  Person B: "Nobody is perfect; you are too hard on yourself."
- **2. Person A:** "If you ask me, we ought to ship all these immigrants back to where they came from."
  Person B: "Do you really think that would solve anything?"
- **3. Person A:** "You aren't God!"
  Person B: "Are you feeling frustrated because you would like me to admit that there can be other ways of interpreting this matter?"
- **4. Person A:** "I think that you take me for granted. I wonder how you would manage without me."
  Person B: "That's not true! I don't take you for granted."
- **5. Person A:** "How could you say a thing like that to me?"
  Person B: "Are you feeling hurt because I said that?"
- **6. Person A:** "I'm furious with my husband. He's never around when I need him."
  Person B: "You think he should be around more than he is?"
- **7. Person A:** "I'm disgusted with how heavy I'm getting."
  Person B: "Perhaps jogging would help."

- **8. Person A:** "I've been a nervous wreck planning for my daughter's wedding. Her fiancé's family is not helping. About every day they change their minds about the kind of wedding they would like."
  Person B: "So you're feeling nervous about how to make arrangements and would appreciate it if your future in-laws could be more aware of the complications their indecision creates for you?"
- **9. Person A:** "When my relatives come without letting me know ahead of time I feel invaded. It reminds me of how my parents used to disregard my needs and would plan things for me."
  Person B: "I know how you feel. I used to feel that way too."
- **10. Person A:** "Person A: I'm disappointed with your performance. I would have liked your department to double your production last month."
  Person B: "I understand that you are disappointed, but we have had many absences due to illness."

ANSWERS for Exercise 1:

- 1. Not in agreement. "for no reason" is an evaluation. Examples of observations without evaluation might be: "Jeevan told me he was angry," or "John pounded his fist on the table."
- 2. YES, an observation was expressed without being mixed together with an evaluation.
- .3. YES, an observation was expressed without being mixed together with an evaluation.
- 4. Not in agreement, "good man" is an evaluation. An observation without evaluation might be: "For the last 25 years my father has given one tenth of his salary to charity."
- 5. Not in agreement, "too much" is an evaluation. An observation without evaluation might be, "Jatin spent over 60 hours at the office this week."
- 6. Not in agreement "aggressive" is an evaluation. An observation without evaluation might be: "Hena hit her sister when she switched the television channel."
- 7. YES, an observation was expressed without being mixed together with an evaluation.
- 8. Not in agreement, "often" is an evaluation. An observation without evaluation might be: "Twice this week my son didn't brush his teeth before going to bed."

- 9. YES, an observation was expressed without being mixed together with an evaluation.
- 10. Not in agreement "complains" is an evaluation. An observation without evaluation might be: "My aunt called me three times this week, and each time talked about people who treated her in ways she didn't like."

ANSWERS for Exercise 2:

- 1. Not in agreement, "you don't love me" is not a feeling. It expresses what the speaker thinks the other person is feeling, rather than how the speaker is feeling. Whenever the words "I feel" are followed by the words "I," "you," "he," "she," "they," "it," "that," "like," or "as if," what follows is generally not a feeling. Examples of an expression of feeling might be: "I'm sad" or "I'm feeling anguished."
- 2. YES, a feeling was verbally expressed.
- 3. YES, a feeling was verbally expressed.
- 4. Not in agreement, "neglected" is not a feeling. It expresses what the speaker thinks the other person is doing to him or her. An expression of feeling might be: "When you don't greet me at the door, I feel lonely."
- 5. YES, a feeling was verbally expressed.
- 6. Not in agreement, "disgusting" is not a feeling. It expresses how the speaker thinks about the other person, rather than how the speaker is feeling. An expression of feeling might be: "I feel disgusted."
- 7. Not in agreement, "like hitting you" is not a feeling. It expresses what the speaker imagines doing, rather than how the speaker is feeling. An expression of feeling might be: "I am furious at you."
- 8. Not in agreement, "misunderstood" is not a feeling. It expresses what the speaker thinks the other person is doing. An expression of feeling in this case might be, "I feel frustrated," or "I feel discouraged."
- 9. YES, a feeling was verbally expressed. However, the word "good" is vague when used to convey a feeling. We can usually express our feelings more clearly by using other words, e.g. in this instance: "relieved," "gratified," or "encouraged."
- 10. Not in agreement, "worthless" is not a feeling. It expresses how the speaker thinks about him or herself, rather than how the speaker is feeling. Examples of an expression of feeling might be:

"I feel skeptical about my own talents," or "I feel wretched."

ANSWERS for Exercise 3:

- 1. Not in agreement. The statement implies that the other person's behavior is solely responsible for the speaker's feelings. It doesn't reveal the speaker's needs or thoughts that are contributing to his or her feelings. To do so, the speaker might have said, "I'm irritated when you leave company documents on the conference room floor, because I want our documents to be safely stored and accessible."
- 2. YES, the speaker is acknowledging responsibility for his or her feelings.
- 3. Not in agreement. To express the needs or thoughts underlying his or her feelings, the speaker might have said, "I feel frustrated when you come late because I was hoping we'd be able to get some front-row seats."
- 4. YES, the speaker is acknowledging responsibility for his or her feelings.
- 5. Not in agreement. To express the needs and thoughts underlying his or her feelings, the speaker might have said, "When you said you'd do it and then didn't, I feel disappointed because I want to be able to rely upon your words."
- 6. YES, speaker is acknowledging responsibility for his or her feelings.
- 7. Not in agreement. To express the needs and thoughts underlying his or her feelings, the speaker might have said, "Sometimes when people say little things, I feel hurt because I want to be appreciated, not criticized."
- 8. Not in agreement. To express the needs and thoughts underlying his or her feelings, the speaker might have said, "When you received that award, I felt happy because I was hoping you'd be recognized for all the work you'd put into the project."
- 9. Not in agreement. To express the needs and thoughts underlying his or her feelings, the speaker might have said, "When you raise your voice, I feel scared because I'm telling myself someone might get hurt here, and I need to know that we're all safe."
- 10. YES, the speaker is acknowledging responsibility for his or her feelings.

ANSWERS for Exercise 4:

- 1. Not in agreement. The word "understand" does not clearly express a specific action being requested. Instead, the speaker might have said, "I want you to tell me what you heard me say."
- 2. YES, the statement clearly expresses what the speaker is requesting.
- 3. Not in agreement. The words "feel more confidence" do not clearly express a specific action being requested. The speaker might have said, "I'd like you to take a course in assertiveness training which I believe would increase your self-confidence."
- 4. Not in agreement. The words "stop drinking" do not clearly express what the speaker wants, but rather what he or she doesn't want. The speaker might have said, "I want you to tell me what needs of yours are met by drinking, and to discuss with me other ways of meeting those needs."
- 5. Not in agreement. The words "let me be me" do not clearly express a specific action being requested. The speaker might have said, "I want you to tell me you won't leave our relationship — even if I do some things that you don't like."
- 6. Not in agreement. The words "be honest with me" do not clearly express a specific action that is being requested. The speaker might have said, "I want you to tell me how you feel about what I did and what you'd like me to do differently."
- 7. YES, the statement clearly expresses what the speaker is requesting.
- 8. Not in agreement. The sentence does not clearly express a specific action being requested. The speaker might have said, "I'd like you to tell me if you would be willing to meet for lunch once a week."
- 9. Not in agreement. The words "show respect for my privacy" do not clearly express a specific action being requested. The speaker might have said, "I'd like you to agree to knock before you enter my office."
- 10. Not in agreement. The words "more often" do not clearly express a specific action being requested. The speaker might have said, "I'd like you to prepare supper every Monday night."

ANSWERS for Exercise 5:

- 1. NO, Person B giving reassurance rather than empathically receiving what Person A is expressing.

- 2. NO, Person B attempting to educate rather than empathically receiving what Person A is expressing
- 3. YES, B is receiving empathically what A is expressing.
- 4. YES, B empathically receiving what Person A is expressing.
- 5. NO. Person B disagreeing and defending rather than empathically receiving what is going on in Person A.
- 6. NO, Person B taking responsibility for Person A's feelings rather than empathically receiving what is going on in Person A. Person B might have said, "Are you feeling hurt because you would have liked me to agree to do what you requested?"
- Person B receiving Person A's thoughts. However, it would have better if Person B had said, "So you're feeling furious because you would like him to be around more than he is?"
- 7. NO, Person B giving advice rather than empathically receiving what is going on in Person A.
- 8. YES, Person B empathically receiving what is going on in Person A.
- 9. NO, Person B assuming that he/she has understood and talking about his/her own feelings rather than empathically receiving what is going on in Person A.
- 10. NO, Person B starting by focusing on Person A's feelings but then shifting to explaining.

49. An Exercise for Listening Skills

The group should be divided into subgroups of three. There will be three roles in each subgroup: speaker, listener, and observer. Everyone will take each role once in this practice, so divide into your subgroup and decide who is going to take which role first.

Objective

The point of the practice session is to give each person the opportunity to learn how to use verbal and non-verbal minimal encouragers and become a better listener.

Instructions to the speaker

Your task is to talk about something that is important to you: your job, your family, a decision, or a question. The practice will be more helpful if you talk about something you really care about, although role-playing is possible. You may find yourself in the midst of discussing something important when the allotted time runs out. If this happens, you could make an agreement with the person listening to carry on later, after work or during a break.

Instructions to the listener

Your task is to practice the skills of the session: eye contact, body language, silences, and verbal minimal encouragers. Don't panic! Just concentrate on following the speaker's train of thought. Try to limit your responses to the listening skills.

Instructions to the observer

Your task is to observe the listener's verbal and non-verbal skills. Observe and count only as many behaviors (eye contact, body posture, verbal minimal encouragers, topic jumps) as you can manage accurately.

Procedure

The first speaker will talk with the listener for three or four minutes. The listener will then discuss the listening experience with the two other members of the subgroup. (To the listener: What was comfortable? Difficult? Did you stay with the speaker?) Then the speaker will share his or her feelings about the listener's listening. (To the speaker: Did you feel listened to? Was it helpful? Did the listener have any habits you found distracting?). The observer will then share observations. This sharing process should take about three or four minutes.

Now everyone change places. Have the listener become the speaker, the speaker the observer, and the observer the listener. Go through the five minutes of talking and listening and five minutes of exchanging remarks twice more so that each person takes each role once. The entire practice session should take about 25 minutes.

When you are finished, form the large group and share your practice experiences. How are these skills relevant to your work? Where else would they be useful? Go around the group so that participants have a chance to share at least one thing they have learned about themselves in this practice session.

50. An exercise for Questions, Reflections, Summarization

Form subgroups of three and practice using question asking as a listening skills. Each member of your subgroup should take turns being the speaker, the listener (who practices the skill of questioning), and the observer.

Instructions to the speaker: In the speaker role, you have to share something that is a real concern to you. Sharing a real part of your life will make this practice both interesting and useful.

Give the listener a chance to practice interactive skills. If you, as the speaker, take all of the practice time in a monologue about yourself, the listener will not have a chance to practice listening skills. So, be sure to pause often to encourage the listener to respond, even though this may seem a bit unnatural.

Try to share information that allows the listener to practice the art of questioning. If you give the complete details of your concern, for example, it may be difficult for the listener to find anything to ask questions about. Or, if your story is completely factual and does not include your personal feelings or opinions, the listener may have difficulty asking questions with a speaker focus. As the speaker in the practice session, part of your job is to help your listener practice listening skills.

Instructions to the listener: Try to concentrate on asking questions, reflecting, and, at the end, summarizing even though this may seem difficult. You may use minimal encouragers occasionally, as long as your primary responses are questions. Vary your responses between open and closed questions and vary the focus of your questions (i.e., on speaker, topic, or others). By using both open and closed questions you will also see how your question and its focus can determine the course of the conversation.

Instructions to the observer: Keep track of the listener's responses. Include the number of open and closed questions used by the listener and the focus of each question; note the use of feeling and factual reflection, and the effectiveness of the listener's summary.

Procedure

The speaker and listener will have a conversation of three or four minutes duration. The observer can also time the conversation, gently announcing "stop" when the time is up. After the conversation, take a few minutes: First, the listener will share thoughts about how they used questions; second; the speaker will comment on his/her experience during the conversation and the listener's use of the skill; finally, the observer will share observations and comment on the conversation. Now trade roles and repeat the practice.

Each listener practice should take eight to ten minutes: three or four minutes for the initial conversation and three or four minutes to review it—to share the listener's and the speaker's impressions and the observer's reactions (l/2 hour). When exchanging observations about a conversation, please give the listener accurate feedback about how he or she used the skills. If the listener is having difficulty asking open questions, reflecting, or summarizing, say so and help him/her learn how to do so better. Remember that the purpose of practice is for the listener to learn the listening skill. Feedback and suggestions from both speaker and observer are essential to the learning process

51. Test your Spiritual Quotient

A high **SQ** or "Spiritual Quotient" is the best predictor of happiness, serenity, good self-esteem, and harmonious and loving relationships. People who know how to translate life's problems and struggles into spiritual issues can often find more gratifying and rewarding solutions to these problems through their spiritual IQs.

1. **When I look at my life I feel:**

(a) Absolutely contented and want things to stay exactly as they are
(b) My life's a mess and it is my parent/spouse/boss's fault
(c) There is nothing I or anyone else can do about it
(d) I want to create the life I choose

2. **Happiness is:**

(a) How my spouse/lover and I got along today
(b) When my mind is quiet
(c) My designation in my organization and my pay cheque
(d) A function of controlling others

3. **When facing a challenging situation, I...**

(a) Face it with an open mind
(b) Put a smile on my face
(c) Turn and run
(d) Pretend it's not happening and hope it will go away

4. **I view change as:**

(a) Inconvenient but unavoidable
(b) An opportunity for growth
(c) A threat
(d) A loss of the familiar

5. **When things don't go my way, I...**

(a) Try to force it around
(b) Speak my mind and complain

(c) Pretend it's not happening
(d) Handle the situation at hand

6. When I feel insecure I...
(a) Hide somewhere safe
(b) Know that is just a feeling
(c) Panic and worry
(d) Force myself to be happy

7. My personality is...
(a) A hopeless mess
(b) Something others have to bear
(c) Something I am stuck with
(d) A work in progress

8. I see others as...
(a) The enemy
(b) Separate from me
(c) Different from me
(d) As myself

9. When I feel out of control, I...
(a) Surrender to the power that knows the way
(b) Try harder
(c) Push back
(d) Give up

10. When I want love I...
(a) Look for it in my relationships
(b) Do whatever it takes
(b) Do whatever it takes to get it
(c) Blame myself for never getting it
(d) Rest in the love that I am

SCORING SYSTEM

Scores for each answer you ticked are given below. Now add up your score.

1.	(a)	3	(b)	1	(c)	2	(d)	4
2.	(a)	3	(b)	4	(c)	2	(d)	1
3.	(a)	4	(b)	3	(c)	1	(d)	2
4.	(a)	3	(b)	4	(c)	1	(d)	2
5.	(a)	3	(b)	2	(c)	1	(d)	4
6.	(a)	2	(b)	4	(c)	1	(d)	3
7.	(a)	1	(b)	2	(c)	3	(d)	4
8.	(a)	1	(b)	2	(c)	3	(d)	4
9.	(a)	4	(b)	3	(c)	1	(d)	2
10.	(a)	3	(b)	2	(c)	1	(d)	4

Here's how to interpret your score: 36-40:

You are spiritually adept and act with spiritual intelligence, through sensitivity, compassion, and understanding.

26-35:

You are a seeker and are striving to strike a balance in body, mind, and spirit.

25 and below:

Your decisions seem to be driven by ego, rather than any spiritual sense

52. Job Motivation

Achieving the ability to believe is within your power. Learn how to believe in whatever you do. Following steps can help you acquire patterns of thinking that can lead you to the belief:

Step 1: Quit your job: Yes, quit your job. But, only mentally. Now you have no job and you are looking for one. You decide to accept the one you just left. Tomorrow will be your first day on the job. For next few minutes, discuss how your attitude tomorrow(first day on new job) will be different than it was today. How about your level of interest, enthusiasm, ambition on first day of this new job? Any different from today's attitude towards job? How? How hard are you going to work the first few days on your new job? Have you been applying yourself like this?

Step 2: Make the decision: You have the ability to choose your attitude in any situation. That is your greatest power- to choose your thoughts! In order to believe in your job, your company, yourself, your philosophy of life, make the decision to believe. Say to yourself," I choose to believe in the way I am using my life"

Step 3: Benefits of belief: Good thoughts and good actions bring good results. Belief is no exception. Write three ways that you would benefit personally by believing deeply in what you do and becoming motivated to do the very best job you know how to do. Share these with Team Members:

1. ____

____

2. ____

____

3. ____

____

Step 4: Reject all negative thoughts: Learn to face unpleasant people and circumstances without letting them affect your belief. Reject all negative thoughts about your work. Discuss negative thoughts about company, work, job, boss, people or your feelings and then discuss how you might benefit by removing such attitudes from your mind.

Step 5: List ways you can do a better job:

1.

2.

3.

4.

5.

6.

7.

53. Your effectiveness in an organization

SPIRO (***Styles Profile of Interaction Role in Organizations***) TEST

SPIRO QUESTIONNAIRE

Rarely=1, Occasionally=2, Sometimes=3, Often=4, Always=5

1. I assure my subordinates of my availability to them.
2. I delay doing things that I do not like.
3. I encourage my subordinates to question me about what should or should not be done.
4. I communicate strong feelings or resentment to my bosses without caring whether this will affect my relationship with them.
5. I collect all the information that is needed to solve various problems.
6. I discuss new ideas with my subordinates without working out details of these ideas.
7. I respect and follow organizational traditions that seem to give organization its identity.
8. I provide my subordinates with the solutions to their problems.
9. I take up my subordinates' causes and fight for them.
10. I admonish my subordinates for not acting according to my instructions.
11. I think of new and creative solutions.
12. I collect information and data, even when these are not immediately needed or used.
13. I help my subordinates to become aware of some of their own strengths.
14. I avoid meeting my bosses and subordinates if I have not been able to fulfill their expectations.
15. I help my subordinates to see the ethical dimensions of some of their actions.
16. I champion my subordinate's causes even at the cost of organizational effectiveness.
17. I think out many alternative solutions to problems before adopting one for action.
18. I overwhelm my subordinates with new ideas.
19. I accept only those bosses' and subordinates' suggestions that appeal to me.
20. I instruct my subordinates in detail about work problems and their solutions.
21. I zealously argue my point of view in organizational meetings.
22. I give clear instructions to my subordinates about what should or should not be done.
23. I try out new things.
24. I spend my time on specific work to be performed.
25. I reassure my subordinates of my continued help

26. I do not express my negative feelings during unpleasant meetings but continue to be bothered by them
27. I help my subordinates to examine the appropriateness of proposed action.
28. I express resentment to the authorities concerned about things that have not been done as promised.
29. I continuously search for various resources from which needed information can be obtained in order to work out solutions to problems.
30. I try out new ideas or methods without waiting to consolidate the previous one.
31. I accept help from others and appreciate it.
32. I encourage my subordinates to come to me frequently to seek my advice and help.
33. I express my feelings and reactions frankly in meetings with my own bosses.
34. I clearly prescribe standards of behaviour to be followed in my work unit.
35. I enjoy trying out new ways and see a problem as a challenge.
36. I work primarily on organizational tasks sometimes at the cost of sensitivity and attention to the feelings of people.

Scoring Sheets

Transfer your scores from SPIRO QUESTIONNAIRE directly into the following scoring sheet.

OK EGO States

PARENT (1)……..+(13)………+(25)………=……….SUPPORTIVE

(3)……..+(15)………+(27)………=……….NORMATIVE

ADULT (5)……..+(17)………+(29)………=……….PROBLEM SOLVING

CHILD (11)……..+(23)………+(35)………=…….INNOVATIVE

(9)……..+(21)………+(33)………=…….CONFRONTING

(7)……..+(19)………+(31)………=……….RESILIENT

NOT OK EGO STATES

PARENT (8)……..+(20)………+(32)………=……….RESCUING

(10)……..+(22)………+(34)….. = …….PRESCRIPTIVE

ADULT (12)……..+(24)………+(36)……… = ……….TASK OBSES SIVE

CHILD (6)……..+(18)………+(30)……… = ……BOEHEMIAN

(4)……..+(16)………+(28)……… = ……AGGRESSIVE

(2)……..+(14)………+(26)……… = ………..SULKING

SPIRO SUMMARY SHEET

ENTER YOUR SCORES IN THE APPROPRIATE BOXES

EGO STATES	PARENT		ADULT	CHILD		
	Nurturing	Regulating		Creative	Reactive	Adaptive
OK	Supportive	Normative	Problem solving	Innovative	Confronting	Resilient
NOT OK	Rescuing	Prescriptive	Obsessive	Bohemian	Aggressive	Sulking
OPERATING EFFECTIVENESS QUOTIENT						

OPERATING EFFECTIVENESS QUOTIENT (OEQ)

NOT OK SCORE

NOT OK SCORE ↓ / OK SCORE →

	3	4	5	6	7	8	9	10	11	12	13	14	15
3	0	100	100	100	100	100	100	100	100	100	100	100	100
4	0	50	67	75	80	83	85	87	89	90	91	92	92
5	0	33	50	60	67	71	75	78	80	82	83	85	86
6	0	25	40	50	57	62	67	70	73	75	77	78	80
7	0	20	33	43	50	55	60	64	67	69	71	73	75
8	0	17	28	37	44	50	54	58	61	64	67	69	70
9	0	14	25	33	40	45	50	54	57	60	62	65	67
10	0	12	22	30	36	42	46	50	53	56	59	61	63
11	0	11	20	27	33	38	43	47	50	53	55	58	60
12	0	10	18	25	31	36	40	44	47	50	53	55	57
13	0	9	17	23	28	33	37	41	44	47	50	52	54
14	0	8	15	21	27	31	35	39	42	45	48	50	52
15	0	8	14	20	25	29	33	37	40	43	45	48	50

For each ego state style, the OEQ scores are given at the intersection of the OK score (in the column) and the NOT OK Score (in the rows). These scores are to be noted on the summary sheet. The table indicates the percentage of potential being used effectively in a particular style. Using the table one can see how reduction in Not Ok Scores improves OEQ. A respondent can thus strive to obtain the highest score (100) by reducing his/ her Not Ok behaviour to maximize the use of his/her potential for the present level of an ego state.

Index